# Sun, Sin & Su

# Sun, Sin & Suburbia

THE HISTORY OF MODERN LAS VEGAS

## Geoff Schumacher

**REVISED AND EXPANDED EDITION**

University of Nevada Press  Reno and Las Vegas

The first edition of *Sun, Sin & Suburbia* was published in 2004 and the second edition in 2012 by Stephens Press. This University of Nevada Press edition is a reprint of the 2012 edition.

University of Nevada Press, Reno, Nevada 89557 USA
Copyright © 2015 by University of Nevada Press
All rights reserved
Manufactured in the United States of America
Design by Sue Campbell

Library of Congress Cataloging-in-Publication Data
A catalog record for this book is available from the Library of Congress
ISBN-13: 978-0-87417-988-0 (paper) —
ISBN-13: 978-0-87417-989-7 (e-book)

The paper used in this book meets the requirements of American National Standard for Information Sciences—Permanence of Paper for Printed Library Materials, ANSI/NISO Z39.48-1992 (R2002). Binding materials were selected for strength and durability.

First Printing
23  22  21  20  19  18  17  16  15
5  4  3  2  1

*For Erin and Sara*

# Contents

**Chapter 12**

# Preface to the Revised and Expanded Edition

The first edition of *Sun, Sin & Suburbia* was published in the fall of 2004 — at the apex of the Las Vegas boom years. Eight years and one devastating recession later, the community had undergone such profound changes that we thought it was time to update the story of modern Las Vegas.

This new edition has been extensively rewritten and updated to reflect developments over the past several years, from the rise of CityCenter to the fall of the economy. Sections have been added to recognize new players and initiatives. Some things that seemed important in 2004 turned out not to be historically relevant, and so they were omitted. A lot of ground is covered in this new edition, but it is not a comprehensive history. Modern Las Vegas is just too big and complex to get that treatment in a single volume.

It's often said that the one constant in Las Vegas is change. A cursory comparison of the first and second editions of *Sun, Sin & Suburbia* gives credence to this adage.

# Introduction: Making a Life in the City of Sun, Sin, and Suburbia

*"Vegas is a town ... where the vast majority of the population arises every morning absolutely delighted to have escaped Hometown, America and the necessity of chatting with Mom over the back fence."*

—DAVE HICKEY, *AIR GUITAR*

*"There may be some who feel that Las Vegas is an abomination and should be destroyed. They would then have to argue, with me at least, that the oil companies are straight, the stock market is not a flimflam, and that our South American policy is not insane. They would even have to argue that the Democratic Party and the Republican Party are more honest than the Mafia."*

—MARIO PUZO, *INSIDE LAS VEGAS*

Several years ago, while perusing the shelves of a used bookstore, I happened upon a 1979-80 edition of *Arthur Frommer's Guide to Las Vegas*. A quick flip through the chapters sparked a swirl of nostalgia about the pre-megaresort city and what dramatic changes had occurred over the past two decades. The guide painted a picture of a Las Vegas that was quite different from today. For example, Steve Wynn's name was mentioned only once in the guide, in passing reference to his ownership of the Golden Nugget. Also, a map of the area did not show the U.S. 95 expressway, and Rancho Drive was called Tonopah Highway.

The guide listed just two hospitals: Sunrise and Southern Nevada Memorial (now University Medical Center), although a few others were operating at the time. There are a dozen major hospitals today and counting. The main movie house in town was the Red Rock Theatres on West Charleston Boulevard, which closed several years ago and was demolished. The guide made no mention of master-planned communities. The Las Vegas Hilton was the state's tallest building, a distinction it lost well before the Stratosphere Tower was finished in the mid-'90s. *Frommer's* listed only one disco, Jubilation, owned by Paul Anka and described as "Las Vegas's answer to Studio 54." A quarter-century later, Las Vegas had forty dance clubs, including one called Studio 54.

The "top ten hotels" in 1980 were MGM Grand (now Bally's), Caesars Palace, Las Vegas Hilton, Desert Inn, Flamingo Hilton, Tropicana, Aladdin, Riviera, Dunes and Sands. Today, four of those hotels had been torn down (Dunes, Sands, Aladdin, Desert Inn), and only one of them (Caesars Palace) would make anyone's top ten list. That's not a criticism, just an acknowledgement that the modern megaresorts have eclipsed the industry leaders of the past.

Of course, Las Vegas residents don't need a musty *Frommer's Guide* to know the place has changed significantly over the past thirty years. Just walk outside and the evidence is everywhere. Clark County's population in 1980 was 463,087. Today, the county population is two million. Those additional people have radically altered almost every aspect of life. Thousands of acres of scrub brush and lizards are now covered with houses, apartment complexes, shopping centers, casinos, bars, restaurants, schools, parks and other accouterments of suburban living. The city has spread from the valley's center in all directions, its momentum slowed only by time, money and mountain ranges. During the '90s, the critics' mantra was that Las Vegas was developing at a rate of two acres every hour.

As dozens of new neighborhoods cropped up at the edges, the urban core suffered. Downtown lost its luster. The tourist numbers on Fremont Street plummeted as the Strip, with its myriad extracurricular attractions, came to dominate visitors' interest. McCarran International Airport expanded to accommodate the growing tourist hordes, which required the acquisition of hundreds of homes to be demolished to make way for new gates and runways, as well as an ever-widening noise corridor. The expansion of U.S. 95 and construction of the Las Vegas Beltway required the demolition of hundreds more homes across the valley. The rush to the suburbs made residential living along some streets unbearable. Long stretches of Decatur Boulevard and Jones Boulevard, for example, once were lined with houses. Today, many of those houses have been torn down or converted into shops and offices.

Of course, the growth wasn't all bad. More than anything, it gave residents more choices in employment, housing, recreation and culture. Tourism remained the city's economic engine but it was now possible to work in an array of interesting and rewarding fields not linked to the resort industry. Housing options widened. One could live in a brand-new tract house on the outskirts or move close to the action, buying an old place downtown and fixing it up. The apartment market offered an array of options, and condos ran from cheap to the pinnacle of jetset leisure. As for recreation, Las Vegas had almost everything imaginable — even that most unlikely of desert pastimes, ice hockey. Perhaps the most significant benefits of growth were the cultural additions, from museums to art galleries, orchestras to ballet companies, rock 'n' roll concert halls to roller coasters. It seemed physically impossible for one person in one lifetime to sample all of the city's fine dining establishments. Las Vegas evolved well beyond its trademark lounges and buffets.

Some say Las Vegas is completely different from other cities. Others say once you venture beyond the Strip, it's basically the same as anyplace else. They're both right. Geography distinguishes Las Vegas from many other cities. It isn't by an ocean, lake or river. It isn't in the mountains, and it doesn't sit amid vast farmland. Its location is notable only because it's near the halfway point of the railroad line between Salt Lake City and Los Angeles.

The city was not founded by any religious or ethnic groups. The nineteenth century Mormon settlers didn't stay long. None of its neighborhoods is primarily Italian or Polish or Chinese. While its black population once was segregated into one area, that practice ended decades ago, and the area in question, the Westside or West Las Vegas, is now a melting pot of race and ethnicity. Areas that are now primarily Hispanic didn't start out that way, but evolved with high levels of immigration and new housing construction that encouraged white flight.

Las Vegas differs from many other cities, especially those back East, in that its history is not woven into the fabric of its culture. Boston is the home of Revolutionary War rebellion. Philadelphia is the birthplace of independence. San Francisco was the cradle of the Gold Rush and later the counterculture. Las Vegas did not contribute in such a way to the American story until more recently, when it became the catalyst for the mainstreaming of gambling.

Las Vegas does share one key characteristic with many other cities: It is associated with a dominant industry. Pittsburgh had steel, Detroit has cars, Hollywood has movies, Las Vegas has gambling. And for a long time Las Vegas's dominant industry made it a unique company town: No other major American city had legal gambling halls. That is no longer true. Gambling in some form is now legal in forty-eight states, and casino-style games are offered in cities such as Atlantic City, Detroit and New Orleans, and on riverboats and Indian reservations across the land.

However, Las Vegas is still the only major city that depends almost entirely on gambling for its livelihood. Gambling, along with the accompanying attractions, remains the beating heart of the economy. A third of Las Vegans work directly for the industry, and another third work for it in indirect ways. The final third percent most likely wouldn't be here without it.

While some Las Vegans don't gamble, they find it difficult to divorce themselves completely from the industry's charms. The casinos host most of the city's best restaurants. They also have movie theaters, concert venues, nightclubs, showrooms, art museums, bowling alleys and even an ice skating rink, making them the city's primary cultural and recreational centers. This fact certainly helps make the case that Las Vegas is different from other cities.

And yet, in many ways, Las Vegas is very much like other places, especially those in the Southwest. Not far from the Strip are residential neighborhoods made up of middle-class suburban houses surrounding parks, ballfields, schools and churches. Shopping centers feature supermarkets, laundromats,

*Sun, Sin & Suburbia: The History of Modern Las Vegas*

hair salons and drugstores, while fast-food restaurants and convenience stores crowd around the intersections of major thoroughfares. It's the usual pattern, except with slot machines in the stores.

Many Las Vegans today have lifestyles that simply do not involve the casinos. With a little effort, a resident can avoid setting foot in a Strip hotel for months at a time. Oftentimes a prolonged absence from the resort corridor ends only when a visiting relative or friend wants a "guide" to see what all the excitement is about.

I can remember when Rainbow Boulevard was a gravel road. Well, at least parts of Rainbow were gravel when I was a boy, and today it's a major thoroughfare. Longtime residents are famous for making comments like this. The gravel road in question depends on how long you've been around. Some old-timers can remember when Decatur was a gravel road, and it developed decades ahead of Rainbow.

For some reason, this question of Las Vegas longevity fascinates us. Most natives are proud they were born in Las Vegas; it doesn't take long after meeting one to learn about his hardscrabble youth when the community was small and it took only ten minutes to drive across town.

I'm not a native. My family moved to Las Vegas from Wisconsin in 1977, when I was in the fifth grade. But when I would tell people how long I'd been there, they'd typically say, "Well, that makes you a native." Not quite, but I *can* say that I lived in Las Vegas longer than more than a million and a half people who came after me.

Plenty of people possess at least a snapshot knowledge of Las Vegas history, whether they learned it in school or picked it up from books, museums, cable television programs or conversations with longtime residents. The key moments tend to come up in conversation from time to time as newcomers wonder aloud just how this city emerged from the Mojave sands. But at the same time, it's often difficult to draw solid lines between the Las Vegas of black-and-white photographs and the modern metropolis. As you drive around the valley, it's a challenge to find remnants of that time before themed resorts and master-planned communities, neighborhood casinos and business parks. Most everything you see has been built over the past thirty years.

Las Vegas history starts with thousands of years of Native American habitation and almost 160 years of continual occupation by people of European heritage. Las Vegas has many stories to tell about its origins, its early settlers, its evolution into the world's gambling capital. But all that pales in comparison to the dramatic changes that have occurred since about 1980. Nonetheless, in order to understand what has happened recently, it's important to be at least vaguely acquainted with what happened before. Although this book focuses on more recent decades, I provide a brief chronology of Las Vegas's early history in the first chapter, in the hope it will help to put recent happenings in the proper context. In researching this book, I constantly found important linkages between more recent historical developments and the city's pioneer days.

It's sometimes difficult to assess Las Vegas's recent history because, in many cases, it's still unfolding. For example, this book contains a chapter about the Summerlin master-planned community, yet the massive development won't be completed for at least another decade. Another chapter discusses the Las Vegas Beltway, though it won't reach its full potential for several more years. Some facts and figures in this book will be outdated by the time it hits store shelves. But that's the nature of most books about Las Vegas, and it only reinforces the vibrant, intriguing, important story that modern Las Vegas has to tell.

A frequently asked question in Las Vegas is, "Do you like it here?" This must be a common question in other cities, but it seems to carry greater weight in Las Vegas, in part explaining the high transience of the population. People come here to live and spend a few months deciding whether they like it. If they do, they stay. If they don't, they may leave. Often it takes longer than a few months for somebody to feel comfortable here. Other cities seem to have much less coming and going. So, do I like Las Vegas? My woefully predictable answer: Yes and no.

*Sun, Sin & Suburbia: The History of Modern Las Vegas*

On the positive side, I like the climate. Las Vegas has terrific weather at least seven months of the year. That's a pretty good percentage if you think about it. Spring and fall are mild. Winter can get chilly but rarely bitterly cold. There is little snow to speak of, maybe some flurries once a year, and rain is infrequent at best. Summers can get intolerably hot — it's a dry heat, as they say, but that doesn't sell when it's 110 with no breeze for two straight weeks. But unless they're in San Diego, who can say they live in a climate that doesn't have a few uncomfortable months? It's also worth noting that Las Vegas is unlikely to endure hurricanes, tornadoes, blizzards, mudslides or devastating earthquakes (although seismologists say the city falls within an earthquake zone). The city is prone to flash floods, perhaps once a year, but they usually aren't too bad if you're smart enough not to drive through deep water. A massive flood control project has minimized the risks for neighborhoods once susceptible to flooding.

Until the recent downturn, I also was very appreciative of Las Vegas's economy. It was booming most of the time I lived there, and the costs of living stayed relatively low. Unemployment was low, wages were relatively good and the opportunity for advancement in almost any field was great. In my twenty-three years of post-college employment in Las Vegas, I was never lacking a good job, and I was able to steadily advance in my field. While not every Las Vegan can tell such a story — the city has its share of homeless and poor, and the recession took a brutal toll on employment — many people can. And those who moved to Las Vegas from parts of the country with deep economic problems tell their Las Vegas success story with a lot more spirit than I would. While young couples in cities such as Los Angeles and San Francisco struggle to find ways to afford an entry-level home, my wife and I were able to partake of that piece of the American dream with relative ease.

From my experience, the public schools in Las Vegas get a bad rap. My two daughters attended local schools, and they had positive experiences. Their teachers ranged from good to excellent, and they all were enthusiastic and well-meaning. The school facilities were in good shape, and extracurricular activities were abundant. Las Vegas schools are underfunded and the teachers underpaid, but they don't seem to crumble under the strain. My kids left the school system sufficiently prepared for university work.

But lest this book turn into a chamber of commerce-approved advertisement for Las Vegas, let's turn to the negative aspects of living there, and there are plenty. For most of the period covered by this book, the over-arching issue was the double-edged sword of growth. While growth brought jobs and culture and money to the community, it also brought headaches. The roads were congested and constantly under construction. The air was dirty. The schools were crowded. The social safety net was full of holes. Historic landmarks and ecological havens were destroyed to make way for the new. The city at times felt chaotic, anarchic, a constant whirl of noises, frustrations and changes. It was difficult to get into a routine, because the environment was always changing. Very little of the city felt permanent, including the people. There was a severe shortage of "community" in Las Vegas, a young city where newcomers are reluctant to put down roots. Lasting friendships are prized because they are rare. Neighbors often don't know each other. They tend to keep to themselves, saying hello at the mailbox and that's about it.

The 2008 recession idled the bulldozers, but it was difficult to detect resulting improvements to the problems cited above. The city still bustled and rankled, with perhaps a greater degree of desperation in the air.

The lack of community connection or pride seems to breed aberrant and self-centered behavior — drivers who race through school zones, run red lights and cut off other motorists with impunity; the guy who revs his Harley in the middle of the night; the neighbor who operates a dangerous meth lab out of his garage. Incivility is hardly unique to Las Vegas, but the fact that so few people feel a connection to the place often is reflected in a more prevalent uncaring attitude. It also has social effects: While low voter turnout is a national problem, newer Las Vegans often seem less interested in politics and issues with which they have no history; contributions to local charities and the arts are meager; and interest in historic preservation, while growing, remains minimal. In the 2002 election, for example, Las Vegas area voters approved extra taxes for transportation projects but soundly defeated measures to help the homeless and expand the library system.

Name a modern social ill, and Las Vegas seems afflicted with a bad case. The rapid growth was a big reason. Politicians constantly struggled to find money to meet the ever-increasing demands for services and programs to properly care for the populace. The needs of one group were constantly balanced against those of another. In the process, the constituencies with the least political clout — the homeless, mentally ill, etc. — tended to get the crumbs left over after the powerful had taken their bites. The Nevada Legislature approved $836 million in tax increases in 2003 — the largest tax increase in state history — and it barely kept pace with the demands of growth.

Urban critic James Howard Kunstler, from Sarasota Springs, New York, was perhaps Las Vegas's toughest critic. His 2001 book *The City in Mind* contained a long rant against Las Vegas. "They say that Antarctica is the worst place on Earth," Kunstler wrote, "but I believe that distinction belongs to Las Vegas, hands down." Condemning those who suggested Las Vegas was a "city of the future," Kunstler wrote: "If Las Vegas truly is our city of the future, then we might as well all cut our own throats tomorrow. I certainly felt like cutting mine after only a few days there, so overwhelming was the sheer anomie provoked by every particular of its design and operation."

Kunstler was well-known for his hyperbolic style. But his attack on Las Vegas felt ill-informed and unfair. After all, Kunstler was most fond of Eastern and Midwestern prewar hamlets that preserved or adopted New Urbanist principles that encourage walking, foliage and a strong sense of place. Western cities grew within a different climate and a different time, making them difficult to compare with Kunstler's ideal. Still, Kunstler's comments were worth considering, in part because he was not alone. James Ellroy, whose 2001 novel *The Cold Six Thousand* was set partly in Las Vegas, went off on the city in a magazine interview: "It's a shit hole. It's a testimony to greed and prostitution and exploitation of women and narcotics and the get-rich-quick fervor that is one of the worst aspects of America."

As the late UNLV history professor Hal Rothman said, Las Vegas "is a hard town that will make you pay for your inability to restrain your desires." The twenty-four-hour lifestyle is an open invitation for alcohol and drug abuse, for promiscuity and compulsive gambling. Gambling addiction happens everywhere, especially with the proliferation of gambling around the world, but nowhere in America is the environment so rich for this devastating problem to flourish. What's so troubling is that Las Vegas collectively does so little to help problem gamblers. While other states and cities with legalized gambling have made treatment and prevention programs a priority, the issue gets back-burner status in the gambling capital of the world.

Las Vegas, then, has its pros and cons, much like any city. Local writer Scott Dickensheets, in an article for *Money* magazine in 2002, said, "Mixed feelings are practically a civic duty if you live in Las Vegas." Whether you like or dislike the place depends largely on what you consider important in life. But it's never that simple. One might expect very religious people to dislike "Sin City," with its morals-challenged mindset, but Las Vegas's significant population of Mormons and fundamentalists calls that assumption into question. One might expect the city's barren desert and extreme summer heat to be too much for natives of the lush Midwest and Northeast, but large numbers of the city's recent emigrants hail from places like Michigan, Wisconsin and New York.

One thing is generally agreed upon: Unless you're a diehard gambler or lounge lizard who can't imagine being anyplace else, Las Vegas is an acquired taste. Before the recession, Las Vegas boasted that anywhere from 4,000 to 8,000 people move there every month. But almost half that many also left each month. Las Vegas is not for everyone, but over the past thirty years it has become steadily more attractive to a wider spectrum of people. Las Vegas matured from a frontier town to a modern metropolis. It added dimensions to everyday life that people have come to expect in a major city. That transformation is largely what this book is about.

I witnessed the rise of Las Vegas, and I witnessed the fall. And then I watched it all from a distance — for a while.

In the spring of 2011, I left Las Vegas. I didn't flee, as some did when the recession hit, but I did end up in a greener pasture. I was offered a job oppor-

*Sun, Sin & Suburbia: The History of Modern Las Vegas*

tunity that was impossible to pass up. After twenty-three years as a writer and editor in Las Vegas, I became the publisher of a group of newspapers based in Ames, Iowa.

After so many years enmeshed in the business, cultural and political spheres of Las Vegas, I had come to view the community as "normal," or at least not as unusual as its reputation suggested. But after I had lived in the Midwest for a few months, I came to realize that Las Vegas is indeed unique. I came to see why people find the city so exciting — and so repugnant.

Some people I met in Iowa were frequent visitors to Las Vegas: for conventions, for a long weekend or to visit family members who had moved there. They tended to enjoy it — as a place to visit. It appealed to them because it's so different from their everyday environment.

Other Iowans seemed to have absolutely no interest in Las Vegas. To them, Las Vegas is everything they abhor. It's congested, noisy, full of hustlers, hookers and temptations they'd rather not deal with. They asked me questions, perhaps curious about whether the mob still lurks in the shadows, but they had no plans to pay a visit.

Most of the revised and expanded parts of this book were written in Iowa. At first I thought this might be a disadvantage, but it didn't turn out that way. Rather, I believe moving 1,500 miles from my subject improved my sense of perspective. I would not presume to compare myself to great writers, but there's a venerable tradition of writing well about places from a distance. Consider Ernest Hemingway, who wrote some of his finest short stories set in Upper Michigan while sitting in a Paris café. Salman Rushdie grew up in India but has lived primarily in England since college. His most-admired novels are set in India. Rushdie has said: "The only people who see the whole picture are the ones who step out of the frame." At the *Los Angeles Times* Festival of Books in 2012, the novelist Steve Erickson remarked, "I had to leave L.A. in my twenties and thirties in order to understand it." I hope this revised and expanded edition benefits, at least a little, from the perspective I gained from looking at Las Vegas from afar.

Alas, I returned to Las Vegas in early 2014, and I changed professions as well. After twenty-five years in the newspaper business, I became the director of content for the Mob Museum in downtown Las Vegas. Among other things, I'm the in-house historian, a position I relish and am humbled by on a daily basis. I have a great seat to observe how Las Vegas grows and reinvents itself again as we push more deeply into the twenty-first century.

# CHAPTER 1

# Downtown: The Revival

While this book focuses on recent history, understanding the dynamics of downtown Las Vegas requires some familiarity with the city's origins. Just about everything happening today in the downtown area has some connection to events that occurred one hundred years ago or more.

The story of Las Vegas's early days is fairly well-documented. The first non-native believed to have set foot in the valley was Mexican scout Rafael Rivera in 1829. His discovery of the valley's plentiful springs led other traders to begin traversing the route, which came to be known as the Old Spanish Trail. After famed explorer John C. Fremont documented his 1844 trip through Las Vegas in a best-selling report, the valley became a popular rest stop for parched traders and immigrants. The first white residents arrived in 1855. They were Mormons sent by Brigham Young to serve traders and mail riders and protect them from bandits, and preach the gospel to the Indians. It was a difficult and unpopular mission, fraught with hardships, dissension and discontent, and less than three years later Young ordered the missionaries to pack up and return to Utah. They left only an adobe fort in their wake. (A small part of the fort, the state's oldest building, still stands within a state park at Las Vegas Boulevard North and Washington Avenue.)

During the remainder of the nineteenth century, Las Vegas was a tiny outpost valued primarily for its water and grass. The Las Vegas Ranch, which encompassed the old Mormon Fort, was the main attraction. Operated by the entrepreneurial Octavius Decatur Gass, the ranch flourished in the 1870s.

23

Gass plowed expansive fields and orchards, raised cattle and planted cotton-wood trees that soon served as cool resting places for weary desert travelers. Archibald and Helen Stewart obtained the ranch from Gass, who had fallen on hard times financially, in 1881, and the couple moved there the next year. After her husband was shot and killed under mysterious circumstances in 1884, Helen Stewart continued to operate the ranch into the twentieth century, serving travelers and miners seeking a civilized respite from their harsh daily existence. With just a handful of people living in the Las Vegas area, she started a school, a post office and a church. Today, Helen Stewart is widely hailed as the "First Lady of Las Vegas."

Las Vegas's fortunes started to change after the turn of the century when U.S. Senator William Andrews Clark, a Montana copper mining mogul, decided to build a railroad through Las Vegas. As roughly the halfway point between Salt Lake City and Los Angeles, Las Vegas was a logical place to locate repair shops to service the trains. It helped that Las Vegas had a good water supply. Clark bought part of Stewart's Las Vegas Ranch in 1902 and railroad construction began in 1904. A tent city emerged in the summer of that year west of the tracks. Owned by J.T. McWilliams, the eighty-acre plot (also purchased from Helen Stewart) soon included saloons, restaurants and markets serving miners from the booming Bullfrog and Rhyolite mining districts. Stanley Paher, in his seminal history, *Las Vegas: As It Began—As It Grew,* described the scene:

"Every general store did a lucrative business, especially in outfitting miners and prospectors who came into town with their burros to rest a few days before heading out again. At Crowell and Alcott's store on Clark Avenue and Railroad Street people could buy everything from a thimble to a plow, including dry goods, thick hams, dry salt pork, lard, bacon or kegs of beer. The clerks kept busy from early morning until late at night."

McWilliams struck first in developing a Las Vegas townsite, and as many as 1,500 people lived there before regular train service rolled through the valley. But Clark got the last laugh. On May 15, 1905, the railroad held an auction of 1,200 lots laid out in a grid pattern east of the tracks. On this unusually hot spring day, a crowd of 2,000, mostly from Los Angeles, snapped up

176 lots (for a total of $79,566). Many more lots were sold on the second day. Canvas tents and other primitive buildings quickly sprung up along Fremont Street, Main Street and other newly staked-out dirt paths. Many businesses in the McWilliams townsite moved to Clark's townsite. Later that year, the McWilliams townsite endured a tremendous fire that left it in ruins. (The McWilliams townsite later became known as the Westside, a poor and primarily African-American neighborhood.)

Though Clark played a pivotal role in the growth of Las Vegas, it is not surprising that few sing his praises today. Clark was, by most accounts, a ruthless businessman and corrupt politician. In a 1907 essay, Mark Twain unleashed a tirade of loathing for Clark: "He is as rotten a human being as can be found anywhere under the flag; he is a shame to the American nation, and no one has helped to send him to the Senate who did not know that his proper place was the penitentiary, with a ball and chain on his legs. To my mind he is the most disgusting creature that the republic has produced since Tweed's time."

Las Vegas prospered initially, although in fits and starts, thanks to national economic problems and floods northeast of town that washed out some of the tracks. It became the county seat for the newly created Clark County in 1909, beating out the mining town of Searchlight for the honor. The following year the railroad began building large machine and maintenance shops in Las Vegas, ensuring the employment of hundreds more men. At the same time the railroad built dozens of small bungalow-style houses for its workers (only a handful of which still stand today). However, the town, which incorporated as a city in 1911, didn't grow much during the 1920s, hampered in part by an acrimonious labor strike in 1922 that prompted the railroad to pull its important repair shops out of Las Vegas. When the Great Depression hit, Las Vegas's population stood at a modest 5,165.

But the prospects of a giant dam being constructed on the Colorado River buoyed the city. Work began on Hoover Dam in 1931, boosting Las Vegas's economy, even though the federal government built its own town, Boulder City, for its workers. Even before the dam's completion in 1935, it and the lake it created became popular tourist attractions.

The legalization of gambling in 1931 did not immediately transform Las Vegas into a vacation destination. Reno was the first city to take full advantage of legal gambling (as well as quickie divorces and marriages). But casino joints along Fremont Street began to flourish in the late 1930s and early '40s as illegal gambling operators were driven out of other cities and took refuge in Las Vegas. The city received another boost during World War II, as the establishment of the Las Vegas Army Air Field (now Nellis Air Force Base) in the northeast valley and the Basic Magnesium plant in Henderson flooded the town with thousands of new residents.

While the first casinos on what later would become known as the Strip opened for business in the early '40s, Fremont Street remained the valley's main attraction, its collage of colorful neon signs prompting the nickname "Glitter Gulch." But in the '50s the Strip overtook downtown as the dominant player in Las Vegas tourism, its sprawling resorts drawing visitors who gambled but also enjoyed lounge acts, swanky restaurants and relaxing swimming pools that the tightly packed downtown casinos did not offer.

Despite increasing competition from the Strip, downtown casino operators did not throw in the towel. Instead, they upgraded their facilities, added hotel rooms and catered to serious gamblers and value-conscious visitors. In the '50s, Binion's Horseshoe Club, operated by Texas maverick Benny Binion, became a favorite of high-stakes bettors and poker players. In 1965, the Mint Hotel expanded to feature downtown's first high-rise at twenty-six stories. In the '70s, a young casino executive named Steve Wynn remodeled and expanded the Golden Nugget, making it as big and luxurious as any Strip resort. Still, for several key reasons, Glitter Gulch fell far behind the Strip in prominence and economic importance. A series of community decisions doomed the downtown casinos to permanent second-class status.

### Hollowing out

Fremont and Main is where it all started, where Las Vegas transformed from frontier rest stop to full-fledged city. And for forty years that intersection was the axis around which Las Vegas rotated. It was the heart of "Downtown," the place where Las Vegans shopped, dined in restaurants, watched movies, bought insurance, attended school and did their banking. It was also where people went if they wanted to gamble, drink and perhaps pay for companionship.

This is no longer true, and hasn't been for several decades. Development has spread across the valley in all directions, and downtown is no longer the community's focal point. Las Vegas doesn't really have a downtown in the way it is understood in other parts of the country. For the most part, people take care of their affairs in or near their neighborhoods, no matter what part of the valley they live in. They have few practical reasons to venture downtown, unless they have a court date or a desire to make demands at City Hall. Redevelopment efforts in recent years have begun to reverse that downward spiral, but downtown Las Vegas is unlikely ever to regain its past glory.

Las Vegas is not unique in this respect. The same can be said of most other Western cities that have developed in the automobile age. America's love affair with the car has dictated urban development patterns across the country, but it has been particularly influential in the more recently emergent West. Author Jim Harrison describes Western cities as "nearly all 'outskirts,'" a description that aptly describes Las Vegas. As a result, the concept of a downtown, where a wide array of public and private entities are packed tightly together so people can walk easily from one place to another, has lost its appeal.

And if anything in Las Vegas resembles an urban core, it is the Strip, not downtown. The Strip is the community's largest employment center. It's where people go for big-time entertainment such as concerts, stage productions and boxing matches. It's the focal point of major events such as New Year's Eve celebrations. It's the venue of choice for labor demonstrations and activists who want to protest injustice. Joel Garreau, in his landmark 1991 book *Edge City: Life on the New Frontier*, confirmed this perspective when he called the Strip "the center of people's perception of what Las Vegas means." Garreau added: "How many visitors to Las Vegas discover that downtown even exists?"

Downtown's decline may have been inevitable, but it's too simple to lay the blame solely on the rise of suburbia and car culture. As with most things, it's more complicated. A careful examination of Las Vegas's development patterns over the past seventy years reveals a string of political and economic decisions that contributed to downtown's diminished importance.

Probably the first strike against downtown came with the construction of Hoover Dam in the early '30s. Before the dam, Las Vegas was fairly concentrated around its railroad hub at Fremont and Main. The dam project prompted the extension of Fremont Street through the building of Boulder Highway, which connected Las Vegas to the dam site and drew development away from downtown. The most notable early development on Boulder Highway was the Meadows Club, an elegant casino that opened in 1931.

World War II military and industrial projects also fragmented valley development patterns. The Las Vegas Army Air Corps Gunnery School, which later became Nellis Air Force Base, drew development to the northeast and North Las Vegas, while a magnesium plant created the suburb of Henderson to the southeast. These large-scale projects, which drew thousands of soldiers and workers to the valley, did fuel construction of several subdivisions adjacent to downtown, but they also spurred residential and commercial development near the military base and industrial plant.

The improvement of the Los Angeles Highway (now Las Vegas Boulevard) was another major blow to downtown. The highway fueled resort development on a scale that downtown casino operators had never imagined. What eventually became known as the Strip started in 1941 with the opening of the El Rancho Vegas. A year later came the Last Frontier. These trailblazers were followed in 1946 by the Flamingo Hotel, which added a new level of sophistication to the Las Vegas resort experience.

One reason for the Strip's development: The properties fell outside the city limits. In the unincorporated county, taxes were lower and regulations looser. Seeing an alarming trend, city leaders tried to annex the Strip in 1946—without success. They tried again in 1950, failing once more to bring this burgeoning area into the municipal fold. The Strip casinos rebuffed the city's attempt by lobbying for the creation of Paradise Township, which could not be annexed without County Commission approval. It stands to reason that if city officials had been successful at that time, they could have done more to ensure downtown remained the centerpiece of the valley's tourism efforts rather than ceding that distinction to the Strip.

It became clear during the fast-growing '50s that the Strip was where the action was and would be for years to come. Several key decisions cemented downtown's fate. The first was the location of what would become McCarran International Airport. The valley's first commercial air service was offered at the Army's air field, but increased military operations in the late '40s forced civic leaders to find a new place for commercial airplanes. They chose a location near the south end of the Strip rather than one more favorable to downtown. McCarran Field opened in 1948 with twelve flights per day.

In 1959, another political decision favored the Strip when the convention center opened on Paradise Road, just east of the Strip. Eugene Moehring, author of *Resort City in the Sunbelt*, summarized the effect of this decision: "This location behind the Thunderbird awarded the Strip hotels a valuable advantage over their downtown counterparts. As larger conventions came to Las Vegas in the '60s and '70s, conventioneers invariably booked rooms in the nearby hotels, and confined their casino play to the Strip. As a result, the area's surging convention business helped boost the expansion of Strip hotel facilities compared to those along the less strategically located streets downtown."

The emergence of Maryland Parkway in the late '50s and '60s as a hub of local activity further diminished downtown's prominence. The first building at the University of Nevada, Las Vegas, campus, dictated by a large land donation at the south end of Maryland Parkway, opened in 1957. Sunrise Hospital, built by Mervin Adelson, Irwin Molasky and Moe Dalitz's Paradise Development Company, opened in 1959. The Boulevard Mall, another Paradise Development project, opened in 1967. Molasky said he took advantage of what he saw as the "logical growth area" for Las Vegas. His company essentially master-planned Maryland Parkway, building shopping centers and then residential neighborhoods to support them. "We were selling a house a day over there," he said of the Paradise Palms subdivision east of Maryland. In theory, the downtown area would have been a logical location for important developments such as the hospital and the mall, but Molasky said politics were a problem at that time within the city limits. "The main thing is that downtown was stagnant," he said. "They didn't put money back into it. They kept the old houses down there. They played a lot of politics in those days. They just wanted to keep the status quo."

These specific projects are only part of the story. A look at the bigger picture suggests some general trends that supersede individual developments. Cheap land as far as the eye could see was a major factor. First, the farther the land was from the city center, the more cheaply it could be obtained. As long as builders had access to utilities, they could enhance the bottom line. Second, the vast stretches of undeveloped land encouraged low-rise, low-density construction. Buildings tended to be one story and spread out. The desire to build in this manner deterred developers from investing in downtown, where lots were small and numerous and complicated ownerships made it difficult and expensive to assemble large parcels. Also, Las Vegas prided itself on a laissez-faire approach to urban planning, which allowed for chaotic, checkerboard development. A stronger commitment to proper land planning may have dictated a more sensible city expansion that would have required large commercial and civic developments to be sited downtown.

## Redevelopment

Downtown Las Vegas still exists, of course, and it continues to attract tourists and locals in large numbers—just not on the massive scale enjoyed by the Strip. Vigorous efforts to redevelop the area around Fremont and Main have proved successful in recent years, and optimism about the future is running high. Besides the casino row, downtown remains the valley's government and legal hub, hosting Las Vegas City Hall, the Clark County Government Center, the Sawyer State Office Building, the Clark County Detention Center and all the local, state and federal courts.

But downtown advocates weren't always so bright and cheery. In the late '80s, downtown appeared to be in deep trouble. The opening of the Mirage Hotel on the Strip in 1989 seemed to signal downtown's imminent demise, at least as a gambling center. The Strip, following the lead of Steve Wynn, had emerged from the doldrums of the '80s with a strong desire to reinvent itself and expand its markets. As the Strip offered a greater variety of attractions, tourists were less likely to visit downtown during their vacations.

*Sun, Sin & Suburbia: The History of Modern Las Vegas*

Meanwhile, the concept of the neighborhood casino began to take hold in a big way. At the time, a large chunk of downtown's customer base was local. When hotel-casinos with buffets, bowling alleys and movie theaters began cropping up in suburban neighborhoods, locals drifted away from downtown haunts in favor of the gambling hall just down the street. The rise of riverboat casinos and Indian reservation casinos in other states further gouged downtown's market share.

Something had to be done to stop the bleeding. The city's first effort began in 1987 when officials approached Bob Snow, a Florida developer, about building a new downtown resort. They enticed him by agreeing to contribute $17 million in taxpayer funds to the project. Two years later Snow purchased the money-losing Park Hotel, on Main Street east of Fremont, and built what he eventually named Main Street Station (the project started as Winchester Station and later was called Church Street Station, the same name as his Orlando facility). Snow's $82 million casino was a step up in luxury compared with most of its downtown competitors. A Victorian theme was carried throughout, and Main Street Station featured elegant appointments such as hardwood floors, stained glass and an expensive antique collection.

But Main Street Station's beauty did not translate into customers. It was a failure almost as soon as it opened on August 30, 1991. Just a month after its grand opening, Main Street Station laid off 150 employees, while dozens of building contractors filed liens against the property. Snow declared Chapter 11 bankruptcy in December 1991, and 200 more employees were laid off a month later. In April 1992 Bank of America announced plans to auction Snow's thousands of antiques, which he had used as collateral for his casino loan. Main Street Station closed in June 1992.

Why did Main Street Station fail? With costly construction overruns, marketers had only $140,000 available to promote the resort's opening, a pittance compared with the investment in other casino openings. Some executives and observers blamed Snow himself, citing his perfectionist approach and his refusal to listen to the advice of seasoned casino operators. Others noted that the resort's 430 rooms were old and nondescript, remnants from the Park Hotel rather than fresh and elegant like the casino. But the primary reason cited was Main Street Station's off-the-beaten-path location, which downtown interests had forced Snow to accept. Snow said at the time that he would have been better off building at his initial downtown location at Ogden Avenue and Fourth Street, but that site might have faced similar problems.

The public consensus was that the city had made a huge mistake by investing $17 million of taxpayer funds in the casino venture. Disgruntled downtown casino operators filed a lawsuit to try to stop the expenditure, arguing that it was unfair to them. They lost the legal battle but their cause was just. A *Las Vegas Sun* editorial published a few days before Main Street Station closed summed up the sentiment:

"The ten-month-old casino is almost a textbook case in how not to spend public money. It took seemingly endless infusions of cash and donations of real estate and—believe it or not, public money to purchase antiques—to get the casino opened. Four months later, it went bankrupt. … Main Street is not the way to use redevelopment funds. You don't rejuvenate a neighborhood by competing with existing businesses across the street. The funds should infuse activities to improve the business climate."

To their credit, city officials learned from their mistake. The next redevelopment effort would be successful, largely because it was a cooperative project aimed at improving the bottom line for everybody. Casino owners came together with city leaders to dream up a better idea. "Our mantra was, 'We need our own volcano,'" recalled Mark Brandenburg, owner of the Golden Gate hotel-casino, referring to the street-side attraction that draws tourists to the Mirage. "Casino owners who had historically been fierce competitors decided they needed to get together and collaborate to build our own volcano."

They hired design companies and evaluated a series of creative proposals. One early contender was "Las Venice," a network of canals along downtown thoroughfares on which tourists could enjoy a leisurely boat ride. Another idea that gained some momentum was a full-size replica of the Starship Enterprise—twenty-three stories tall and 600 feet long, with a ride, restaurants and convention facilities. "That was taken seriously," Brandenburg recalled. "Seriously enough that one of our board members and our mayor went to Paramount Studios to have a conversation about it."

Unsatisfied with the ideas on the table, Wynn, owner of the Golden Nugget, invited design guru Jon Jerde into the discussion. Soon the brains behind Horton Plaza in San Diego came up with the idea of putting a canopy over five blocks of Fremont Street and offering a dazzling light show overhead. The street would be closed to automobile traffic, creating a pedestrian mall—in essence, a foyer for the casinos. Fremont Street had found its volcano.

The $70 million Fremont Street Experience, funded with public and private dollars, debuted in 1995, and it immediately put downtown back on the map. The light show brought visitors downtown, but that was just one part of the project. Perhaps more important, Fremont Street was freshened up. Although controversial in some circles, police officers and private security were ever present on the quasi-public street to shoo away panhandlers and enforce regulations. Downtown redevelopers set up commercial kiosks to add variety to the street and scheduled public events to attract customers.

It is not far-fetched to argue that the Fremont Street Experience saved the Glitter Gulch casinos. Former Las Vegas Mayor Jan Jones, an aggressive advocate of downtown redevelopment in the '90s, said if the attraction had not been built, "Fremont Street would have died a slow, painful death. People were looking to move out. Downtown would have died. It would have been over. It would have become a seedy, challenged area." Brandenburg agreed: "I don't think anybody who's been in business downtown would tell you that we would still be here today if it weren't for the Fremont Street Experience." Bill Boyd, CEO of the Boyd Gaming Group, owner of the Fremont and California hotel-casinos downtown, said his properties did well even during difficult times, but he agreed that without the Fremont Street Experience, some casinos might have closed. "We turned it around with the Fremont Street Experience," Boyd said.

Even Main Street Station enjoyed a revival. Boyd Gaming bought the moribund property for $16.5 million in 1993. It built a pedestrian bridge connecting it to the California and combined its marketing, reservations, accounting and payroll functions with its other downtown resorts. Boyd benefited from the extra rooms for its sturdy customer base of Hawaiian tourists, while the casino's Triple 7 Brewpub became a popular lunch spot for downtown executives.

Brandenburg noted that most people don't realize what an amazing accomplishment the Fremont Street Experience was. "Few understand or appreciate the difficulty of getting a number of different competing businesses together. We had to function by committee, and then work with the city in a public-private partnership. To me this should be a case study for business schools." Brandenburg said the competitors were able to come together because they all saw the writing on the wall. "They all bit their tongues at the appropriate times and decided they needed to compromise because they knew if they didn't build this, they would dry up and blow away."

Sadly, Fremont Street's rising redevelopment batting average suffered at the dawn of the new century due to another less-than-successful project: Neonopolis. The $100 million movie theater, shopping and dining complex at Fremont and Las Vegas Boulevard was intended to be downtown's answer to the Strip's increasing variety of amenities beyond the casino floor. But much like Main Street Station, Neonopolis sputtered out of the gate. The three-story structure opened with less than half its shop and restaurant space occupied, and after a few months some of its more promising shops pulled out. Restaurants on the ground floor within sight of Fremont Street drew decent traffic, but the complex's inward-looking design failed to attract large numbers of curious Fremont Street pedestrians. Some locals who supported Neonopolis's restaurants and movie theater were turned off a few months after the opening when the city imposed a fee to park in the taxpayer-funded garage.

Meanwhile, it became increasingly obvious that the Fremont Street Experience light show needed an overhaul. Technological progress had shot past the millions of light bulbs that created the streaking jets and patriotic shows appearing on the canopy. In 2003, the casino operators invested $17 million to upgrade the light show so that high-resolution, television-like images could be displayed overhead. The new-generation attraction, which debuted in the summer of 2004, lured tourists and locals alike to eagerly crane their necks to watch light shows unfold as if they were being projected on the heavens.

## Beyond Fremont Street

Downtown redevelopment first focused on ensuring that the Fremont Street casinos were on a solid financial footing. But the larger goal of city officials all along has been to revitalize the wider downtown area. The sprawling, suburban metropolitan area needed a true downtown, advocates believed, a place where young professionals and creative people could congregate and live more urban—and urbane—lives.

In discussing the downtown of today, it's important to define what we're talking about. Everybody has a different idea of what constitutes downtown. We all can agree that Fremont Street—"Glitter Gulch"—is downtown. Most agree that downtown incorporates the grid of streets (including Fremont) that the railroad first platted when it started selling lots in 1905. Beyond that narrow definition, however, people are likely to have divergent opinions on downtown's boundaries.

The most logical and beneficial definition is broad, encompassing a vast swath of older areas of the city built mostly but not entirely before 1950. Downtown includes the old Las Vegas High School neighborhood, east of Las Vegas Boulevard between Charleston Boulevard on the south and Bonanza Road on the north; the John S. Park and Huntridge neighborhoods, south of Charleston and east of Las Vegas Boulevard to Maryland Parkway; West Las Vegas, the once-redlined and segregated black part of town north of Bonanza and west of Interstate 15; the affluent Scotch 80s and McNeil Estates neighborhoods west of I-15 and south of Charleston; Rancho Circle and Rancho Bel Air, the exclusive gated communities on Rancho north of Alta Drive; the cultural corridor along Las Vegas Boulevard North, which includes the Las Vegas Library, Cashman Field Center, Reed Whipple Cultural Center, Neon Museum, Las Vegas Natural History Museum and Old Mormon Fort State Park; the so-called homeless corridor along North Main Street, where Catholic Charities, Salvation Army, Shade Tree and other social service agencies are based; and last but not least, Symphony Park, the former Union Pacific rail yard west of Main Street where the Clark County Government Center, Smith Center for the Performing Arts and Las Vegas Premium Outlet Mall are located. In short, downtown is not strictly a geographic question. It is an idea and a way of life. Living, working and recreating downtown are different experiences than in the suburbs.

Redeveloping downtown beyond Fremont Street has been an agonizingly slow process. Thankfully, a string of relatively small successes has commanded patience and fueled optimism. Major coups for downtown have come in the form of government projects that, in bleaker times, might have been inclined to flee to the suburbs. These include the Clark County Government Center, the Lloyd D. George Federal Court Building on Las Vegas Boulevard at Lewis Avenue, the new Las Vegas City Hall and the massive Clark County Regional Justice Center. Construction flaws and cost overruns plagued the latter project, but once it finally opened for business in 2005, it cemented downtown's status as the hub of legal affairs in Southern Nevada.

Redevelopment has two basic components: 1) the preservation, rehabilitation and repurposing of historic structures and 2) new development. Efforts to preserve historic neighborhoods and buildings have met with mixed success. The city created its Historic Preservation Commission in 1991, and it has been an aggressive advocate. But it wins some and loses some. The city tried unsuccessfully to create a historic preservation district in the old Las Vegas High neighborhood, east of Las Vegas Boulevard. The neighborhood once was home to the city's upper middle class, and many homes are significant examples of early and mid-twentieth century architectural styles. But over the years many houses in the neighborhood have been converted to offices, particularly law firms, and some business-minded owners are not keen on the building restrictions that come with historic preservation guidelines. As a result, the City Council has declined to approve some historic designations. Some structures within the neighborhood, particularly the art deco high school built in 1929, are listed on historic registers, but the neighborhood's character is at risk of being lost to progress. A campaign to preserve the John S. Park neighborhood, south of Charleston and east of Las Vegas Boulevard, proved more successful. Over the objections of just a couple of property owners, the City Council approved adding a layer of historic protection to the neighborhood. That designation paid off handsomely for John S.

Park residents, who saw their property values increase and young families buy homes in the neighborhood.

Another successful case of historic preservation was the city's move in 2002 to obtain title to the old federal building at 300 Stewart Avenue. Built in 1933, the building once hosted the federal courts and the city's main post office. The 1950 Kefauver hearings, probing mob involvement in the gambling business, were held there. After a sluggish start, the city finally transformed the neo-classical structure into a museum focusing on the history of organized crime in America. An early plan had envisioned a modest local museum opening there in 2005. A more ambitious plan later emerged, and the Mob Museum opened in 2012.

For every preservation victory there seems to be a defeat, and perhaps the saddest example is the steady loss of a subdivision of sixty-four cottages the railroad built for its workers from 1909-1911. While one cottage has been relocated to the Clark County Museum in Henderson to be put on permanent display, only a handful remain on their original lots today, and the prospects are dim that they will be there much longer. Downtown's economic revival has made the land beneath the cottages desirable to those who would build law offices and business plazas.

The city also enjoyed no success preserving the Moulin Rouge hotel-casino. When the Moulin Rouge opened in 1955 on Bonanza Road, it was the first resort in Las Vegas to serve both white and black customers. The Moulin Rouge was a popular nightspot, its showroom featuring an array of top-shelf African-American entertainers, and their performances attracted big-name celebrities, black and white. Thanks to its bold attempt to buck racist policies in Las Vegas, the Moulin Rouge appeared on the cover of *Life* magazine.

The Moulin Rouge had a brief heyday, however. It was open just six months before closing its doors under mysterious circumstances. To this day, speculation runs rampant as to why the resort was shuttered, some suggesting its finances were poorly managed, others ominously citing pressure from segregation-minded casino owners. In any case, it earned a treasured place in Las Vegas history, one worthy of preservation. Parts of the property opened and closed under various owners during the ensuing decades, but it never reached its early potential. In more recent years, its motel rooms were rented as apartments. Historic elements of the resort, such as its signage, showroom and mural-backed bar, remained intact, though, and efforts to preserve them continued for years. In early 2003, a promising group of entrepreneurs announced plans to protect the historic elements and open a museum while building a modern new resort on the fifteen-acre property. A damaging fire in May of that year posed a setback, but the development group vowed in 2004 to proceed with its plans. Another fire in 2009 finally ended hopes of reviving the Moulin Rouge. Today, the resort's iconic sign is all that remains, preserved in the Neon Museum.

### Sixty-one acres

Of course, these and other projects are fairly small potatoes compared with the big daddy of downtown redevelopment, once known as "Oscar's sixty-one acres." Well-known attorney Oscar Goodman succeeded Jan Jones as mayor in 1999, and he made downtown redevelopment his top priority. About a year later, he executed a land trade that brought the vacant sixty-one-acre parcel west of the Plaza Hotel under the city's control. The city traded seventy-one acres in the Las Vegas Technology Center in the northwest valley to Lehman Brothers for the downtown parcel, which had been the longtime site of the Union Pacific rail yard. Goodman quickly dubbed the site the "jewel of the desert," and said its development would be the key to downtown revival.

In 2001, the city sought to hire a "master developer" for the sixty-one acres. This company, following city criteria, would spearhead development of the site. Four candidates came before the council, and each presented a detailed proposal for the acreage. One plan focused on an academic medical center, while another proposed television and movie studios. The council selected Southwest Sports Group, a Dallas company that proposed a minor-league baseball stadium as the parcel's centerpiece. Goodman said he voted for the Dallas company because of its experience with similar projects but emphasized that his vote did not constitute support for a minor-league stadium. This put the city in an odd position, because Southwest Sports Group was not ready to budge on the stadium issue.

Originally, Goodman, a sports fan, pitched the idea of building a professional sports stadium on the site, but efforts to attract a major-league franchise to gambling-centric Las Vegas did not pan out. (League officials weren't interested in bringing a team to Las Vegas while sports bets were being taken down the street. Goodman asked the casinos if they would stop taking bets on certain sports or local teams but they declined.) Goodman opposed building a minor-league baseball stadium on the site, insisting that Las Vegas is a "major-league city." As a result, the city and Southwest Sports Group eventually parted ways, and city officials took over the master developer role for the sixty-one acres, hiring consultants to help with the detail work.

The city soon settled on three key components: an academic medical center, a performing arts center and an urban village. Goodman traveled to Cleveland, Ohio, home of the respected Cleveland Clinic, to persuade executives to build a medical research facility on the sixty-one acres. The city and clinic jointly invested several hundred thousand dollars to study the feasibility of such a venture. The Cleveland Clinic later balked at the proposal, but its withdrawal did not squelch plans for a medical center on the site. At the same time, the city set aside a small piece of the property for a performing arts center. Las Vegas was one of the largest cities in America without such a stand-alone venue to host Broadway productions, large concerts and other cultural events. In 2003, a car rental tax increase was authorized to help raise money for the venture. Former Mayor Jan Jones believed the performing arts center would be an important anchor for downtown. "It's a good location—equidistant from all parts of the valley," she noted. The third element of the plan was a pedestrian-friendly urban village, with high-rise condos at its core.

While the city moved toward developing the sixty-one acres, other projects cropped up around it, most notably the Las Vegas Premium Outlets, an upscale open-air mall developed by Chelsea Property Group. The $95 million mall opened in the summer of 2003 and instantly drew crowds of locals and tourists alike by offering discounts on the hottest brands. Also, the World Market Center, a giant home furnishings convention venue, enjoyed a promising start, drawing thousands of industry decision-makers for several big shows each year. The center added a second building in 2007 and a third in 2008, creating a complex of showrooms totaling five million square feet. Finally, the Molasky Corporate Center, an energy-efficient, sixteen-story office building, opened in 2007. It houses, among other tenants, the the Southern Nevada Water Authority.

## Smith Center for the Performing Arts

After several fits and false starts, the city's plans for the sixty-one acres finally evolved into a project called Symphony Park. As before, the centerpiece would be a performing arts center, filling a gaping hole in the Las Vegas cultural scene. Although Las Vegas obviously had no shortage of entertainment venues in its hotel-casinos, it was the largest city in America without a stand-alone performing arts center.

Civic efforts to build such a facility started taking shape as far back as the mid-'90s. At one point, plans called for it to be built in the suburban enclave of Summerlin. For a time, two separate projects were envisioned. But a performing arts center didn't build any momentum until city leaders invited advocates to locate it on a choice five-acre parcel in Symphony Park. The city added bonds from its redevelopment fund, and a two percent tax on car rentals was levied in 2005 to help fund the project. The project's prospects were solidified that same year by a massive donation from the Donald W. Reynolds Foundation, headed by longtime newspaper executive Fred Smith. Smith initially committed $50 million to the center, and two years later gave $100 million more. Altogether, the contribution equaled almost one-third of the project's $470 million price tag. But the Reynolds Foundation was far from the only private contributor: Fifty-seven people gave $1 million or more to the project.

Ground was broken in May 2009, and the construction project generated 3,500 jobs at a time when they were sorely needed in Las Vegas. In fact, during the depths of the recession, the Smith Center was one of the only large construction projects in Las Vegas.

The Smith Center opened on March 10, 2012, with a black-tie spectacle featuring an array of major-league talent on stage and the cream of Las Vegas dignitaries in the audience. Hosted by television star Neil Patrick Harris, the event included performances by pop divas Carole King and Jennifer Hudson, country legends Willie Nelson, Merle Haggard and Martina McBride, classic rocker John Fogerty, violinist Joshua Bell and several Broadway and dance performances. The show went on for three hours, brilliantly reflecting the vast range of talent destined to play the new venue.

Indeed, the Smith Center immediately introduced a much-needed dose of diversity to the Las Vegas entertainment scene that the casinos never would be motivated to provide. The facility offers two primary venues, the 2,050-seat Reynolds Hall, which features touring Broadway productions and other high-profile performers, and Cabaret Jazz, a 260-seat theater offering a more intimate environment for live music. The center is home base for the Las Vegas Philharmonic and Nevada Ballet Theatre.

Another key component is the Smith Center's focus on arts education. Among other endeavors, it has a partnership with the Kennedy School for the Performing Arts to increase arts education in the community, and local philanthropist Elaine Wynn, ex-wife of casino owner Steve Wynn, donated $5 million to create the Elaine Wynn Studio for Arts Education.

Renowned architect David M. Schwarz designed the Smith Center, and his elegant and sophisticated design has drawn raves. When the facility opened, Steve Bornfeld of the *Las Vegas Review-Journal* praised its "art deco/Hoover Dam-inspired exterior" and said the building "visually lifts downtown Las Vegas onto its shoulders and carries it forward." Bornfeld highlighted the center's Carillon Tower: "Climbing seventeen stories into the downtown sky, it is the center's capstone, housing a four-octave carillon of forty-seven hand-crafted bronze bells—nearly 30,000 pounds of them—that will ring with a promise a cultural nexus brings a city."

But Bornfeld reserved even more enthusiasm for the performance spaces inside. Reynolds Hall, he wrote, is a "symphony of elegance in brown and beige. Contradictory as it sounds, the horseshoe-shaped venue marries immensity to intimacy, creating a cozy colossus inspired by centers from New York's Carnegie Hall to Milan, Italy's La Scala." The stage, he said, is "wide, deep and dramatic," while the orchestra pit can hold "a hearty ninety-eight musicians."

The two-level Cabaret Jazz, meanwhile, is the Smith Center's ode to intimacy. "U-shaped and radiating warmth, it is an intriguing layout in that the upper level, creating a double-decker viewing area, lends it a sense of mini-grandeur rare for most jazz outposts," Bornfeld wrote. "Atmosphere can match artistry here."

As much as anyone, two men are responsible for the Smith Center's completion and success: Don Snyder and Myron Martin. Snyder, a former bank and casino executive, chaired the Smith Center board, while Martin, who had managed UNLV's Performing Arts Center, served as chief executive.

Snyder's first exposure to the performing arts center idea came in the mid-'90s when he attended a meeting of community leaders called by casino owner Steve Wynn. In an interview with Steve Green of *Vegas Inc* in 2011, Snyder recalled: "Steve Wynn stood up and said we were the largest community in North America that doesn't have its own performing arts center. 'We need to change that,' he said." Snyder agreed to become a member of the original board of directors. He recalled that a consultant brought in to work with the board said it could take twenty years to get the project done. Snyder and others scoffed. "It doesn't take us twenty years to do anything in Las Vegas. In fact, we can build buildings and tear those buildings down in a twenty-year period." But Snyder soon realized a civic project of this nature does tend to take longer than a strictly commercial endeavor. Snyder stuck it out, and he led the efforts to secure huge commitments of public and private dollars. His connections in the business community and his insistence that the project be run like a business both contributed to its success. Ninety percent of the funding was in place before construction began, which is highly unusual for such a project.

As for Martin, he spearheaded the project with a constant focus on enthusiastically educating whoever would listen about the Smith Center's cultural importance. Martin's vision for bringing a vast range of artistic performance to Las Vegas—far beyond what any Strip resort would consider—helped to build support from donors and average citizens alike.

It is no exaggeration to say the Smith Center is one of the great achievements in Las Vegas history. Not only was it completed during a devastating

*Sun, Sin & Suburbia: The History of Modern Las Vegas*

economic period, but no corners were cut in the process. The quality, scope and vision that infuse its design and execution give Las Vegas a performing arts center that is among the world's finest. It was accomplished not by one person with a vision and a checkbook—the typical Las Vegas narrative—but through a true community effort. What's more, the Smith Center likely will drive further economic development in downtown Las Vegas, just as such centers have done in other communities. Snyder, who has seen some pretty amazing things during his several decades in Las Vegas, compared the Smith Center with Hoover Dam in terms of its far-reaching impact. "Other than Hoover Dam, I don't know of any project that has touched the community as broadly and deeply as this one will," he said.

While the comparison to Hoover Dam might be a tad dramatic, it seemed a sure bet that the Smith Center would accelerate the downtown renaissance. Bornfeld: "Like a large stone splashing into a still pond, its effects will ripple outward toward the rest of Las Vegas."

## Lou Ruvo Center for Brain Health

Next door to the Smith Center is the most intriguing work of architecture in Las Vegas. The Lou Ruvo Center for Brain Health, which opened in 2009, was designed by famed Los Angeles architect Frank Gehry. Gehry is as controversial as he is admired. To those who see buildings purely as functional spaces for living and working, Gehry's unorthodox designs may be strange, perhaps even offensive, to their tastes. The public's reaction to the $80 million Ruvo Center was no exception. The twisted metal facade, made up of 18,000 individually cut stainless-steel panels, was celebrated by those eager to see something creative and different amid the banality of so much Las Vegas design. But more practical-minded Las Vegans thought it was weird and unnecessary.

Regardless of the building's appearance, what was happening inside met with universal approval. The study and treatment of Alzheimer's, Parkinson's, Huntington's and Lou Gehrig's diseases held the promise of prevention and cures for some of the most horrifying maladies of the modern age. Operated by the respected Cleveland Clinic, the center is the brainchild of Las Vegas businessman Larry Ruvo, who named the center for his father, who suffered from Alzheimer's.

In 2012, *Review-Journal* reporter Paul Harasim reported on the Ruvo Center's research, noting that it was "carrying out more clinical trials of drugs to use against Alzheimer's and other neurocognitive diseases, twenty, than any other center in the country." The center had earned an international reputation and attracted respected researchers, from its director, Dr. Jeffrey Cummings, to Nobel Prize laureate Dr. Stanley Pusher, who chaired the center's scientific advisory board.

Credit for the Ruvo Center's success, however, was attributed to the passion of its founder, Larry Ruvo, who was motivated by his family's trying experiences when his father began suffering from the disease. Harasim explained: "It took nearly eighteen months of doctor visits and misdiagnoses in Las Vegas during the 1990s before Ruvo's father, Lou, was diagnosed with Alzheimer's in California. And as Angie Ruvo, Lou Ruvo's wife and caregiver, struggled to care for him, she ruptured disks in her back, forcing her to have surgery that has left her barely able to walk." As a result, Larry Ruvo has guided the center to focus more time and energy on the caregivers and families of Alzheimer's patients, not just laboratory work.

The Lou Ruvo Center for Brain Health holds out the enticing prospect that Las Vegas could become known for something far more meaningful to humanity than fun and games.

## Mob Museum

What kind of museum would you go to in Las Vegas? For better or worse, people don't visit Las Vegas to contemplate modern art. The Guggenheim gave that a good try at the Venetian and it didn't fly. And tourists aren't all that interested in scholarly exhibits documenting the region's dusty origins. They're looking for something with a little more flavor.

Enter the Great Idea: a museum about the mob. Who isn't fascinated by the mob?

The idea was championed by Las Vegas Mayor Oscar Goodman, who, back in his days as a legal eagle, defended mobsters in many high-profile cases.

He, as well as anyone, understood the public's insatiable interest in organized crime.

When the city of Las Vegas took possession of the historic three-story federal building at 300 Stewart Avenue, officials knew they wanted to turn it into a museum. At first, it was going to be a museum about Las Vegas history. But the project poked along until Goodman and others conceived the ingenious plan to focus on organized crime's central role in the city's history. That got people's attention.

Of course, not all the attention was positive. Some thought the idea was crazy. Others complained that the mob should not be glorified by museum treatment. Goodman quickly responded that the mob would not be celebrated: "The bottom line is—and nobody knows this better than I do—law enforcement won. The mob is not here, and that's one of the reasons I became the mayor. I didn't have any clients left."

As the project developed, its scope expanded in two ways. First, rather than focus solely on the mob's role in Las Vegas, museum designers decided to cover the mob's history across the country. Second, the museum's secondary name, the National Museum of Organized Crime and Law Enforcement, signaled that it wouldn't just be an ode to the bad guys.

In addition, the project was given a shot of credibility when Dennis Barrie was named creative director. Barrie played prominent roles in the creation of the International Spy Museum in Washington, D.C., and the Rock and Roll Hall of Fame in Cleveland. In each case, Barrie successfully delivered the sizzle with the steak—exhibits appealing to a popular audience that retain their historical accuracy and objectivity.

The $42 million museum, funded by a stew of federal, state and city dollars, opened on February 14, 2012—the eighty-third anniversary of Chicago's St. Valentine's Day Massacre, a famously horrific episode in mob history. Visitors were introduced to an interactive and multimedia experience, with touch screens and video presentations to go with more traditional exhibits. One exhibit explained how money was skimmed from the casinos, while another surveyed how Hollywood has portrayed the mob.

Reactions to the museum were generally positive.

"The museum mixes attraction and repulsion, sentimentality and hard-edged realism, relish and disgust," wrote *New York Times* critic Edward Rothstein. "Like a gangster movie, it seduces us with these figures on the one hand, and with the other reminds us of the demands of justice." Rothstein noted that the "emphasis is ultimately placed not on the mysterious appeal of the mob but on the fight against it. The museum's heart is a splendidly restored courtroom where the Senate's Special Committee to Investigate Organized Crime in Interstate Commerce held its seventh hearing in 1950."

John L. Smith, *Las Vegas Review-Journal* columnist and author of several books about organized crime figures, spotted a few actual mobsters, presumably retired, at the museum's grand opening. Although Smith refrained from critiquing the various exhibits, he stressed that most of the tax dollars poured into the project were used to preserve a historic building. "Instead of standing empty or crumbling into ruins, it sparkles with a new purpose and can't help but increase the vitality of the downtown economy," he wrote.

In a column for *Vegas Seven* magazine, Las Vegas historian Michael Green, who consulted in the museum's development, staunchly defended its cultural value: "Few outsiders and too few insiders even try to understand Las Vegas in depth. But if tourists and locals visit this museum, they will see Las Vegas acknowledging and analyzing the good and bad of its past, and how that past connects to other places and developments. Then they might even want to learn more than the museum can tell them."

## Neon Museum

Another major accomplishment in 2012 was the long-awaited opening of the Neon Museum on Las Vegas Boulevard North. A "boneyard" of dozens of old neon signs had resided since the mid-'90s on the site a few blocks north of Fremont Street, serving as a popular backdrop for photographers and film-makers. But advocates wanted to transform the dirt lot full of metal and glass into a more cohesive environment to present the storied history of a form of illuminated signage synonymous with Las Vegas.

The turning point for the project came in 2005 when news surfaced that the La Concha Motel on the Strip was going to be torn down. Preservation-minded citizens realized the motel's 1950s Googie-style lobby would be perfect to serve as the visitors center for the Neon Museum. A $300,000 grant from the Las Vegas Convention and Visitors Authority helped to move the lobby to the neon boneyard site.

Another aspect of the Neon Museum: the nine refurbished signs on display in the downtown area. Highlights include the Hacienda Horse and Rider sign, originally installed at the Hacienda Hotel in 1967, and Aladdin's Lamp, originally built for the Aladdin Hotel in 1966.

## Fremont East

It seemed like Fremont East happened overnight. For decades, there was East Fremont Street, the couple of blocks of sketchy retail businesses east of Las Vegas Boulevard—just beyond the clutches of the orderly and carefully managed Fremont Street Experience pedestrian mall. Tourists, most of them not knowing what they were getting into, ventured into East Fremont, curious about what lay beyond the casino canopy. But rarely did they return with much except maybe a tattoo, a cheap pair of sunglasses or a candy bar from the 7-Eleven convenience store. Then, rather suddenly, East Fremont stepped into a phone booth and emerged as Fremont East, an up-and-coming entertainment district catering to local hipsters pining for a place to call their own.

It didn't really happen overnight, of course. In 2002, the city identified East Fremont as a good place to foster a district full of bars, restaurants and clubs that didn't rely on gambling to pay the bills. The city's plan, which included an extensive renovation of the streetscape, germinated for a while before local entrepreneurs decided to take a chance that the concept would catch fire. One of the major pioneers was the arrival in 2004 of the Beauty Bar, a popular chain that features live music. The Las Vegas Beauty Bar, which holds its shows in an open-air patio behind the bar, is often packed for perfomances by the hottest indie rock bands.

The "bohemian chic" Downtown Cocktail Room, owned by Michael and Jennifer Cornthwaite, opened in 2007 and proved to be a popular after-work and weekend hangout for young professionals. The bar's website describes the desired attire for its customers: "As an individual, not a bum, a cheesy tourist or a want-to-be rock star."

Perhaps the biggest step forward for Fremont East was the opening of Emergency Arts, a two-story warren of small businesses, art studios and nonprofits—a "creative collective" —in a former medical building. The Beat, a coffeehouse fronting Emergency Arts, soon became a gathering place for downtown's growing cadre of advocates and fans.

Another major contributor to the Fremont East vibe was the remodeled and rebranded El Cortez hotel-casino. One of the oldest continuously operating casinos in Las Vegas, once part-owned by Bugsy Siegel, the El Cortez underwent a radical reinvention to complement Fremont East.

Other businesses followed those leaders, and Fremont East became a popular destination for locals and tourists seeking a more urban, organic experience. Although Fremont East was gentrifying, it still had to deal with the realities of its former identity, as homeless people, drug addicts and assorted troublemakers in the surrounding streets continued to filter through. But by and large, the city's original vision for the area came into being.

## Living downtown

While these individual projects were important for a sustainable downtown revival, there was something equally vital: housing. It's common sense. As it stands, tens of thousands of people work downtown each day, then get in their cars and head home to the suburbs at night—and for the most part stay out there on weekends. If downtown businesses are going to thrive, they need bodies coming through the door—and not just from nine to five weekdays. That's where housing comes in.

The downtown housing stock is sparse and aging. It consists largely of low-rent apartments, daily/weekly motels, public housing complexes and older neighborhoods of questionable quality and safety. Pockets of affluence, such as Rancho Circle, the Scotch 80s and McNeil Estates west of Interstate 15, are the exception. Some neighborhoods have been troubled but are showing signs of progress, such as John S. Park and Huntridge south of Charleston Boulevard. One big problem is the shortage of housing in the middle ground between low and high. You can live either in a dilapidated apartment complex full of desperadoes or a million-dollar ranch house in a guard-gated community.

By contrast, housing in the suburbs covers all economic strata and provides a variety of styles and locations. During the 1990s and early 2000s—before the real estate collapse—Las Vegans enjoyed few things more than buying a house before it was built, choosing the lot, the number of bedrooms and the carpet color, then watching as it was constructed and complaining to the contractor about the things that weren't done right. Downtown does not offer that possibility. What appeals to a relatively small segment of the population, however, is the chance to buy a promising fixer-upper at a good price and then renovate it, increasing its value in the process. This fairly common practice back East is slowly coming into vogue in Las Vegas, especially downtown. Homeowners in McNeil Estates, John S. Park and Huntridge, to name just three up-and-coming neighborhoods, are making improvements to complement their tall trees and mature landscaping.

Investing in a house downtown is not for everybody, of course. It tends to attract young people of a certain stripe: for example, those who do not intend to have children attending neighborhood schools anytime soon. A casual perusal of school district test scores and discipline records shows that the suburban schools far outdistance the aged inner-city campuses. It may sound haughty, but parents who might be interested in a downtown fixer-upper tend not to want to gamble on sending their impressionable youngsters to downtown schools. If they can afford private school, that might change the equation.

An added challenge is the threat of crime. Downtown's new settlers are a hearty bunch, because burglaries and other criminal activities are much more likely to occur downtown than in the suburbs. George Knapp, a veteran KLAS Channel 8 reporter and columnist for the *Las Vegas Mercury* and *CityLife* weekly newspapers, has detailed his frustrations with downtown crime. In a December 4, 2003, column, Knapp related that his centrally located house had just been burglarized, the sixth time that year that his property had been a victim of crime. "They entered in the wee hours, stole my wallet, credit cards and keys," he wrote. They also took his girlfriend's Chevy Suburban parked outside. This all occurred in near-silence as Knapp slept in the bedroom. "Some of my neighbors have gone to great trouble to put together a 'neighborhood plan,' a document that touts the impressive history of this 'hood and which states that it remains a great place to live," Knapp wrote. "I really wish I could believe that. I would like to believe the hype that the downtown area really is being invaded by upscale yuppies and well-heeled couples, and that better days are just around the corner. But the only thing around my corner seems to be punks and gangbangers, and I'm sick of it."

A few years after that column was published, Knapp moved to the outskirts of Las Vegas.

Knapp had worse luck than others. Many new downtown homeowners are vocal advocates of the lifestyle, touting how close they are to everything and that the houses all look different. They relish the historic significance of their homes and condemn the "soulless suburbs." At the same time, they are eager for further downtown redevelopment, as the area has a dearth of supermarkets and other basic ingredients of neighborhood existence. It's an ironic element of downtown life that you have to get in your car and drive well out of your neighborhood to buy ingredients for dinner.

With no space for single-family homes, the city has focused on building vertically rather than horizontally. The trend started with affordable new apartments, intiated in 2000 with the opening of Campaige Place, a 320-unit efficiency apartment complex at Stewart Avenue and Eighth Street developed by the Tom Hom Group of San Diego, California. The attractive and colorful complex, designed by noted architect Rob Wellington Quigley, stands in stark contrast to its rundown surroundings. It filled up quickly with downtown denizens eager for clean, fresh lodging and a degree of security. In 2003, the City Center Apartments opened at Bridger Avenue and Eighth Street. The four-story, 300-unit complex appeals to a slightly higher economic level than Campaige Place, offering everything from studios to two-bedroom apartments at market rates. Both complexes emphasize security, with access to the units and amenities restricted to residents and their guests.

Loft-style apartments represented the next wave of new housing. Aimed at drawing yuppies and creative types to the fledgling downtown arts district, three projects were announced in 2003: L'Octaine, a fifty-one-unit loft complex at Las Vegas Boulevard and Gass Avenue developed by the Tom Hom

*Sun, Sin & Suburbia: The History of Modern Las Vegas*

Group; the fifteen-story SoHo Lofts, 112 luxury apartments at Las Vegas Boulevard and Hoover Avenue developed by Sam Cherry and Harris Rittoff; and the Holsum Lofts, a conversion of a bakery. Developer Jeff LaPour transformed the fifty-three-year-old bakery on Charleston Boulevard just east of I-15 into ten live/work spaces above a large showroom and art gallery. LaPour highlighted the building's industrial character and retained the distinctive Holsum neon sign out front. While L'Octaine and SoHo took off, Holsum ultimately did not become a residential project. Instead, it is a retail center. Unfortunately, the conversion of Holsum is not likely to be repeated many times in downtown Las Vegas. Unlike other cities, where old commercial and industrial buildings are often renovated and repurposed, Las Vegas simply does not have many such buildings to convert.

## First Friday and the Arts District

Development is the driving force downtown, but another aspect of the area's revival is its growing identification with the arts. Talk of a downtown arts district dates to the early '90s, with hipsters flocking to the Enigma Café on Fourth Street for poetry readings and its eclectic menu. But the movement took off in 1997 with Wes Isbutt's opening of the Arts Factory. A commercial photographer by trade, Isbutt converted an old industrial building at Charleston and Main into a series of artist studios and galleries. The building eventually filled up with artists, photographers and architects eager for a creative and affordable place to work. But while the Arts Factory got the ball rolling, the Arts District gained its identity in 2002 with the creation of First Friday, a monthly open house for downtown culture venues. First Friday was the brainchild of Cindy Funkhouser, who owned an antique shop on Casino Center Boulevard, a few blocks from the Arts Factory. Funkhouser got the idea from a trip to Portland, Oregon, which holds a similar event called First Thursday. It didn't take long for the event to catch on locally, and soon hundreds of people were showing up each month to look at new art (and maybe buy some), listen to live music, eat at downtown restaurants and enjoy conversation with the gathered tribe of culture mavens. An array of downtown venues leapt at the chance to participate, partly out of idealistic support for the arts, partly in hopes of increasing business. The Arts District evolved mostly south of Charleston, where aging commercial buildings housing secondhand furniture stores and thrift shops could be affordably converted into studios and galleries.

Funkhouser's idea caught the attention of city officials, who had long wanted to nurture a downtown arts district. The city operated a trolley that transported people to dozens of venues hosting First Friday events. Showing his support, Mayor Oscar Goodman recited poetry at First Friday. The city worked with First Friday organizers to expand the event to include a street festival, complete with food vendors, live music and poetry tents. As the city became more involved in the monthly festivities, turnout increased, but those preferring a more organic experience grew wary of where things were headed.

In the summer of 2011, First Friday took its first-ever hiatus. During that two-month break, Funkhouser stepped away from the event she had created, citing rising expenses, and sold it for $50,000 to a new set of owners: four Zappos.com executives and a fifth investor. The new operators promised they would make First Friday bigger and better than ever. They immediately expanded marketing of the event, improved parking options and incorporated activities in the Fremont East entertainment district. Initial concerns—who are these people? what are they going to do to our event? is First Friday going corporate?—were alleviated to an extent by the new owners' devotion to the event's original purpose and the fresh ideas they introduced. One particularly innovative twist was to bring some of the ideas of the hugely popular Burning Man Festival, held each year in the remote Black Rock Desert of Northern Nevada, to the Las Vegas Arts District. In March 2012, First Friday's main attraction was Lucky Lady Lucy, a wooden effigy of a showgirl that was set aflame in a vacant lot amid a wild flurry of music and dance.

"We're all pretty stoked about a changing of ideas, a changing of perspective," Arts Factory owner Wes Myles (formerly Isbutt) said on Nevada Public Radio. "It's a fairly well known fact that things had gone a little awry in the past couple of years."

Progress in the Arts District has been frustratingly slow, often one step forward and two steps back. Which begs the question: Can Las Vegas build a vibrant arts district that compares with the more renowned arts enclaves across

*Sun, Sin & Suburbia: The History of Modern Las Vegas*

the country? Not likely. Las Vegas simply does not attract the large numbers of creative and educated people who make those places special. What's more, the constructed landscape does not offer the highly urbanized setting that has incubated such districts elsewhere. Still, the slow but persistent evolution of the Arts District, combined with the infusion of money and new ideas into First Friday, suggest sustained forward progress for a city once known for importing all of its culture.

## Glitter Gulch

Influential segments of the community believe a vibrant downtown is important, that Las Vegas will be a lesser place if it lacks an urban center full of trendy restaurants and bars, art galleries and, above all, warm bodies with more than crumpled drink coupons in their wallets. This movement is occurring largely outside the traditional downtown nucleus of Fremont Street, which, to many, is separate from the hipster/arts element that is slowly embracing downtown. But the fact remains that as Glitter Gulch goes, so goes downtown. Downtown is unlikely to survive in any desirable form without the casinos serving as the primary economic engine. The Fremont Street Experience seems to have ensured the survival of the downtown casinos. But it has not yet proved to be a catalyst for significant casino growth or expansion. With a few modest changes, the Fremont Street casinos cover basically the same footprint as they did ten years ago, and surprisingly similar to twenty years ago.

But if it hasn't grown per se, Glitter Gulch *has* changed. Just as the Strip is constantly reinventing itself, most of the downtown casinos are making improvements and trying new things.

In 2002, Don Barden of Detroit purchased Fitzgeralds, rescuing the casino from bankruptcy and becoming the first African-American to own a Las Vegas casino. Barden spent $2.5 million on improvements and emphasized cross-marketing opportunities with his Fitzgeralds properties in Tunica, Mississippi, Black Hawk, Colorado, and Gary, Indiana. When Barden died in 2011, his estate sold Fitzgeralds to fellow Detroiters Derek and Greg Stevens. The brothers soon announced they were changing the name of the hotel to The D Las Vegas, with the D representing downtown's revival, and investing

$15 million in improvements. Among them: a 100-foot outdoor bar and a one-way escalator to the casino's second floor.

MGM Mirage sold the Golden Nugget, downtown's largest and most luxurious resort, in 2004. The Poster Financial Group, headed by young dot-com millionaires Tim Poster and Tom Breitling, paid $215 million for the downtown property along with the Golden Nugget in Laughlin. The creators of Travelscape.com (they later sold the brand to Expedia.com) intended to use their Internet savvy to enhance their marketing efforts. Poster and Breitling's takeover of the Golden Nugget was documented by a television reality show, *The Casino*. The Nugget's new owners also hoped to capitalize on the star power of one of their local investment partners: tennis star Andre Agassi.

The youngish new owners expressed unbridled enthusiasm for downtown's future and intended to bring money and energy to the task of reviving the Golden Nugget. They definitely attracted attention, but their tenure at the resort was brief. In 2005, they sold it to Landry's Restaurants Inc. Between 2006 and 2009, Landry's spent more than $200 million to expand and renovate the hotel, including adding two aquariums, one of which features a slide through a tank containing sharks. The improvements helped to secure the Golden Nugget's status as downtown's premier resort and create a palace rivaling the best places on the Strip.

Tempering these positive stories was the abrupt closure of Binion's Horseshoe, among the most famous casinos in the world, in January 2004. Binion's, once one of the most profitable gambling halls in Las Vegas and host to the popular World Series of Poker, had been struggling ever since Benny Binion's daughter, Becky, bought out her siblings and took over the 366-room property in 1998. Becky Binion Behnen was not a skilled casino operator, and she alienated regular customers and tourists alike. Locals were miffed when she closed the casino's popular coffee shop, where cheap eats were available and Benny Binion once held court, meeting and greeting the city's movers and shakers. Perhaps the worst move from a publicity standpoint was her sale of the casino's famous display of $1 million in cash. Millions of Las Vegas visitors had been photographed with the kitschy display. Behnen also imposed lower

*Sun, Sin & Suburbia: The History of Modern Las Vegas*

limits on table games, which flew in the face of the casino's long-standing reputation for taking all bets, no matter how big.

Just weeks after the closure, Harrah's Entertainment came to the rescue, buying the fallow property for $50 million. Harrah's interest centered on taking control of the well-known Binion's Horseshoe name and the World Series of Poker. Harrah's, one of the nation's largest gaming companies, wasn't particularly excited about operating the downtown property, but it nevertheless reopened the casino on April 1 and held the annual World Series of Poker there in May, with a record purse and number of participants. Harrah's sold the Horseshoe property to MTR Gaming Group of West Virginia, but agreed to manage the hotel-casino for one year. Harrah's eventually cut all ties with the downtown casino but took the Horseshoe name and World Series of Poker with it. MTR retained the "Binion's" name and made some modest improvements to the aging property, but it sold out to TLC Casino Enterprises in 2008. A year later, TLC decided to close the 365 hotel rooms.

If a dark Binion's Horseshoe wasn't bad enough for downtown's mood in early 2004, the Castaways hotel-casino made things worse when it closed a few weeks later. Situated several blocks east of the Fremont Street Experience, the Castaways opened in 1954 as the Showboat, and arguably was the city's first neighborhood casino. It was a popular place well into the '80s, best known for its 106-lane bowling center, which hosted televised professional tournaments for decades. It also held boxing, professional wrestling and roller derby events in its sports pavilion, which later was converted to a bingo hall. The Castaways was hit hard when new neighborhood casinos such as Sam's Town and Boulder Station sprouted nearby. It didn't help that residential growth moved westward in the valley instead of east and north. But industry observers suggested that was only part of the problem. They drew parallels between mismanagement of the Horseshoe and mistakes made by Castaways managers. First, the 447-room hotel-casino failed to significantly respond to the challenge posed by the new neighborhood casinos. It rested on its laurels rather than raising the bar. And later, as the demographics of the valley's east side changed, taking on a heavy Latino flavor, the casino failed to appeal to its newfound customer base.

While the prospects for rejuvenating the Horseshoe seemed bright, optimism about the Castaways' future was dim. Its location—close to downtown but not in downtown, and far from the suburbs—seemed like a losing proposition to many potential operators. Local investors suggested the location would be better suited for a Walmart store or some other retail center. One local gaming concern was willing to take a chance on the Castaways, on the premise that it could revive the property by marketing it 100 percent to the valley's Hispanic residents, as well as Hispanic tourists from California, Arizona and Mexico. Randy Miller, Rich Iannone and Rich Gonzales, owners of the Bighorn casino in North Las Vegas and the Longhorn casino on Boulder Highway, said they envisioned a Spanish-speaking work force, signs in Spanish, Mexican music and televised international sporting events. The plan had potential but it never got off the ground, and Station Casinos took ownership. The Castaways was imploded in 2006 and the property went undeveloped for several years.

Back in Glitter Gulch, one of the more encouraging announcements came in 2011 when the owners of the Golden Gate, the oldest hotel-casino on Fremont Street, said the property would undergo a $12 million expansion and renovation. The old-school casino, with origins dating to 1906, updated the rooms and expanded the property. The owners—the Stevens brothers along with local stalwart Mark Brandenburg—saw signs of a "significant turnaround downtown" and decided to jump on the bandwagon. "There's no question that the downtown renaissance was a big part of our decision to go forward with this expansion," Brandenburg told the *Review-Journal*.

Across the street, the long-shabby Plaza Hotel, owned by the Tamares Group, underwent a $35 million renovation starting in 2010, highlighted by a new steakhouse called Oscar's, named for former Mayor Oscar Goodman. In a clever move, the renovation used furnishings and materials that had been intended for the Fontainebleau resort on the Strip. When the Fontainebleau construction was suspended in 2009, those materials became available at bottom-dollar prices.

Another downtown casino that hit a rough patch was the Lady Luck, a block north of Fremont Street near the mob museum. The Lady Luck closed in 2006, ostensibly so it could be completely remodeled as part of a larger project to transform Third Street into an entertainment district just off Fremont. A couple of restaurants and bars opened across Third Street—including the popular Triple George Grill—but the remodeling of the hotel did not occur, and the Henry Brent Company sold the property to CIM Group out of Hollywood in 2007. The Lady Luck sat idle during the depths of the recession, and city leaders grew impatient as the unsightly property accumulated trash and weeds. In 2009, Mayor Goodman called it a "disaster" and a "carcass." Finally, in 2011 the CIM Group announced its plans for the property, highlighted by a new name: the Downtown Grand. CIM removed the Lady Luck sign and started work, promising to spend $100 million and open in 2013.

The combination of the Fremont Street Experience light show upgrades, the refurbishing and expansion of downtown casinos under new ownership and the various developments beyond the casino core seemed an ideal recipe for a downtown renaissance. However, it's awfully easy to get caught up in downtown boosterism and forget the larger economic realities of Las Vegas. First of all, as much as Fremont Street improves, it still can't compete on most levels with the Strip, where hundreds of millions are spent each year to ensure its place atop the planet's list of resort destinations. Second, neighborhood casinos continue to get bigger and better, some of them comparing favorably with Strip properties for entertainment, dining and nightlife. They aren't slot joints anymore but full-fledged resorts, yet another strike against downtown. Third, the growth of Indian casinos in California has tended to have a bigger impact on places such as downtown Las Vegas, Laughlin and Reno than on the Strip.

Fourth, pre-recession promises that the urban core of Las Vegas would fill with high-rise condos—creating a natural customer base for downtown casinos and retail outlets—never came to pass. It's unlikely downtown will ever look anything like the high-rise clusters of Manhattan or Chicago. Las Vegas remains a Western city where the car is king, and where living downtown is simply not a consideration for the large majority of residents. New downtown development is encouraging but spotty at best. A casual drive through the urban core reveals that sleek new buildings are the exception to the rule.

Demographics also are telling. In 2002, the median household income in the 89101 ZIP code, which encompasses the bulk of downtown, was $20,815. By contrast, the citywide median income was $44,069, and suburban ZIP codes soared between $50,000 and $70,000.

Still, Boyd Gaming learned years ago that its downtown casinos could succeed by catering to specific customers who appreciate what it offers. Boyd has all but locked up the Hawaiian tourist market at its downtown casinos, bringing charter flights from the islands on a regular basis. The California's restaurant menus and gift shops serve the needs and desires of Hawaiian visitors. "Hawaiians are people who like to be recognized," Bill Boyd explained. "They like to see people they know. They like that familiarity. They're not as comfortable at the larger Strip places. We have done everything to make Hawaiians feel at home. The dealers wear aloha shirts. Our managers go to Hawaii five or six times a year and have parties for customers and market our properties." Boyd said the biggest selling points of downtown are convenient parking, reasonably priced food, intimate casinos and the ability to easily walk from one casino to another. "That's a niche that a larger Strip place can't have," he said.

Downtown, in other words, is not a vestigial appendage of the Las Vegas resort industry, doomed to extinction. It serves an important purpose, appealing to certain elements of the tourist and local markets—and, beyond Fremont Street, to that segment of the population seeking a more urban lifestyle. Downtown's future looks bright, as long as you keep things in proper perspective.

### Enter Zappos

When Oscar Goodman stepped down as Las Vegas mayor in the summer of 2012, he passed the torch of downtown revitalization. But the recipient was not the new mayor—his wife, Carolyn. Instead, it was Tony Hsieh, the chief executive officer of Zappos.com.

Hsieh is a classic Internet success story. Entrepreneurial since he was a young boy, he coasted through Harvard, but he showed more interest in money-making opportunities than in his classes. After graduating in 1995, he and a classmate started a business creating websites. But they soon realized a

*Sun, Sin & Suburbia: The History of Modern Las Vegas*

side project to distribute banner advertising across the web held greater potential. Their company, LinkExchange, grew quickly, and Hsieh and friends sold it to Microsoft in 1998 for $265 million.

Hsieh was twenty-four years old.

Suddenly flush with cash, Hsieh created a Silicon Valley investment firm, Venture Frogs, to invest in start-up tech companies. One of the projects he bet on was Zappos.com, an online shoe retailer, in 1999. Zappos struggled to get off the ground, but the passion of its founders, along with Hsieh's unwavering support, helped it to turn the corner. Hsieh eventually became the company's CEO, and Zappos grew dramatically. It recorded $8.6 million in sales in 2001, a figure dwarfed by the $70 million collected in 2003 and $184 million in 2004.

In 2004, Zappos moved from the Bay Area to Henderson, with the goal of improving its call center operations. Expanding its retail offerings beyond shoes into clothing and other items, Zappos registered $1 billion in sales in 2008. A year later, Amazon bought Zappos for $1.2 billion, with the understanding that Hsieh would continue to guide the company.

In November 2010, Hsieh announced that Zappos would be relocating its headquarters from Henderson to downtown Las Vegas. The city agreed to sell the old city hall at 400 Stewart Avenue, as well as two adjacent parking garages and another building, to Resort Gaming Group for $25 million. In turn, Resort Gaming planned to renovate the buildings and lease them to Zappos. The renovations were expected to cost up to $40 million.

The deal's announcement yielded rave reviews. "You have to be impressed with what the city has already done—the Lou Ruvo Center, World Market Center, the Smith Center—but this is going to be the first large, nongaming employment center downtown," local fiscal analyst Jeremy Aguero told the *Las Vegas Sun*. "It's the first step forward into really making downtown Las Vegas a place where people want to live and work at the same time. I can't think of a better fit, to be perfectly honest."

When the Las Vegas City Council approved the deal the following month, Mayor Goodman said, "This is a transaction that is going to affect forever the social fabric of our community."

Although Goodman was leaving office having already made great progress with downtown revitalization, the Zappos deal was like hitting a home run in the bottom of the ninth. It's important for a lot of reasons, but topping the list is that Zappos is not merely an "attraction" like the Smith Center or the Mob Museum. It's a large employer in a high-profile industry. It will draw thousands of people into downtown every day—local people for whom downtown will become an integral part of their lives. Some will move downtown, perhaps accelerating the building of middle-class housing near the urban core.

The presence of Zappos also is likely to boost development of the Fremont East entertainment district, which is within easy walking distance. The emergence of Fremont East was a major factor in Hsieh's decision to relocate. He told reporters that the tech community thrives on the mix of bars, clubs and coffee shops starting to sink roots in the district.

Originally, Hsieh had thought about building a self-contained corporate campus like those of Apple, Google and Nike. One idea was to partner with the Silverton hotel-casino in southwest Las Vegas. The Zappos campus would be self-contained on the Silverton site but employees would have access to the casino's amenities. But a different strategy germinated during a walk through Fremont East with Andrew Donner, chief executive of Resort Gaming Group. At the time, plans called for the old city hall to be torn down and a sports arena built in its place. Cordish Companies, out of Baltimore, had exclusive rights. But when the arena project stalled, Donner approached the city with a new idea. City officials negotiated with Cordish to move its arena plan to Symphony Park, opening the door for Zappos.

"When this opportunity came up to move downtown, we started to rethink [the corporate campus plan] and actually started thinking, 'Let's not be like other companies. Let's not be insular and only care about our employees,'" Hsieh told the Las Vegas City Council. "So, for me what's really exciting is we're not building a campus. We want to help contribute and help build a community and really integrate into a community around our campus."

The Zappos move could have the game-changing effect of an automaker opening a manufacturing plant in a struggling Southern town. Zappos is

*Sun, Sin & Suburbia: The History of Modern Las Vegas*

planning for growth. When it moves downtown, it will bring about 2,000 employees, but it foresees that figure eventually increasing by several thousand.

In his best-selling 2010 book, *Delivering Happiness*, Hsieh made no mention of his plans to colonize downtown Las Vegas. The idea sprouted while the book was in production, but it was not made public until after it was released. In any case, the book provides some insights into Hsieh's philosophies about business and life that bode well for downtown's future. Zappos was built on customer service (free shipping!) and its revered company culture, which revolves around a fun and rewarding workplace where employees enjoy free vending machines and a legitimate voice in what happens. Zappos is regularly lauded as one of America's best places to work.

By moving the Zappos headquarters to downtown Las Vegas, Hsieh promised to infuse the area not only with economic growth, but with Zappos's core values. This means thousands of smart, creative people who are comfortable with an environment characterized by growth, change and "a little weirdness." "One of the things that makes Zappos different from a lot of other companies is that we value being fun and being a little bit weird," Hsieh wrote in *Delivering Happiness*. "We don't want to become one of those big companies that feel corporate and boring. We want to be able to laugh at ourselves. We look for both fun and humor in our daily work."

Weirdness is encouraged, Hsieh wrote, because it promotes innovation. "When you combine a little weirdness with making sure everyone is also having fun at work, it ends up being a win-win for everyone: Employees are more engaged in the work that they do, and the company as a whole becomes more innovative."

Risk-taking is also a hallmark of Zappos culture. "We want everyone to not be afraid to take risks and to not be afraid to make mistakes, because if people aren't making mistakes then that means they're not taking enough risks," Hsieh wrote. "Sometimes our sense of adventure and creativity causes us to be unconventional in our solutions (because we have the freedom to think outside the box), but that's what allows us to rise above and stay ahead of the competition."

When Zappos moves downtown, its employees will strive to make an emotional connection to the area. Hsieh was an early adopter, moving into a twenty-third-floor condo in The Ogden high-rise and becoming a regular at The Beat coffeehouse and Downtown Cocktail Room in Fremont East. In 2012, he bought the old 7-Eleven building at the entrance to Fremont East for $4.1 million. The building also houses the Downtown Cocktail Room, The Griffin bar and two restaurants. Plans for the convenience store space were still being formulated.

But the company's tribal mindset—"We watch out for each other, care for each other, and go above and beyond for each other," as Hsieh wrote—likely will be tested by municipal politics and neighborhood realities such as poverty, drugs and crime. The passion that underlies everything Zappos does should be welcomed downtown, but it's not guaranteed that all the various constituencies will contribute to the revolution.

It also remains to be seen whether Hsieh's management savvy can be applied to the field of urban design. Millions of dollars will be spent to renovate the old city hall and, eventually, to expand beyond its confines. This is new territory for the technology company, and its creative culture is likely to meet with roadblocks it is not accustomed to encountering. Still, the potential is high that Zappos will change downtown Las Vegas in profound and lasting ways, creating an environment that will attract other companies—tech and otherwise—eager to participate in this renaissance. Speaking in March 2011 with *Las Vegas Sun* reporter Joe Schoenmann, Hsieh threw out several developments he'd like to see downtown, including a charter school, a business incubator, affordable housing and innovative ways to boost the live music scene, such as subsidizing downtown casinos to host performers. The common thread is to create an environment conducive to attracting the "creative class" to Las Vegas.

"To get the kinds of people and businesses here to make it happen, you're not going to do that with just the Strip," Hsieh told the *Sun*. "If that's all Vegas offers, they won't come here."

A few months later, Schoenmann was invited to listen in as thirty Zappos employees—Zapponians—gathered at Hsieh's house for a brainstorming

*Sun, Sin & Suburbia: The History of Modern Las Vegas*

session on the downtown move. It was just one meeting in a long series intended to discuss everything from bars and restaurants to education and housing. While his employees ambitiously hashed out the details, Hsieh offered an overview: "It's about bringing a real sense of culture and community to downtown Las Vegas. It's about revitalizing a town, and we're super-excited about it."

In December 2010, not long after the downtown deal became public, Hsieh posted a link on his Twitter page to a *New York Times* article and said it was "very relevant to Zappos' move to downtown Las Vegas." The article was about a physicist named Geoffrey West and his effort to apply scientific principles to urban planning. West's computations conclude that the larger the city, the more efficient and productive its residents will be. "What the data clearly shows ... is that when people come together, they become much more productive," West told the *Times*.

However, many newer cities, such as Phoenix and Las Vegas, have been running in the opposite direction, emphasizing suburban seclusion and sprawl over urban proximity and interaction. The data show that this suburban model reduces productivity.

West acknowledges that a problem with big cities is people don't always want to interact with other people all the time. He "describes the purpose of urban planning as finding a way to minimize our distress while maximizing our interactions," according to the *Times*.

Clearly, Hsieh is thinking hard about how Zappos will adapt to the downtown environment, as well as the effect it will have on the area and its diverse populace. In an interview with Paul Carr for the *Huffington Post*, Hsieh likened his company's relocation to the *Sim City* video game. "For us it's like playing *Sim City* in real life," he said. "One tagline we've come up with is 'from *Sim City* to Sin City.'"

In the same article, Hsieh noted that there are practical questions when you take ownership of a building such as city hall. "There are jail cells in there," he told Carr. "We're thinking of turning them into nap rooms, or maybe a speakeasy."

No matter what, when Hsieh and his Zappos family make the move in 2013, they undoubtedly will have a transformative effect. Zappos is an international brand with a dedicated following, so if Zappos says downtown Las Vegas is cool, millions of people will think so too. And in the long run, if Zappos proves to be a sustainable online retailer—never a given in this roller-coaster age—it could attract other digital companies to downtown Las Vegas. It may be difficult to imagine today, when downtown is still, charitably speaking, a work in progress, but Zappos has the potential to be the first building block of a much-needed new economy for Las Vegas.

"At Zappos, we've historically thought of our brand in terms of the 'Three Cs': clothing, customer service and company culture," Hsieh told the *Sun*. "Now we want to add a fourth C: community. We want to be a part of revitalizing downtown Las Vegas."

It would be prudent, however, not to overstate either Hsieh's power to transform downtown or his company's idealism. In June 2011, Zappos and Resort Gaming Group asked the city to sell them the building for $18 million instead of the previously approved price of $25 million. They asked for the discount, they said, because of the extensive renovations the aging building requires. City leaders had little choice but to approve the lower price. After all, they had already lavished praise on the deal as a game-changer for downtown. Still, the request left a sour taste, especially because of an e-mail from a Zappos executive threatening to pull out of the deal if the city didn't acquiesce.

"Without the proposed modifications to the" agreement, Chris Nielsen wrote to City Manager Betsy Fretwell, "Zappos.com, Inc. is unlikely to finalize a transaction ... for the City Hall property."

The idea of Zappos not following through was too devastating for city officials to imagine. Councilman Steve Ross summed up the city's predicament. "The only risk I see," he said, "is not making this happen."

Clearly, Zappos was playing hardball, knowing the city was in no position to call the company's bluff. Some cynics wondered why Zappos didn't go further and demand the building for free.

Aside from a bit of hardball negotiating, Hsieh has revealed no cracks in his dedication to fueling a downtown renaissance. He, along with co-investors, purchased the rights to First Friday, the monthly arts district festival. He contributed $2 million to the Smith Center for the Performing Arts. He helped to fund a tech library in the Emergency Arts cultural building. Perhaps more important: He's encouraging other Silicon Valley tech companies to relocate to downtown Las Vegas, and he's providing seed money to employees and others who want to start downtown-based businesses.

The infusion of money, energy and creativity that Hsieh hopes to generate promised to reinvent the downtown area in a way that previous redevelopment efforts could only dream about. Because of Hsieh's standing in the digital industry, he's looking for people from New York, Seattle and Silicon Valley to join him. As *Las Vegas CityLife* writer Amy Kingsley cleverly observed, "The irony of all this is that it may be easier to convince someone from San Francisco or New York that downtown has potential than it is to convince a resident of Summerlin."

It's reasonable to compare Hsieh with entrepreneurs who have made deep impressions on Las Vegas in the past. Two that immediately come to mind are Howard Hughes and Steve Wynn. But Hsieh begs to draw a distinction. While Hughes and Wynn were individual visionaries, possessing my-way-or-the-highway egos, Hsieh is a different breed. His method is to bring smart people together to find solutions organically rather than to rely entirely on his own genius. He insists that whatever Zappos accomplishes downtown will be the handiwork of a large group of people. "These are other people's passions," he said of the range of projects in which he's involved. "I'm just helping to integrate all of them together."

This collaborative ethos may differentiate Hsieh from Wynn and Hughes, but he hopes to echo Hughes in one respect. When Hughes came to Las Vegas in the late '60s, he invested several hundred million dollars in casinos, real estate and other ventures. But more important, Hughes's confidence in the city's future convinced other individuals and companies to invest in Las Vegas. Hsieh, too, could leave his most enduring mark by serving as the pied piper of downtown investment.

# CHAPTER 2

# The Strip: 1941–1988

*"Tourists who have never seen a gaming device in their lives pour into the Strip hotels off the searing desert highways by the thousands all day and all night and, after that first startled stare, begin to succumb to the sorcery of fashionable mass gambling."*

—KATHARINE BEST AND KATHARINE HILLYER
*LAS VEGAS PLAYTOWN U.S.A.*, 1955

*"The sad truth is that without gambling, Nevada wouldn't need a governor— just a night watchman."*

—ED REID AND OVID DEMARIS
*THE GREEN FELT JUNGLE*, 1963

The Strip originally was known as Route 91, or the Los Angeles Highway. Its main purpose in 1940 was to transport gamblers to downtown Las Vegas, where all the casinos were. In addition to a few minor businesses, there was a small nightclub operating on the highway, the 91 Club, but it wasn't much competition for the neon signs and gambling tables of Fremont Street.

This situation, however, was about to change. Encouraged by Las Vegas business leaders, California hotel operator Thomas Hull came to town and saw an opportunity to try something a little different. Rather than break into the competitive Fremont Street scene—and pay city taxes—he bought thirty-three acres (at $150 per acre) outside the municipal limits along the Los Angeles Highway, at the intersection with San Francisco Street (now Sahara

Avenue). He built a ranch-style resort and casino. The El Rancho Vegas opened on April 3, 1941, a date that probably should be celebrated annually in Las Vegas.

The El Rancho Vegas offered more than merely a place to sleep and play cards. In addition to sixty-three bungalow-style rooms, a small casino and gasoline station, Hull's property had restaurants, retail shops, a swimming pool, horseback riding and lounge shows. He brought in big-name entertainers to perform. From the start, Strip resorts sought to satisfy all their customers' needs and desires.

Hull's success with the El Rancho Vegas was one of the factors that spurred another out-of-town businessman, Texas movie theater mogul R.E. Griffith, to build a resort on the Los Angeles Highway. In 1941, Griffith purchased 175 acres (which included the 91 Club) south of the El Rancho Vegas, and constructed the Last Frontier, which opened on October 30, 1942. With the help of architect son-in-law William Moore, Griffith took the Las Vegas resort concept to the next level. While his sprawling property was similar in many ways to Hull's, it was more elegant and detailed. A Western motif carried throughout the resort, accurately reflecting the Last Frontier's slogan, "The Old West in Modern Splendor." In *Resort City in the Sunbelt*, historian Eugene Moehring describes what the resort's early customers encountered:

"The décor was deliberately extravagant, awarding the resort instant notoriety. The main building contained a trophy room lined with large stuffed animals; inside was the Carrillo Bar immortalizing the Cisco Kid's famed sidekick, actor Leo Carrillo (a frequent patron). The Horn Room and Gay Nineties Bar were illuminated by lighting fixtures shaped in the form of wagon wheels suspended by chains hanging from the ceiling. ... In the guest rooms, cow horns adorned every bed."

If the El Rancho Vegas was the first resort-style hotel in Las Vegas, the Last Frontier was the first resort with a strong theme. Their importance to the shaping of the Strip cannot be overestimated. They shatter the popular perception that Bugsy Siegel "invented" Las Vegas a few years later with the opening of the Flamingo Hotel.

*Sun, Sin & Suburbia: The History of Modern Las Vegas*

For several years, partly because of the overwhelming impact of World War II, the El Rancho Vegas and Last Frontier were the only resorts on the Strip. Another reason was that Fremont Street thrived in the '40s. Several new casinos opened, including the El Cortez, Pioneer Club and Golden Nugget, and others expanded. At that time, downtown was undaunted by the slowly emerging Strip.

## The Flamingo: Fact and fiction

The next entrepreneur to invest in a Strip resort was Billy Wilkerson, founder of the *Hollywood Reporter* newspaper and a successful nightclub and restaurant operator in Los Angeles. Wilkerson was a compulsive gambler, losing hundreds of thousands of dollars in Las Vegas and in illegal games closer to home. He decided the only way to stem his chronic losses would be to "own the house," according to a biography, *The Man Who Invented Las Vegas*, by Wilkerson's son. His first gambling-related venture was a failing hotel in Lake Arrowhead, near Big Bear Lake, three hours from Hollywood. While Wilkerson was successful in reviving the mountain resort, his main interest was backroom card games. The small illegal operation soon grew into a full-fledged casino, but only temporarily. In 1940, authorities raided the hotel and shut it down.

Wilkerson concluded that to get into the casino business, he would have to go to Las Vegas. In 1944, he leased the El Rancho Vegas for six months, but he wasn't satisfied with its rustic flavor. Wilkerson wanted to be able to attract the Hollywood crowd to the desert, and that would require a more sophisticated resort than the city then offered. In early 1945 Wilkerson purchased a parcel several miles south of the Last Frontier for $84,000.

The goal from the outset was to bring Hollywood style and a luxury resort experience to Las Vegas. "His vision called for Paris, not the Western frontier," his son, W.R. Wilkerson III, wrote. "His hotel would offer first-class accommodations, along European lines. Luxurious and elegant, it would be designed to attract an upscale Beverly Hills clientele. Each hotel room would be decorated with sumptuous appointments and top-quality fixtures."

Wilkerson had another innovative idea, fueled by his knowledge of what makes hardcore gamblers tick: Make the casino the centerpiece of the resort.

"No guest would be able to move around the hotel without passing through the casino," Wilkerson wrote. "There would be no windows. 'Never let them see daylight,' he commanded." He also made chairs available to gamblers, who at that time typically stood at the green felt tables. The final touch was the name. He chose the Flamingo, reflecting the "beauty, grace and elegance" of the distinctive pink bird.

Needing help with the operation of a large casino, Wilkerson hired Gus Greenbaum and Moe Sedway from the highly successful El Cortez. While the two had shady pasts linked to organized crime, they knew how to run a gambling hall. The estimated price tag for construction was $1.2 million, a lot more than Wilkerson had at his disposal. He obtained a $600,000 loan from the Bank of America and got $200,000 from his friend Howard Hughes (in the form of prepaid advertising in the *Hollywood Reporter*), but he was still $400,000 short. Efforts to raise more money through high-stakes gambling proved fruitless, yet Wilkerson forged ahead, breaking ground in November 1945.

A third of the way into construction, Wilkerson ran into difficulties. Although the war was over, lingering restrictions made construction materials expensive. In addition, Wilkerson continued his fiendish gambling habits, losing tens of thousands of dollars. Construction ceased in January 1946. A month later, New York organized crime boss Meyer Lansky put together a scheme to buy into Wilkerson's project and spend $1 million to get it finished.

Wilkerson resumed building the Flamingo, but one day a familiar face from Hollywood showed up on the construction site: Benjamin "Bugsy" Siegel. Siegel was to be Lansky's representative on the Flamingo project, a task he initially did not want. Although Siegel had been involved with downtown Las Vegas casinos for several years, he would have preferred to maintain his playboy lifestyle in Los Angeles and avoid the heat and dust of Las Vegas. At first, Siegel deferred to Wilkerson's expertise on the Flamingo project. He learned the business from Wilkerson and completed assignments for him, proving particularly useful in obtaining building materials from the black market. But the right-hand man role did not last long, as Siegel began to make decisions on his own and reverse Wilkerson's directives to contractors.

Soon, Siegel was boasting publicly that the Flamingo was his idea, and privately he demanded more hands-on involvement. Eventually Wilkerson agreed to split the project, with Siegel handling the hotel part and Wilkerson all the rest. Separate contractors were hired for each piece, and Siegel launched his infamous spending spree that caused the Flamingo budget to balloon.

In June 1946, Siegel, with the project's organized crime bosses behind him, essentially pushed Wilkerson out of the Flamingo. Although Wilkerson technically remained a major shareholder, his creative participation in the project ended. Siegel, acting as the Nevada Projects Corporation, proceeded to bring in his own people, including contractor Del Webb, who would go on to play a large role in Las Vegas as a casino operator and developer.

Massive cost overruns ensued as Siegel and his girlfriend, Virginia Hill, demanded expensive construction changes and insisted on the finest materials and decorations. Siegel's expenditures alarmed his bosses, who tended to more conservative investments. Desperate to start bringing in revenue, Siegel rushed completion of the Flamingo and moved up the opening date by two months, to December 26, 1946. Although the hotel would not be finished and patrons would have to stay at other Las Vegas resorts, Siegel pressed ahead with the Christmastime opening.

It was a disaster, but it wasn't all Siegel's fault. Terrible weather in Los Angeles grounded charter flights to Las Vegas that could have brought an array of celebrities to the opening. A few celebrities arrived by car, and the night's entertainment was top notch: Jimmy Durante, Xavier Cugat and his band and George Jessel as master of ceremonies But other problems caused by the rushed opening marred what otherwise could have been a huge event. The lack of hotel rooms put the Flamingo in the red from the start, and Siegel closed it down in late January 1947. Siegel's costs had now run as high as $6 million.

On March 1—Wilkerson's original opening date—Siegel reopened the Flamingo, with ninety-three rooms now ready, and soon began to turn a profit. But the positive numbers came too late for Siegel, who had lost the confidence of his mob superiors. On June 20, 1947, he was shot to death in his girlfriend's Beverly Hills house. Greenbaum and Sedway quickly took over the Flamingo, eventually turning it into a highly profitable casino.

In popular lore—even among some historians and many Las Vegans who should know better—Siegel is credited as the founding father of Las Vegas, the creator of the resort concept that remains the primary modus operandi on the Strip. But in reality, Siegel was neither a visionary nor a good casino operator. Wilkerson deserves more credit than Siegel for vision, while Greenbaum and Sedway should be credited with making the Flamingo successful. David Schwartz, author of *Suburban Xanadu: The Casino Resort on the Las Vegas Strip and Beyond*, summarized Siegel's contribution to Las Vegas: "He essentially hijacked another man's project and nearly drove it into the ground."

Nevertheless, the Flamingo represented a paradigm shift for Las Vegas. While it cemented the Strip as the community's future economic engine, it also altered the idea of what kind of visitor the city was aiming to attract. As Eugene Moehring explained: "The Flamingo liberated Las Vegas from the confines of its Western heritage and established the pattern for a 'diversity of images' embodied in future resorts like the Desert Inn, Thunderbird, Dunes, Tropicana, and Stardust." In his architectural history, *Viva Las Vegas*, critic Alan Hess wrote of the Flamingo: "It created a significant new sophisticated market for Las Vegas; it opened the Strip to a wider range of images in the service of making appealing places; it broke Las Vegas out of the public relations mode of a Western town of modern splendor and set it on its way to being a mirror of the spectrum of American popular culture."

### The '50s: Super-boom

The '90s were a tremendous growth period for Las Vegas, but it can't be emphasized enough that the '50s were bigger. The Strip really became a strip in the '50s, as a laundry list of soon-to-be-iconic casinos spread across the desert floor, with a variety of other businesses sprinkled in between. It also marked the period when organized crime became entrenched in the Las Vegas casino business.

The Flamingo set a new standard for the Strip, and most subsequent resorts tried to emulate it. The first was the Thunderbird, which opened in 1948. Although it had a Western/Native American motif, the Thunderbird was more modern and sophisticated than the harsh rusticity of the original El Rancho Vegas and Last Frontier.

The Desert Inn took the Flamingo's elegance to new heights. But while the Flamingo was patterned after a Hollywood nightclub, the Desert Inn took its inspiration from Palm Springs. Wilbur Clark, who had been involved in various Las Vegas casinos in the early to mid-'40s, started building his dream resort about the same time that Wilkerson and Siegel were building the Flamingo, but he too ran into money problems that delayed its completion. With financial assistance from organized crime figures out of Cleveland, led by the legendary Moe Dalitz, Clark completed the Desert Inn and opened on April 24, 1950. It was an immediate success, drawing crowds of well-dressed customers. The D.I.'s centerpiece was the Sky Room Bar, which, from its third-story perch, offered panoramic views of the resort property and the Las Vegas Valley in three directions. The Desert Inn featured the Strip's first golf course, which, starting in 1953, hosted the Tournament of Champions professional tournament. It also included the Desert Inn Estates, where the valley's movers and shakers built palatial homes.

Other resorts sprung up in rapid succession. The North Africa-themed Sahara and the architecturally sleek Sands opened in 1952. The Royal Nevada, the Dunes, the renovated New Frontier, and the Riviera, the Strip's first high-rise at nine stories, all opened in 1955. The family-friendly Hacienda opened in 1956, and the Tropicana, sporting an elegant Miami Beach vibe, opened in 1957. The Stardust, the first Strip hotel with 1,000 rooms, opened in 1958, absorbing the failed Royal Nevada.

The Stardust represented another sea change on the Strip, as it eschewed the chic appeal to high-rollers in favor of the mass market. The Stardust stood ready to provide affordable lodging to the unwashed masses. The Stardust was noteworthy not for its architectural touches, which were few, but for its huge, colorful sign. It was the Stardust that epitomized the concept of the "decorated shed," as defined by authors Robert Venturi, Denise Scott Brown and Steven Izenour in their architectural classic *Learning from Las Vegas*. The Stardust sign prompted other Strip resorts (as well as downtown clubs) to revamp their signs, making them bigger and brighter.

The '50s construction boom on the Strip basically ended with the Stardust, as the city had reached a plateau. Properties such as the Dunes and Riviera ran into financial problems and shuffled management, while the Royal Nevada closed. The ingenious solution was to turn Las Vegas into a convention mecca. A publicly funded convention center opened in 1959 on the site of a defunct horse track, and marketing campaigns were launched to attract business travelers. Soon, the resorts were able to fill their rooms in the middle of the week and during traditionally slow periods of the year.

Despite the absence of new resorts, the Strip hit its stride in the early '60s. This was the era of the Rat Pack playing the Copa Room at the Sands. Hollywood also did its share to boost Las Vegas, producing several iconic Las Vegas films, including the Rat Pack-led *Ocean's Eleven* (1960) and Elvis Presley's *Viva Las Vegas* (1964). Both were practically propaganda films for Las Vegas cool. Other high-profile entertainers regularly performed in Strip showrooms and lounges, and the Beatles performed at the convention center in 1964.

## The big picture: Why it worked

A hundred books have been written about the Strip over the past fifty years but it wasn't until 2003 that an author provided a clear and convincing big-picture explanation for why this barren scrap of roadway became a universally known and desired destination. The writer was David Schwartz, director of the Center for Gaming Research at UNLV, and the book was *Suburban Xanadu: The Casino Resort on the Las Vegas Strip and Beyond.*

Schwartz explained that Strip casinos were America's postwar solution to the prevalence of illegal gambling dens. Allowing gambling to occur in a small, distant desert outpost, far from urban centers, was "tolerable and even desirable." At mid-century, Schwartz said, illegal gambling was going on "seemingly everywhere in cities large and small," and this spurred a strong anti-gambling wave in the country. Reformers were particularly concerned about the emergence of slot machines in retail outlets and their ability to corrupt women and children. Law enforcement authorities were concerned that organized crime syndicates controlled most of the illegal gambling rackets. The solution was to crack down on the illegal gambling operations and allow an outlet for the nation's insatiable gambling passion. "The distant isolation of casinos on the Strip, which early promoters probably considered their greatest drawback, was paradoxically its salvation," Schwartz wrote. "Because the 'wide-open' action of the Strip was located at a safe distance from the teeming masses of urban America, there was no great outcry over it. Few do-gooders complained about Strip casinos' impact on public morality or individual finances." This "containment of gambling" meant that, "by default, the state of Nevada had solved the national debate over gambling policy. Gamblers would no longer contribute to urban corruption and gambling; rather, those with the means to travel to the desert could now be parted with their money in sunny, state-regulated casinos." What's more, this "solution" guaranteed that Nevada would enjoy a virtual monopoly on legal gambling for decades to come.

The rise of the Strip paralleled the explosion of suburbia across the nation, Schwartz noted. Unlike the cramped downtowns of Las Vegas and Reno, the Strip, with its large parking lots, sprawling layouts and multiple amenities, felt familiar and comfortable to suburbanites. Schwartz drew parallels between the social structure of suburbia and the culture of vacationing on the Strip. He debunked the reputation of Strip resorts as "lawless underworld jungles," noting: "Even in its headiest boom years in the early 1950s, the Strip was as ordered an environment as the shopping malls and subdivisions that developers were building throughout the nation." He also contrasted the "hard-sell focus on gambling" in the downtown settings with the "soft-sell approach" on the Strip. "In Strip casino resorts, vacationers tried their luck in between jaunts to 'their' resort's yacht on Lake Mead, the swimming pool, and the dinner theater," Schwartz wrote. "In their suburban setting, casino resorts offered a complete vacation experience that Reno gambling halls, no matter how astute their owners or how beneficial their payouts, could not. The soft-sell approach of casino resorts made patrons feel it was almost their responsibility to 'be a sport' and gamble a little—after all, it was the least they could do for the resort that had given them such a superlative vacation value."

The strength of *Suburban Xanadu* is that Schwartz cut away the glitz, mob drama and showgirls and put the Strip's development in a more useful context.

He concluded that their obvious differences aside, Strip resorts grew much like other suburban developments across America, but they "just happened to include a casino."

While Schwartz offered a compelling new perspective, it would be the height of naivete to suggest that the rise of the Strip in the '50s and '60s was solely a product of demographic trends and postwar development patterns. Schwartz offered a welcome alternative to previous writers obsessed with organized crime's colorful role in Strip history, but the two perspectives need not be mutually exclusive.

A contrast is offered by the analysis of Sally Denton and Roger Morris in their 2001 book, *The Money and the Power: The Making of Las Vegas and Its Hold on America, 1947-2000*. Denton and Morris focused on organized crime's role in Strip development, painting a picture of a casino industry aswirl in corruption. The authors described a vast organized crime network with Las Vegas as its capital and famed kingpin Meyer Lansky as its leader. Las Vegas's prosperity, they wrote, always had a price—the millions skimmed off the top of the casino take and delivered to out-of-state mob bosses. "Much of the cash went directly to numbered accounts in Switzerland, where it would be relaundered back through banks and financial institutions in the Bahamas and then to the United States, often as construction loans to Las Vegas casinos and the other Syndicate-financed enterprises of hospitals, golf courses, shopping centers, housing subdivisions, and movie production companies," Denton and Morris wrote. In sketching the rise of new resorts on the Strip, they documented the notorious figures who financed each project, sometimes secretly, sometimes not. "It was these men and their money that produced the brightly lit spectacle of the new Las Vegas," they wrote. Denton and Morris's version of Strip history echoed the work of Ed Reid and Ovid Demaris in their 1963 exposé *The Green Felt Jungle*. "The big guessing game in Las Vegas is 'Who owns whom,'" Reid and Demaris wrote. "Though there are many big hoodlums in Las Vegas operating openly as licensed owners in plush Strip casinos, there are many more who operate behind legitimate or semilegitimate fronts. One front can be divided among a half-dozen hoodlums from as many states."

The truth about Strip history almost certainly lies somewhere between these two perspectives. There is no question the Strip was a hotbed of organized crime activity in those early decades, and that the illicit interests of mob figures such as Meyer Lansky, Moe Dalitz and Jimmy Hoffa influenced development patterns. At the same time, these organized crime leaders did not operate in a vacuum. They were not powerful enough to dictate national social and demographic trends or popular tastes. Most of their customers were regular citizens with no obligations to the underworld. For the Strip to succeed, its mob financiers and the architects, marketers and managers they hired could not function outside the ebb and flow of American life. If, as Schwartz argues, Strip resorts had much in common with suburban shopping malls and therefore appealed to middle-American tastes, those facts are no less true because the mob ran them.

## Jay Sarno: Visionary

Jay Sarno's name should be better known in Las Vegas. Sarno created Caesars Palace and Circus Circus, two Strip landmarks built in the '60s that represent the revival of the themed resort on a grand scale.

Sarno, a native of St. Joseph, Missouri, made his initial fortune by building the Cabana motor hotel chain in cities across the country. During frequent stops in Las Vegas—like Flamingo brainchild Billy Wilkerson, Sarno liked to gamble, often to excess—he was unimpressed with the city's preoccupation with Old West and desert motifs. He felt he could do better. This manifested itself in Caesars Palace, an ancient Rome theme representing the epitome of luxury and decadence. Unlike previous efforts in Las Vegas, Sarno intended for the theme to carry through the entire resort. In the Bacchanal restaurant, for example, beautiful servers fed diners grapes and gave them massages. Caesars stationery looked like weathered parchment.

Though not architecturally trained, Sarno was involved in most every design choice at Caesars Palace. A.D. Hopkins wrote in *The Players: The Men Who Made Las Vegas*, that "Sarno loved ovals, and according to his former wife, he never built a rectangular bar in any motel. He thought they inhibited conversation and that they had a cold feeling about them. He even had dice tables built with specially rounded corners."

*The Strip: 1941–1988*                                                                 77

Opening in 1966, at a cost of $24 million, Caesars Palace quickly became the Strip's most popular and iconic resort. It took full advantage of the city's growing convention trade, regularly filling its 25,000 square feet of meeting space.

Sarno took the profits from Caesars Palace and poured them into his next vision: Circus Circus. When it opened in 1968, Circus Circus truly reflected its name. As gamblers placed their bets in the casino, trapeze acts performed over their heads, while an elephant was taught to pull a giant slot machine handle.

Unlike Caesars Palace, Circus Circus was not immediately successful. The circus acts proved distracting for dealers and gamblers alike, and the absence of hotel rooms proved to be a strategic error. Sarno was so certain the spectacle would appeal to tourists that he charged $2 to get in the door. And despite its presumed family orientation, Sarno tried to bring high-rollers to Circus Circus, which didn't work. The bizarre nature of Circus Circus was the inspiration for one of writer Hunter S. Thompson's most famous lines in his best-selling 1971 book, *Fear and Loathing in Las Vegas*: "The Circus Circus is what the whole hep world would be doing on Saturday night if the Nazis had won the war."

Schwartz, in *Suburban Xanadu*, argued that Circus Circus struggled initially because Sarno failed to learn from his own experience with Caesars: "Despite its attractions, a unique theme alone could not guarantee a casino success; the most important elements of a casino resort remained the interconnected hotel, restaurants, entertainment venues, and casino. When these elements were not present, no matter how overstated the theme, the casino did not stand a chance in competing against full-fledged casino resorts."

In 1974, Sarno turned over the casino to William Bennett and William Pennington, who transformed his twisted vision into a financial windfall. Their solutions were fairly simple. They tamed the raucous circus acts and moved them away from the gamblers. They cleaned out the less-than-honest carnival games. They eliminated the admission fee. And rather than catering to high-rollers, they aimed squarely for the middle-class family market. Circus Circus became one of the most successful properties in Las Vegas, catapulting Bennett and Pennington to the forefront of the casino industry well into the '90s. By 2012, Circus Circus was among the Strip's most weathered resorts but continued to fill the "affordable" niche for its owner, MGM Resorts International.

Sarno had plans for another themed Strip resort, the 6,000-room "Grandissimo," but he never got the financing for it. As a result, his tenure as king of the Strip was relatively shortlived and ended on a sour note. Sarno died of a heart attack in 1984, his later years marred by excessive gambling, health problems and frustration that he couldn't get the Grandissimo off the ground. Nevertheless, time has proved that Sarno was a visionary, as numerous hyper-themed resorts inspired by his creations opened on the Strip in the '90s.

## Kerkorian: Bigger is better

Although Caesars Palace was a huge hit, the Strip's next major resort developer, Kirk Kerkorian, did not use it as a model. Kerkorian, in fact, was the landlord of Caesars Palace, and used part of that investment to finance his first Strip resort. But at least at first, his instincts told him the Strip was ready for something different.

Kerkorian's life is a classic American rags-to-riches saga. He was born in 1917 in Southern California's San Joaquin Valley, where his father farmed on several ranches. But a 1920s recession hit his father's business hard, and the family moved to Los Angeles, where Kerkorian helped run the family produce trucking business. Kerkorian was a tough kid who ran with a gang and dropped out of high school. He followed his brother into the boxing arena, where, as an amateur, he posted an impressive 29-4 record.

Paralleling the passion of eventual casino competitor Howard Hughes, Kerkorian found his place in the world as a pilot. He obtained his commercial license in 1941, joined Canada's Royal Air Force and flew risky transatlantic missions during the war. Afterward, Kerkorian began flying charters in his twin-engine Cessna, including frequent trips to Las Vegas carrying high-profile figures such as Bugsy Siegel. In 1947, he bought Los Angeles Air Service and then became an airplane dealer. He bought old planes, refurbished them and sold them at a profit. After renaming the company Trans International

Airlines, he began passenger service in 1959. Kerkorian did well in the air service business, selling his interest in TIA in 1968 for $104 million.

In the meantime, Kerkorian had developed a keen interest in Las Vegas, where he was a high-rolling gambler dating to the late '40s. He invested in the Dunes Hotel in 1955, which did not prove fruitful and confirmed for him that if he was going to invest in Las Vegas, he needed to control the operation. In 1962, he paid $960,000 for eighty acres across the street from the Flamingo Hotel, which he initially leased to the developers of Caesars Palace and sold to them two years later at a huge profit. In 1967, Kerkorian bought the Flamingo and an eighty-two-acre parcel on Paradise Road, where he planned to build his first Las Vegas resort. Securing a $30 million bank loan—not enough to cover the project's entire cost—Kerkorian sold stock in a new corporation to complete the job. With the assistance of architect Martin Stern Jr., he built the International Hotel and opened it in 1969, with Barbra Streisand as the headlining performer. The International arguably was Las Vegas's first megaresort, at least by the modern definition. Contrasting with other resorts, the thirty-story International was sleek and understated, though huge with 1,500 rooms and a 30,000-square-foot casino. Its Y-shaped design became the standard for Las Vegas resorts for decades to come.

But nothing was understated about the showroom entertainment at the International, where Elvis Presley, donning bejeweled jumpsuits, drew packed audiences. After years of making movies, Presley used the International to return to live performance. Despite a dramatically altered rock 'n' roll landscape, Presley was an immediate hit, attracting diverse audiences during his twice-yearly engagements in the International's 2,000-room showroom. Over the next eight years—sadly, the last eight years of his life—Presley performed 837 times at the hotel, and every show was a sellout.

Aided by Elvis, the International was a success, but Kerkorian sold it in 1970. Both the International and Flamingo were transferred to Hilton Hotels Corporation, which ran them successfully for many years. The International was renamed the Las Vegas Hilton, operating under that name until 2012, when it became the LVH.

Kerkorian, however, was not done with Las Vegas—not by a long shot. As soon as he sold the International and Flamingo, he began laying plans for the MGM Grand. Securing an ideal site at the Strip and Flamingo Road, near Caesars Palace and the Flamingo, Kerkorian spent $104 million on the twenty-six-story, 2,100-room resort. Opening in December 1973, the MGM Grand was considered the most luxurious place in town. Adopting a classic Hollywood theme—at the time Kerkorian had a controlling interest in MGM Studios—the hotel-casino "walked the same fine line between grandeur and populism as the old movie palaces," wrote Alan Hess in *Viva Las Vegas*. The focal point of the property, however, was the giant, eight-lane porte cochere, which replaced the neon sign as the resort's image-setting feature.

In *Suburban Xanadu*, Schwartz explained that the MGM Grand was the prototype for almost everything that came after it on the Strip. "The MGM Grand was, like the International, a glimpse into the future of the casino resort: a large casino surrounded by thousands of hotel rooms geared toward the convention trade and international patronage. These casinos were not only bigger but also more self-contained than the original nightclub-and-bunga-low resorts of the 1950s. One literally did not see sunlight after parking and entering the building—it was possible to spend a weekend eating, shopping, lounging in a spa, and being entertained without leaving the same building, and without leaving the vicinity of the casino."

## Late '70s, early '80s: Caution and anxiety

Aside from the MGM Grand's opening, the Strip focused more on expansion than on new resorts in the '70s. In most cases, the resorts converted from low-rise motels to high-rise towers. Caesars opened a fifteen-story tower in 1973. The Las Vegas Hilton and the Flamingo both added rooms. Circus Circus added a fifteen-story hotel. Also expanding in the '70s were the Tropicana, Desert Inn, Aladdin, Dunes and Hacienda. The growth of the convention business played a large role in the expansion trend.

But while the Strip's business grew in the '70s and the resorts expanded to accommodate the additional visitors, the increasingly corporate atmosphere did not lend itself to innovation. Hal Rothman, in *Neon Metropolis*, described this mindset: "The corporations had plenty of cash, but they lacked verve and flair. They weren't entertainers and they felt uncomfortable with the excesses and eccentricities built into the fabric of gaming. They made decisions by committee, sanitizing the look and feel of the city and keeping both eyes firmly fixed on the quarterly earnings report. Corporate thinking built the towers that put Bugsy Siegel's pool, the pinnacle of his vision of leisure, in the shade all day long."

Bill Thompson, writing in *The Maverick Spirit*, elaborated on Rothman's analysis: "Concerned with the bottom line, corporate managers had introduced cost-conscious accounting practices into their operations. Fearful of making expensive mistakes, they shunned innovation and tended to standardize their gambling product. In a word, they had bureaucratized an enterprise that had been attracting customers who had hoped to find magic in their lives."

A more charitable view is that the late '70s and early '80s were an inevitable transition period for the Strip. A lot of things were happening outside the ethereal realm of dreaming up Next Big Thing resorts. For one, federal and state authorities were pushing the mob, once and for all, out of the industry—a highly volatile and perilous process. The highest-profile case involved Stardust, where the dramatic saga of Frank "Lefty" Rosenthal—played by Robert De Niro in the movie *Casino*—unfolded during this period.

On a parallel track, the corporatization of the casino industry was occurring, and the transformation took time and effort. The man who played a large role in launching the corporate era, reclusive billionaire Howard Hughes, proved to be a terrible casino operator. His properties lost money and he spent little on improvements, leaving no significant legacy on the Strip after his death in 1976. Over the next ten years, his heirs gradually sold off his half-dozen Strip casinos to different buyers.

Meanwhile, Kerkorian, a savvier corporate mogul, had problems of his own. On the morning of November 21, 1980, fire engulfed his colossal MGM Grand. By day's end, eighty-seven people had died and hundreds more had been injured. It was, and remains, the biggest tragedy in Las Vegas history. Kerkorian boldly rebuilt the resort and reopened it just eight months later, but the episode delayed his grand plans for Las Vegas.

In addition, outside forces generated anxiety along Las Vegas Boulevard. The primary reason manifested in 1978 when casinos opened in Atlantic City. New Jersey voters decided in 1976 to legalize casinos in the long-popular seaside getaway, which had fallen on hard times in the '60s as it lost ground to newer vacation spots, including Las Vegas. Schwartz, in *Suburban Xanadu*, noted that cheap air travel contributed to Atlantic City's decay. "As more and more people could afford to hop on a plane to Nevada, Florida or the Caribbean, fewer found a vacation in Atlantic City's aging hotels attractive," he wrote. In an effort to revive Atlantic City's economy, local business leaders lobbied to legalize gambling there. Voters endorsed the proposal in 1976. The first casino, Resorts International, opened two years later and was immediately jammed with gamblers, prompting an explosion of casino development along the boardwalk.

At first, Las Vegas resort executives were arrogantly nonchalant about the potential impact of Atlantic City casinos. But it soon became clear that they had a legitimate competitor to deal with. During the '80s, Atlantic City, capitalizing on giant urban areas just a short bus ride away, actually earned more gross gambling revenue than Las Vegas. But rather than invest in Las Vegas, several local casino operators pursued a piece of the Atlantic City action. One of those was Steve Wynn, who parlayed his success with the Golden Nugget in downtown Las Vegas into a resort project in Atlantic City.

On a more practical level, Strip resort bosses were hampered in the early '80s by a deep national recession that hurt tourism and led to high interest rates, a strong deterrent to construction of new resorts. Thompson explained: "For the first time in over thirty years, Nevada's gambling revenues went down in terms of constant-value dollars, and the slippage continued into the middle of the decade. Consequently, there was little interest in building new properties or making major new infusions of capital into the Las Vegas casino industry."

By the mid-'80s, as Atlantic City expanded, state lotteries grew and movements started to open casinos on Indian reservations and Mississippi riverboats, the Strip needed an infusion of fresh thinking and new money. Fortunately for the city, this would occur in a huge way.

# CHAPTER 3

# The Strip: 1989–2012

*"Rather than developing methodically, Las Vegas's Strip grew*
*by experiment, mistakes, wild visions, pragmatic solutions,*
*and chaotic collage."*

—ALAN HESS,
*VIVA LAS VEGAS*

The conventional wisdom holds that the Mirage Hotel changed everything on the Strip. That when it opened on November 22, 1989, it represented a paradigm shift in the way Las Vegas attracted and catered to tourists. That it triggered an unprecedented boom period in Las Vegas.

To a large extent this is true.

Unquestionably, the Mirage raised the bar for Strip resorts, and its owner, Steve Wynn, did a masterful job of publicizing his new tropical-themed property. The Mirage's success triggered a renewed confidence in the gaming industry that Las Vegas could grow far beyond its modest ambitions in the '80s. But it's a little unfair to other Strip casinos to suggest that the Mirage represented something completely new. Long before the Mirage opened its doors, Strip resorts featured elegant restaurants, posh suites and flamboyant stage productions. Wynn simply took the best of what he learned from others in the casino business and put it all together in one cohesive place. The Mirage represented the next step in a natural evolution for the Strip, and Wynn, considered the P.T. Barnum of gaming, was the right person to take advantage of it.

That's not meant to slight Wynn. On the contrary, Wynn is rightfully credited with having the guts to take the plunge where others hesitated. As the previous chapter notes, in the '80s corporate casinos were in a cautious mood, coping with national recessions and wringing their hands over the spread of gambling to Atlantic City and Indian reservations. Wynn was not fazed by these challenges. Like the Strip's legendary developers, from Billy Wilkerson to Jay Sarno to Kirk Kerkorian, he realized that timidity doesn't get you anywhere in the casino business. "Steve Wynn was willing to say, 'I will build even in the face of New Jersey and these other things," said Bill Thompson, a University of Nevada, Las Vegas professor and frequent writer and commentator on the casino industry. "He was willing to say, 'I will risk putting the money out.'"

It didn't hurt that Wynn's resort opened on the cusp of one of the biggest economic booms in U.S. history. The Strip construction frenzy of the '90s paralleled a period when the stock market skyrocketed, the dotcom industry flourished and fortunes were made on the flimsiest of business plans. By the time the dotcom bubble burst, the Strip had found a more secure place in the public consciousness and in the minds of Wall Street investors. The proof came on September 11, 2001, when terrorists struck New York City and Washington, D.C. Las Vegas experienced a precipitous drop in tourism, but fears that Las Vegas might never recover from the terrorist attack were quelled just a few weeks later as hotel rooms and casino floors began to fill up again with tourists.

The conventional wisdom that the Strip became something completely new and different in the '90s also suggests that taking this step required outsiders to come in and show the old-timers how to do it right. In reality, it was almost entirely local talent that transformed the Strip—casino operators such as Wynn, Bennett and Kerkorian who had cut their teeth in Las Vegas in the '60s and '70s, learning the business and waiting for the right opportunity to leap forward.

Start with Wynn. He came to Las Vegas in the late '60s and got his start with a minor investment in the Frontier Hotel. He then became a liquor distributor. He built his reputation as a gaming maverick in the '70s largely on the success of his management of the Golden Nugget in downtown Las Vegas. Under Wynn, the Golden Nugget expanded and reinvented itself, becoming the fanciest address in Glitter Gulch. Many high-rollers and big-name entertainers, including Frank Sinatra and Kenny Rogers, opted for Wynn's downtown pleasure palace over the sprawling resorts of the Strip.

Wynn's management of the Golden Nugget created his twin reputations: the positive spin focused on his attention to detail in delivering a high-quality experience for customers; the negative spin focused on his micromanagement of hotel-casino operations and harsh treatment of employees. In *Super Casino: Inside the 'New' Las Vegas*, author Pete Earley described Wynn's approach at the Golden Nugget: "He ordered his custodians to paint the white line on the curb in front of the casino daily because it got scuffed so often. He designed the uniforms for the security guards and ordered specially made pistols for each guard that resembled old Wild West .45 revolvers. If he spotted a burned-out light bulb, he threw a fit."

But Wynn's ambitions could not be contained on Fremont Street. He first dabbled in Atlantic City, building an elegant Golden Nugget-branded resort there, but the Strip was his destiny, and it came in the form of the Mirage, a 3,000-room "megaresort" built with junk bonds that, with its erupting volcano, aquariums, dolphin habitat, luxury suites and Siegfried and Roy show, gained international attention. It also was an immediate financial success, grossing more than $1 million per day (just enough to pay its enormous debt and operational costs).

Wynn is duly credited with launching the Strip's '90s boom, but Bennett was right on his heels. In the early '70s, Bennett had turned Jay Sarno's nebulous vision for the Circus Circus into a highly successful enterprise. Where Wynn catered to the upper crust, Bennett appealed to middle America with nickel slot machines, cheap food and gaudy fun. At the same time that Wynn was building the Mirage, Bennett was erecting Excalibur—a giant resort with an Arthurian castle theme. Unlike Wynn, Bennett was a cost-conscious developer. He built the Excalibur as cheaply as possible using existing company resources. Although the Excalibur, with 4,000 rooms, was bigger than the Mirage, it cost hundreds of millions less to build. "Steve Wynn was very,

very different," UNLV's Thompson said. "He was doing it on other people's money, not his own, so he didn't think in terms of cost savings. He thought in terms of the best product. He overspent."

The Excalibur opened seven months after the Mirage, and it too was an instant success. Catering to a different audience, the Excalibur carried its kitschy theme throughout the resort. Earley described the operation: "It had the look and feel of a family theme park. Guests were called 'lords' and 'ladies,' employees were dressed in medieval costumes, the hotel's hallways were lit with fixtures shaped like torches, even the telephone operators dropped 'ye olde English' into their speech."

The Mirage and Excalibur were both wildly successful, and equally responsible for launching the '90s boom. However, Wynn's vision eventually carried the day, as ensuing Strip megaresorts tended to be more like the Mirage than the Excalibur. "Steve Wynn ushered in a quantum leap in quality deliverance for the Strip," Thompson said, noting that the Circus Circus company did not completely buy into this philosophy until it opened Mandalay Bay in 1999—long after Bennett had left the company.

The third local casino man who jumped on the '90s bandwagon was Kerkorian. He had built the city's first megaresort, the International (later called Las Vegas Hilton), in the late '60s, and the Strip's first luxury megaresort, the MGM Grand (now Bally's), in the early '70s. With the great success of Wynn's Mirage and Bennett's Excalibur, Kerkorian took the opportunity to make another big mark on the Strip. Kerkorian chose to revive the "MGM Grand" name with his new megaresort, and to once again build the city's largest hotel. With 5,005 rooms, a huge casino floor and an adjacent 330-acre amusement park, the MGM Grand was a $1 billion colossus, a city unto itself at Tropicana Avenue and Las Vegas Boulevard South.

With such a huge property, Kerkorian did not have the luxury of capturing just one segment of the Las Vegas market. He sought to attract high-rollers and fanny-packers alike—bridging the gap between Wynn and Bennett. The formula worked. The MGM Grand quickly joined the growing pack of highly successful Strip megaresorts.

*Sun, Sin & Suburbia: The History of Modern Las Vegas*

The MGM Grand's 1993 opening coincided with the second wave of resorts built by Wynn and Bennett. Interestingly, Wynn built Treasure Island partly to capture some of Bennett's middle-class market. Bennett, meanwhile, built the pyramid-shaped Luxor in an effort to attract some of Wynn's higher-end customers. In the end, both proved as successful as the Mirage and Excalibur, filling to capacity and helping to expand Las Vegas's tourist base. The final months of 1993 generated unbelievable buzz for the city, as the Luxor opened October 9, Treasure Island opened October 27 and the MGM Grand opened December 18.

As 1994 dawned, the "new Las Vegas" had become a spectacle like never before, drawing a wave of national and foreign journalists eager to marvel at the new attractions and skeptically assess the phenomenon. The dominant theme these writers dug out of their visits was that Las Vegas offered all of the gambling tables and slot machines a visitor could ever want, but the resorts no longer depended solely on gambling for their livelihood. Las Vegas was an "adult Disneyland," as enticing for its visual spectacle and entertainment options as for the chance to win a jackpot. Describing the Luxor, *Time* magazine correspondent Kurt Anderson echoed this theme: "The joint has acres of casino space—but the slots and blackjack tables are, astoundingly, quite separate from and mostly concealed by the Disneyesque fun and games. The bells and whistles are more prominent and accessible than the casino itself, and are not merely a cute, quick way to divert people as they proceed into the fleecing pen." Published on January 10, 1994, just weeks after the opening of the MGM Grand, Anderson's cover article, "Las Vegas, U.S.A.," made the point that Las Vegas was no longer "its own highly peculiar self," but had become part of the American mainstream. It had shed its noirish mobbed-up image in favor of appealing to the masses.

"Vegas in none of its various phases (ersatz Old West outpost in the 1930s and '40s, gangsters-meet-Hollywood high-life oasis in the '50s and '60s, uncool polyester dump in the '70s and '80s) was really an accurate prism through which to regard the nation as a whole," Anderson wrote. "Now, however, as the city ricochets through its biggest boom since the Frank-and-Dino Rat Pack days of the '50s and '60s—the tourist inflow has nearly doubled over the past decade, and the area remains among America's fastest growing—the hypereclectic 24-hour-a-day fantasy-themed party machine no longer seems so very exotic or extreme. ... Las Vegas has become Americanized, and, even more, America has become Las Vegasized." As part of its mainstreaming, Anderson noted, Las Vegas had cleaned up its act, shifting from R-rated to PG. "The place is no longer considered racy or naughty by most people," he wrote.

Anderson identified the key factor that distinguished the '90s on the Strip: In order to fill tens of thousands of new hotel rooms, the resorts had to expand their customer base. In order to tap new markets, especially the giant baby boom generation, they had to de-emphasize gambling and offer the kinds of attractions that had families lining up for Disney World, Sea World, Six Flags and other popular family vacation spots. The tactic proved highly successful

Bu not everybody was pleased with the shiny new image. Marc Cooper, in a November 1993 *Village Voice* article entitled "Fear and Lava," bemoaned that Las Vegas was being "swept away by a lava flow of respectability and Family Values. Anxiously gathered at the foot of the Mirage volcano was this herd of beefy middle Americans, almost all dressed in short pants, T-shirts and baseball caps, and enough of them wearing those pastel-colored fanny packs around their waists that the city looked as though it was immersed in a continuing convention of colostomy patients. If Bugsy Siegel had walked by at that moment, half of these lookie-loos would have called the feds. If so much as one old-time Vegas showgirl had shimmered by in boas and pasties, this assembled decency league would have stoned her to death."

Alan Feldman, vice president of Mirage Resorts, told Cooper that the city's newfound interest in the family market wasn't intended to hook kids on gambling. "The fallacy about what's really going on here is the concept of the family," Feldman said. "Family is the 'F' word here. A casino is no place for kids. Las Vegas is not going after kids. But we have to find a new public for Las Vegas, and the biggest untapped pool are those people who won't travel without their kids. So we're giving a little something for the kids to do too. What we're really after is what Disney said. He's not after the kids, but rather

*Sun, Sin & Suburbia: The History of Modern Las Vegas*

the kids inside all of us. We are building adult theme parks. We are playing in the tour and travel market now, not just the gambling market."

The openings of the Mirage, Excalibur, Luxor, Treasure Island and MGM Grand were only the beginning of the Strip's '90s boom. Casino construction, expansion and renovation in the resort corridor continued throughout the decade and well into the 2000s. Since 1989, twenty-one major hotel-casinos have opened on or near the Strip: the Mirage in 1989; Excalibur and Rio in 1990; Luxor, MGM Grand and Treasure Island in 1993; Hard Rock in 1995; Monte Carlo and Stratosphere in 1996; New York-New York in 1997; Wynn's third Strip megaresort, Bellagio, in 1998; Mandalay Bay, Paris and Venetian in 1999; the new Aladdin (now Planet Hollywood) in 2000; the Palms in 2001; the Wynn in 2005; the Encore and Palazzo in 2008; the Aria at CityCenter in 2009; and the Cosmopolitan in 2010. The national economic downturn hit the Strip hard, resulting in one older casino closed and several planned projects stalled, but not one of those twenty-one resorts shut its doors.

## The evolving Strip

The marketing approach of the early '90s did not age well as the city approached the new millennium. Middle America started to lose its luster for Strip casino execs, who all but abandoned heavily themed "architainment" concepts in favor of elegant, modern designs. With the national economy flush with baby boom wealth and dotcom riches, resort companies set their sights on high-rollers and those who appreciated the good life. To that point, Wynn's Bellagio was the most luxurious resort ever built on the Strip, and the most expensive at $1.6 billion. And although it suggested an Italian theme, that was more an ambiance than a main attraction. "It is obviously the pursuit of excellence come to life," Wynn told *Vanity Fair* magazine shortly before the Bellagio's opening. Rather than a gaudy volcano or pirate show as the nongaming centerpiece, the Bellagio boasted a beautiful eleven-acre lake, a botanical garden and an art gallery featuring Wynn's collection of master-pieces. Mandalay Bay, the brainchild of Circus Circus Enterprises executive Glenn Schaeffer, became a swanky hip hangout. Mandalay Bay appealed to a younger crowd than many Strip resorts and hosted a House of Blues restaurant and concert venue that booked some of the world's hottest pop, rock and blues performers. It also snagged a piece of the luxury market, giving the posh Four Seasons chain the first five floors of its hotel. Shelden Adelson's Venetian rivaled the MGM Grand in size and the Bellagio in luxury.

While never forsaking gambling, Strip resorts began to concentrate not on cheap buffets, free lounge acts and all-purpose gift shops, but high-end restaurants, live entertainment and shops that rivaled the world's best. The Strip became a true "resort destination," offering all the luxuries and extravagances found in the best hotels. The resorts invited celebrity chefs to re-create the restaurants they had developed in New York, Los Angeles and San Francisco. Artful theater productions were staged, such as the musical *Chicago* at Mandalay Bay and the Cirque du Soleil productions *Mysteré* at Treasure Island and *O* at Bellagio. And rather than offering the usual handful of jewelry stores and generic fine clothing shops found in most Las Vegas casinos, the megaresorts brought in brand-name retailers from all over the world and set them up in large indoor malls such as the Forum Shops at Caesars Palace, the Shoppes at the Venetian and Desert Passage at the Aladdin (now the Miracle Mile Shops at Planet Hollywood). Shopping became a significant piece of the entertainment pie for Las Vegas visitors.

The Strip also played host to an array of exotic creatures in the '90s. The Mirage started the trend with its dolphin habitat and Secret Garden mini-zoo, but other resorts soon followed suit. An enterprising tourist could flit from resort to resort, seeing lions, elephants, dolphins, sharks, penguins, flamingos and other birds—none of them native to the Mojave Desert, of course. The Shark Reef at Mandalay Bay featured an amazing diversity of sea life.

The number of live music venues and nightclubs also increased dramatically during the '90s. The MGM Grand Garden and Mandalay Bay Events Center hosted large concerts, competing with the Aladdin Theatre for the Performing Arts, which for decades was the only venue on the Strip for arena-sized music acts. The Joint at the Hard Rock and the House of Blues at Mandalay Bay hosted regular performances by rock, rhythm and blues, country and pop performers, including most of the biggest names—as well as cutting-edge acts—in the business. Those venues, holding fewer than 1,500 people, sometimes charged $400 and more for a ticket to see the likes of the Rolling Stones, David Bowie and Rod Stewart. *Rolling Stone* magazine published an article in 1997—before the House of Blues opened—titled, "Against All Odds, Vegas Rocks," detailing Las Vegas's newfound popularity with touring artists. "Once upon a time, 'goin' Vegas's was the ultimate rock & roll put-down," writer David Wild explained. "That was the way critics derided Bob Dylan's 'Street Legal' tour back in the '70s. In 1997, rockers of all stripes—Dylan included—aren't leaving Las Vegas but are happily heading to this prime desert destination. Forget Seattle—Vegas is the new hip scene."

Caesars Palace built the 4,000-seat Colosseum specifically for Canadian pop diva Celine Dion, who inked a long-term performance contract. In 2004, pop legend Elton John debuted a special periodic Colosseum show of his own, receiving rave reviews. Comedian Jerry Seinfeld was another regular. Caesars reported that revenues from the Colosseum performances were exceeding expectations by millions of dollars. More important, the Colosseum shows brought thousands of people into the resort.

The nightclub scene exploded in the late '90s, with venues at the Hard Rock (Baby's), Luxor (Ra), MGM Grand (Studio 54), Rio (Voodoo Lounge) and Mandalay Bay (Foundation Room, Rumjungle) leading a large pack catering to Gen X dance scenesters. A reborn lounge scene soon followed, with well-known architects and interior designers retained to create the perfect modern or retro vibe. Almost every major Strip resort had at least one nightclub and/ or lounge by 2003, though the nightclub business proved more volatile than other aspects of the resort industry, with venues quickly rising and falling in popularity depending on the ficklest of trends and management decisions. The clubs became popular hangouts for movie, music and sports celebrities, from Paris Hilton and Tiger Woods to Britney Spears and Michael Jordan. And it was no coincidence that both daily local newspapers revived gossip columns to cover them. Norm Clarke, the *Review-Journal*'s longtime gossip guru, became something of a celebrity himself by relentlessly chronicling the late-night shenanigans of the famous and infamous in Las Vegas.

In 2012, the Strip nightclub scene remained robust, despite some predictions that it was a fad, eventually to be replaced by something else. About forty nightclubs attracted mostly young, well-dressed crowds of tourists and locals to dance, drink, see and be seen.

One of the most intriguing trends in the late '90s was the Strip's dabbling in the rarified world of fine art. At first the idea seemed absurd: What self-respecting Las Vegas tourist would spend money and time to contemplate Monet, Warhol and Picasso when there were roller coasters to ride and mock pirate battles to enjoy, not to mention gambling tables and slot machines to beat? The Liberace Museum drew crowds but no one would confuse its kitschy rhinestone displays with fine art. But oddly enough, some visitors showed interest in Las Vegas's odes to high culture. Steve Wynn started the trend at the Bellagio, where he carved out a modest space for an art gallery to house his $300 million collection, ranked among the world's finest compilations of modern art. When lines began snaking out the gallery door, Bellagio executives enlarged the space. The Venetian took the art idea a step further in 2001, partnering with the Guggenheim Museum in New York on not one but two museums. The larger one, Guggenheim Las Vegas, did not succeed, as its first exhibit, a retrospective look at "The Art of the Motorcycle," failed to bring in sufficient patrons. The space was closed at the end of the exhibit and was converted for another use. But the smaller museum, Guggenheim Hermitage, displaying painting masterpieces from the Guggenheim collection in New York and the Hermitage collection in Russia, proved to be a hit—at least initially.

East Coast art snobs were outraged by the idea of classic works hanging in a casino, but Guggenheim officials argued for the democratization of art appreciation. In Las Vegas, observers saw the Bellagio gallery and Venetian museum as encouraging signs that Las Vegas was maturing culturally. Jake Highton, a Reno-based professor and world traveler, praised the Strip's new art venues during a visit in 2003. Writing in the *Sparks Tribune*, Highton condemned Las Vegas generally as exemplifying "what's wrong with America," but he was brought to tears by "seeing the works of famed artists in the most unlikely of places." He wrote, "Art, like music, is a universal language. It speaks magnificently amid the kitsch of Las Vegas." The Guggenheim Hermitage museum closed in 2008, unable to compete with the profit-obsessed demands of a casino. Some members of the local arts community also said the museum suffered because it was treated as an afterthought by the New York-based Guggenheim Foundation. Whatever the causes for its closure, during its seven years in business the museum attracted more than one million visitors.

After the Palms opened in 2001, the Strip took a little breather from the anxiety and anticipation of resort openings. It was one of those occasionally necessary periods when casino executives took a step back and examined how things were panning out. During this time, the September 11, 2001, terrorist attacks occurred, temporarily damaging Las Vegas tourism, and then the national economy fell into recession. And one of the Strip's new megaresorts faltered, as the Aladdin wound up in bankruptcy court. The Aladdin's poor returns were not, however, attributed directly to a case of overbuilding on the Strip. Rather, analysts blamed the poor design of the resort's Strip entrance, which deterred tourists rather than enticing them through the doors, among other poor management decisions.

But while shiny new resorts did not emerge for a few years, existing properties kept busy, embarking on significant expansion and renovation projects. They added hotel rooms, enlarged convention centers, enhanced shopping areas and refined dining and entertainment options. While most communities would kill for the hundreds of millions invested on the Strip during this "quiet" period, some Las Vegans wondered whether there was a problem.

## The modern era

Wynn's ambitious return to the Strip helped ease those concerns. After the Bellagio's opening, Wynn was forced from his perch atop Mirage Resorts in 2000 by a corporate takeover. The company merged with Kerkorian's MGM Grand to become MGM Mirage Incorporated. Wynn, who made several hundred million dollars in the deal, turned around and bought the land-rich Desert Inn at a bargain price of $270 million, vowing to build a resort even more elegant and amazing than Bellagio. After originally calling it Le Reve, Wynn changed the name to Wynn Las Vegas in 2003, in part because people were having trouble correctly pronouncing the French phrase for "The Dream," in part because his name is so well known. The $2.7 billion Wynn Las Vegas opened in 2005, kicked off with a memorable television ad showing

Wynn standing perilously atop the resort. "I'm Steve Wynn. This is my new hotel, the only one I've ever signed my name to," he said as the camera pulled back to reveal him standing on top of the fifty-story structure.

But Wynn no longer stood head and shoulders above his Strip rivals in terms of visionary thinking. In Wynn's absence, Glenn Schaeffer at Mandalay Resort Group assumed the role of Strip creative leader. Under Schaeffer's leadership, Mandalay Bay emerged as the hottest spot on the Strip, offering something for everyone from high-rollers to hipsters to families. In early 2004, Schaeffer opened THEhotel at Mandalay Bay, an 1,118-room tower that blazed new ground for a Strip resort: It was gambling-free. Instead of slot machines, THEhotel's lobby was stylishly appointed, the textured walls adorned by original modern art from masters such as Andy Warhol, Jasper Johns and Richard Serra. Built with conventioneers and business travelers in mind, THE hotel echoed the cosmopolitan air of posh hotels in New York, San Francisco and Hong Kong. The suites are large, high-tech and designed for work as well as rest. Each has two rooms, one a bedroom for personal use, the other functioning as an office where business can be conducted and small meetings held. While the casino is just a short walk away, the understated elegance of THEhotel contrasts sharply with the aural and visual cacophony of the Strip.

Schaeffer invested $250 million in THEhotel for one reason: to complement Mandalay Bay's new 1.4 million-square-foot convention center. With casinos opening around the globe, gambling was no longer Las Vegas's primary calling card. Conventions, however, were a growing industry, and Las Vegas offered a sweet deal: ample and quality convention facilities combined with its vast entertainment options after the day's speeches and seminars are over.

The Las Vegas Convention and Visitors Authority promoted Las Vegas on two levels, as a leisure destination and as a convention and trade show site, with separate advertising campaigns for each market. For the leisure visitor, the latest slogan was "What happens here, stays here," which soon took on a life of its own as a pop culture reference. For the business crowd, it was "We work as hard as we play." Las Vegas welcomed five million convention and trade show attendees in 2003, representing fifteen percent of the visitor total. Manny Cortez, then the director of the LVCVA, said he wanted to increase that figure to twenty or twenty-five percent. The two key reasons: 1) convention attendees tend to spend more money than leisure visitors when they come to town and 2) the expansion of casinos in other states and countries demands that Las Vegas continuously seek out new markets. Officials believe Las Vegas could snag additional convention and trade show business away from other cities. Surveys show attendance tends to go up when annual events rotating among various cities come to Las Vegas.

Another contender for Wynn's throne entered the scene during his temporary exile. George Maloof got his start in 1994 by building the Fiesta hotel-casino on North Rancho Drive. The Fiesta became highly successful by maximizing the time-honored formula for attracting local customers: cheap food, good service and, most important, favorable slot machine odds. Maloof was an almost daily presence on the property, getting to know customers and taking care of them in ways that Las Vegas casino executives had not done in decades.

Maloof parlayed his success with the Fiesta, which he sold to Station Casinos, into the Palms, a $268 million resort on Flamingo Road just off the Strip. With the Palms, Maloof adopted a hybrid approach: locals-friendly casino by day, youth-oriented hotspot by night. Opening in 2001, the Palms quickly became the place to see and be seen in Las Vegas. Celebrities flocked to the resort's chic clubs and upscale restaurants, while well-heeled locals enjoyed top-flight amenities without the hassles of the Strip. "The vision was to create a place with a balance between locals and tourists," Maloof told the *Las Vegas Sun* amid the Palms' second anniversary celebration, during which some observers were calling him a "young Steve Wynn." Maloof said, "The building was designed in a way that they weren't bothering each other—each has their own area, their own time of day when they are there."

The Palms actively competed with the Hard Rock and Mandalay Bay to attract younger customers—the 21-to-35 crowd that may have shunned Las Vegas had those three resorts not identified an opportunity. Maloof's pop culture savvy was evident in this regard. The Palms hosted a season-long taping of the MTV reality series *Real World* in a luxury suite. The series brought massive publicity to the Palms, and, since its broadcast, the suite has been popular with celebrities and other well-heeled visitors. The Palms also hosted the fiftieth anniversary celebration of *Playboy* magazine, and its Brenden Theaters complex was the site of the annual CineVegas International Film Festival. In 2004, Maloof recorded a first in Las Vegas resort history by opening a tattoo parlor in the Palms. In 2005, Maloof opened a second building, the Fantasy Tower, which, until 2012, included a Playboy Club. The Palms also added a concert venue, The Pearl, which competes with the Hard Rock and House of Blues for popular music acts, and a recording studio that has been used by many high-profile musicians.

### Implosion fever

One of the unfortunate aspects of the '90s boom on the Strip was the loss of numerous historic structures. Las Vegas has always favored the future over the past, and this was reflected in the buzz during the '90s surrounding the next implosion. From 1993 to 2001, the "implosion capital of the world" demolished seven resorts, all in dramatic fashion. In each case, large crowds gathered and television crews posted cameras in multiple locations, turning the highly technical act of leveling a high-rise structure into a spectacle. In most cases, bigger, more inspired hotel-casinos have risen from the ashes.

An implosion works like this: Hundreds of pounds of dynamite are placed in strategic locations in the building and detonated in a sequence that brings it down quickly and with minimal impact on surrounding areas. The only effect beyond the property line is a huge dust plume that blankets a few square miles of the city for several hours.

The first implosion occurred on October 27, 1993, when the Dunes Hotel crashed to the ground. The choreographer of this visually striking implosion was Wynn, who bought the sprawling property at Las Vegas Boulevard and Flamingo Road to erect the Bellagio. The implosion is best remembered for the well-lighted slow tumble of the distinctive Dunes neon sign.

Next up was the Landmark, which came down November 7, 1995. Begun by other investors and completed in the late '60s by reclusive billionaire Howard Hughes, the Landmark was never a successful casino, although its trademark space-age design was a staple of the Las Vegas skyline. Footage of its demolition appeared in the Tim Burton film *Mars Attacks!* The Las Vegas Convention and Visitors Authority purchased the Landmark site for use as a parking lot.

A year later, on November 26, 1996, down came the Sands. Once the hip playground of Frank Sinatra's Rat Pack, the Sands fell on hard times in the early '90s as it failed to keep pace with the new wave of megaresorts. The Sands site is now home to Sheldon Adelson's Venetian. December 31, 1996, marked the demise of the Hacienda. The Hacienda was never one of Las Vegas's most glamorous hotels, but it long stood as the Strip's southern anchor. Perhaps the most famous entertainer to perform there regularly was comedian Redd Foxx, who plied his X-rated humor on stage when he wasn't playing his PG role on TV's *Sanford and Son*. The Hacienda implosion, a New Year's Eve spectacle, paved the way for Mandalay Bay.

On April 27, 1998, the old Aladdin tumbled. The wedding place of Elvis and Priscilla Presley, the Aladdin was always financially troubled. It once belonged to mobsters, and at one time entertainer Wayne Newton had a piece of the action. An estimated 20,000 people watched it fall. It was replaced with a newer, bigger Aladdin (later renamed Planet Hollywood) and a shopping mall.

The El Rancho was leveled on October 2, 2000. The implosion was the most necessary and least hyped of the bunch. The hotel had taken the name of the Strip's original resort but had no other relation to it. It had been the Thunderbird, with local owners allegedly fronting for Meyer Lansky, and then the Silverbird, but it had been closed for eight years when it was torn down. The vacant, dilapidated structure was an eyesore, a safety hazard and haven for the homeless until Turnberry Associates, which was building pricey high-rise condos next door, bought the site. Turnberry originally planned to build a London-themed casino on the El Rancho site, but did not do anything with it for several years.

An implosion on October 23, 2001, crumbled a fourteen-story tower of the fabled Desert Inn. Wynn had purchased the D.I. and closed it shortly after to make way for his new resort, Wynn Las Vegas.

After a several-year hiatus, the implosions resumed. The Boardwalk, a relatively minor and nondescript Strip hotel, crumbled on May 9, 2006, clearing space for part of MGM's massive CityCenter project. The Stardust was leveled on March 13, 2007, and the Frontier fell on November 13, 2007. Among the oldest casinos still standing on the Strip, both crumbled to make room for newer, bigger resorts. The Frontier was to become the Plaza, built by an Israeli company. But the national recession put that project on long-term hold. Boyd Gaming started building Echelon Place on the Stardust site. But its construction soon was suspended indefinitely. Boyd no doubt kicked itself for tearing down the Stardust when it did. If it had had some inkling of the impending economic nosedive, it could have kept the Stardust operating instead of generating no revenue whatsoever from the desolate north Strip property.

Many preservationists groan about the Strip's boorish disregard for history, but experience has shown that Las Vegas must constantly reinvent itself and top its previous feats to stay competitive. With growing pressure from rival gambling meccas at home and abroad, that philosophy isn't about to change anytime soon.

## Strip philosophers

For at least fifty years, Las Vegas has fascinated writers. They have endeavored to describe it as something more or less than a typical American city. In colorful and often bloated language, they have tried to explain Las Vegas's "spirit" and its "meaning." They have employed Las Vegas as a symbol of how the culture is headed one way or another. Las Vegas is credited with being either heaven or hell on Earth. These amateur psychiatrists have Las Vegas lie down on the couch and then shrink its neon-encircled head.

The majority of descriptions are negative in nature, focusing on clichés such as zombified slot machine players, the absence of windows and clocks in the casinos, and how rarely gamblers go home winners. The more positive takes tend to emphasize that an appreciation of Las Vegas must be a guilty pleasure. Occasionally the writers are perceptive, and their attempts to identify Las Vegas's place within the larger culture feel right. Las Vegas, or at least the Strip, is indeed unique, and it has played a significant role in shaping the physical landscape of the wider American culture over the past several decades.

*Sun, Sin & Suburbia: The History of Modern Las Vegas*

More often, however, the writers are hacks who embarrass themselves with their purple prose and inane generalizations.

Tom Wolfe is one of the more perceptive writers. He may have started the trend of painting Las Vegas in a larger-than-life context. Before he began writing novels such as *The Bonfire of the Vanities* and *A Man in Full*, Wolfe was a celebrated practitioner of the New Journalism, responsible for best-selling nonfiction works such as *The Electric Kool-Aid Acid Test* and *The Right Stuff* that gave a literary flair to otherwise conventional reportage. One of Wolfe's earliest productions of New Journalism was an *Esquire* magazine article about Las Vegas. The article, published in 1964, was titled, "Las Vegas (What?) Las Vegas (Can't Hear You! Too Noisy) Las Vegas!!!!" Wolfe's manic style fit perfectly with the city's over-the-top nature. However, some of the things he wrote about in the early '60s would qualify as rank cliché today. For example, Wolfe described the zombified slot players:

"One of the indelible images of Las Vegas is that of the old babes at the row upon row of slot machines. There they are at six o'clock Sunday morning no less than at three o'clock Tuesday afternoon. Some of them pack their old hummocky shanks into Capri pants, but many of them just put on the old print dress, the same one day after day, and the old hob-heeled shoes, looking like they might be going out to buy eggs in Tupelo, Mississippi. They have a Dixie Cup full of nickels or dimes in the left hand and an Iron Boy work glove on the right hand to keep the calluses from getting sore." As accurate as Wolfe's description may have been, it's been repeated a thousand times over the past forty years.

But Wolfe wrote something more interesting about Las Vegas in an introduction to a collection of his articles, *The Kandy-Kolored Tangerine-Flake Streamline Baby*, published in 1965. He argued that the visual icons of Las Vegas were the work of "proles" operating "outside of the aristocratic tradition." "The usual thing has happened, of course," he explained. "Because it is prole, it gets ignored, except on the most sensational level. Yet long after Las Vegas's influence as a gambling heaven has gone, Las Vegas's forms and symbols will be influencing American life. The fantastic skyline! Las Vegas's neon sculpture, its fantastic fifteen-story-high display signs, parabolas, boomerangs, rhomboids, trapezoids and all the rest of it, are already the staple design of the American landscape outside of the oldest parts of the oldest cities. They are all over every suburb, every subdivision, every highway."

Hal Rothman, a University of Nevada, Las Vegas history professor, took a bold stab at characterizing the city in his 2002 book, *Neon Metropolis: How Las Vegas Started the Twenty-first Century*. Confirming Wolfe's thesis, Rothman described Las Vegas as a "triumph of postindustrial capitalism," a "spectacle of postmodernism" and "the first city of the twenty-first century." He said Las Vegas is "America in the new millennium," and that "like Disneyland, Las Vegas encapsulates what we are." He continued: "Las Vegas is the therapeutic ethos of our time run amok, our sociopsychological promise to ourselves to be eternally young writ large on the landscape of aging self-indulgence." Rothman contended that "Las Vegas now symbolizes the new America" and is "the place to be as the new century takes shape." Rothman's language, however hyperbolic, mostly rang true. Undeniably, America was becoming more like Las Vegas, and Las Vegas was becoming more like America. (Rothman, an insightful chronicler of modern Las Vegas, died in 2007 of Lou Gehrig's disease. He was just forty-eight years old.)

One of the more egregious efforts to "explain" Las Vegas was *Zeropolis: The Experience of Las Vegas*, written by French philosopher Bruce Begout and published in 2002. At first, Begout seemed to be on the right track, echoing Rothman's thesis that American culture increasingly takes its cues from Las Vegas. "Each trip we take to a shopping center is a shadow cast by Las Vegas habits and customs," he wrote. But as Begout explored Las Vegas, he could not contain an urge to utter vicious generalizations about the city. For example, disgusted by the Mirage volcano, he wrote: "Once what hits you in the first few hours has faded, the city very quickly becomes wearisome. There is little to see beyond the casinos and the themed hotels, and even less to do. All the shows are essentially alike, variations on amusement park fare."

Of course, for every Las Vegas critic, another writer reveled in the city's stimuli. Richard Corliss, writing in *Time* magazine in 2003, explained his love for Las Vegas: "Las Vegas is the great fictional city. It's a page-turning novel told in a million lives and 120,000 hotel rooms; an epic movie with casino chips for special effects; a tragedy of addiction and a burlesque with the smoothest showgirls around." He added, "Gambling is the only night out that offers the hope of returning your investment." Marc Cooper, in his 2004 book *The Last Honest Place in America*, appreciated Las Vegas because it is "the American market stripped completely bare, a mini-world totally free of the pretenses and protocols of modern consumer capitalism."

This international preoccupation with analyzing Las Vegas is both exhilarating and maddening. On the one hand, Las Vegans are constantly reminded that the whole world is watching their city—loving it, hating it, studying it. Walk down the Strip and you're likely to see somebody jotting down observations or filming a documentary. This constant attention is, for a tourism-dependent city, far better than the alternative. On the other hand, the frequent assessments of Las Vegas are often oversimplified and wrong. Reporters who come to Las Vegas tend to get careless with the facts. Perhaps their note-taking is shoddy because of all the dazzling distractions the city offers.

The underlying problem is the desire to summarize Las Vegas in a sentence or a paragraph. It can't be done. The city has become too big and complicated to describe in even five hundred words, however well-wrought. Or, and this may be closer to the truth, the city is too normal, especially to locals, to warrant such lofty inspection. David Schwartz, in *Suburban Xanadu: The Casino Resort on the Strip and Beyond*, elaborated on this local view of Las Vegas. Noting that "the glitter of the Las Vegas Strip is hardly conducive to clear-headed social analysis," he wrote: "To us, 'the casino' is not a sybaritic den of vice, but a place to work or go for entertainment: to see a movie, play bingo, hit the buffet, or gamble. In short, casinos form a normative part of the social and economic landscape, and they are usually neither dangerous nor exciting."

That is not to say Las Vegas is boring, but the most useful writing about the city sheds the clichés, the hyperbole and the quickie generalizations in favor of more thoughtful and honest observation.

## CityCenter

When the economy faltered in 2008, Boyd Gaming abruptly suspended work on its massive $4.8 billion Echelon Place project. Construction was just getting started, so Boyd was able to pull the plug before it had invested too much money. MGM did not have the same opportunity with its even bigger CityCenter project. When the economy collapsed, it already had plunged hundreds of millions into the most ambitious resort complex in Las Vegas history. Shutting down construction would have been a disaster on several levels. So MGM pressed forward with the $8.5 billion CityCenter amid the toughest economic climate since the Great Depression.

Financial challenges ensued, as tight lending markets made it difficult for MGM to secure sufficient funding for the gargantuan project. Needing some help, MGM brought in a partner, the oil-rich Arab nation of Dubai, to finance CityCenter. Later, as the economy continued to deterioriate, Dubai's confidence in the project wavered. In March 2009, MGM was preparing for the possibility of filing for bankruptcy protection, which could have shut down or delayed construction and thrown more than eight thousand people out of work. Ultimately, in late April, MGM and Dubai, along with eight different banks, came together on a funding plan and bankruptcy was averted, in part thanks to the help of the majority leader of the U.S. Senate, Nevada's Harry Reid, who made calls to bankers in support of the project.

The effort to save CityCenter was a remarkable undertaking requiring hundreds of people worldwide working round-the-clock to restructure the whole deal. The *Review-Journal*'s Howard Stutz summarized the scope of the endeavor:

"The work involved dozens of MGM Mirage corporate employees, who were assisted by hundreds of outside advisers from nearly two dozen outside firms weighing in from both U.S. coasts and around the world. ... Some of the advisers were given makeshift offices in Bellagio suites that were commandeered by the company and stripped of their luxury items. Secondary corporate offices at Mandalay Bay were utilized, as were offices in the temporary CityCenter headquarters behind New York-New York. ... Hundreds of seemingly nonstop telephone conference calls were held at all hours of the day and night."

The financing for CityCenter was a high-wire act from the start. MGM started building the project before it had secured all the money it needed. Before the national economic collapse, there was little concern that the credit could be secured. What's more, the CityCenter design was a work in progress, resulting in huge cost overruns. "The complexity and scale of the project have yielded frequent design changes that increased the budget and delayed the execution of final-price agreements with its contractors," the *Las Vegas Sun's* Liz Benston reported in 2009. "CityCenter has ballooned in cost by as much as $5 billion within four years, virtually doubling projections."

CityCenter was conceived in 2004, well before the economic downturn, at a time when Las Vegas business leaders saw no limit to what the city could do and become. It was the brainchild of MGM Chief Executive Officer Jim Murren, an urban planner by training who envisioned a sort of "city within a city"—a downtown for the Strip. The project would encompass six high-rise buildings on seventy-six acres, all of it aimed at the high-end customer. The centerpiece was the 4,000-room Aria hotel-casino, accompanied by the Mandarin Oriental, Vdara and Harmon nongaming hotels, the Veer Towers condo and the Crystals shopping mall. Each building was designed by a different name-brand architect, and several of them earned honors for energy efficiency.

In addition to the financial problems, CityCenter's construction triggered controversy, as six workers died on the work site. While accidents are a possibility on any construction project of this size, the CityCenter project came under scrutiny for lax safety practices. The *Las Vegas Sun's* investigative reports examining the CityCenter construction fatalities earned the newspaper a Pulitzer Prize in 2009.

Also, the Harmon Hotel was scaled back from forty-seven floors to twenty-seven after it was discovered that faulty construction would not safely support a taller structure. As concerns mounted, Harmon construction was halted entirely. By 2011, amid fears that the unfinished building could collapse in an earthquake, officials started debating whether to repair or demolish it.

Although two buildings opened a couple of weeks earlier, for all intents and purposes CityCenter debuted on December 16, 2009, with the usual pomp and fireworks marking the opening of the Aria. Reporters marveled at the high-end and high-tech accommodations, and the natural lighting within the casino—unheard of in earlier times—got a lot of ink. Large pieces of public art by high-profile artists also drew attention.

Reaction to CityCenter ran in both directions. Paul Goldberger, architecture critic for *The New Yorker* magazine, remarked that CityCenter represented an elevation of Las Vegas design from the days of kitschy themed resorts. Regarding Aria, Goldberger wrote: "It's a serious, detailed building, with facades that zigzag in a sawtooth composition and elegant grillwork that lends texture and also provides some deflection of the desert sun." But while Goldberger lauded CityCenter's modern architecture, he questioned whether it could compete with the city's plethora of themed resorts. "Caesars Palace and its progeny are crass but iconic," he wrote. "The CityCenter buildings are sophisticated, but you wonder, finally, if they are all that memorable."

Writing in *L.A. Weekly*, critic Hugh Hart was generally impressed by CityCenter. "There's not a stitch of kitsch to be found in the resort town's latest iteration of destination buildings," he wrote. "Hewing to sustainable practices and materials, the futuristic urban canyon seems to have crash-landed on the Strip, making Las Vegas Boulevard's retro-themed structures look positively quaint by comparison."

The primary criticism of CityCenter focused on its initial promise to be a "city within a city." Early on, the public was left with the impression that CityCenter would be a welcoming, pedestrian-friendly gathering place that would serve the needs of the thousands of condo and hotel dwellers in the area. But that's not how it turned out. "CityCenter is laid out not for pedestrians but as a machine for moving vast numbers of cars efficiently," Goldberger wrote. "There are wide ramps coming off the Las Vegas Strip, auto turnarounds, and porte cocheres—all good for traffic flow but hardly what you would call urban open space. ... There is no pleasant place to walk, except inside the buildings. ... It still isn't much of a center, or much of a city."

Alan Hess, longtime Las Vegas architecture critic, panned the first impression left by CityCenter. "The entrance has all the pleasantness of an airport terminal," he told the *Las Vegas Sun*. "There's a lot of concrete and ramps and other things that turn pedestrians off, and a sense of being channeled into an entryway."

Besides the architectural and urban design criticisms, CityCenter also suffered from the bursting of the real estate bubble, which made it difficult to sell the project's condos at anticipated prices. Further, the Crystals shopping mall, occupied almost entirely by super-high-end shops, struggled from a shortage of visitors who could afford to shop there. But it was too early to assess CityCenter's success. As Jeremy Aguero, a local financial research consultant, noted, CityCenter opened "during the worst economic downturn in Southern Nevada's history. ... That seems to me to be an unfair landscape for a long-term judgment."

Amid the struggles, Jim Murren gained wide respect for successfully navigating incredibly choppy waters to get CityCenter financed, built and opened. His vision and perseverence earned him a place among the pantheon of dreamers who have done something unprecedented in Las Vegas.

## The Cosmopolitan

The Cosmopolitan caught Las Vegas by surprise. When the $3.9 billion resort opened on December 15, 2010, the recession had already been punching the city in the face for two years, and CityCenter, the mammoth resort complex next door, had gotten off to a sluggish start. What's more, the Cosmo, as it soon became known, had an ugly conception. The first developer, Bruce Eichner, lost the half-built resort to foreclosure in 2008, leaving the property in the hands of Deutsche Bank. Despite the global economic crisis, the bank decided to forge ahead. The odds seemed long that the Cosmo would make a big splash.

And yet the resort, designed by architect David Rockwell, brought a fresh, cool vibe to the Strip, and locals and visitors alike quickly took notice. Although the Cosmo spent money on a surreal and provocative advertising campaign ("Just the right amount of wrong"), word of mouth proved to be equally effective in drawing crowds to the ultra-modern property.

Maybe Las Vegas shouldn't have been so shocked by the Cosmo's fast rise. After all, several months before it opened, John Unwin, the creative-minded CEO, had promised to deliver a different sort of place. "We're building a resort on the fifty-yard line on the Strip, and bringing retail and restaurants that are new to Vegas," Unwin told the *Las Vegas Sun*. "We're not a product of a merger, acquisition or expansion. We're building a new culture that's going to be part of our genetic code."

A veteran of the boutique hotel business, Unwin looked for ways to distinguish the Cosmo from its upscale competitors. One way was to offer large rooms with dramatic views of the Strip, more like the urban lofts of New York or Tokyo than the crackerboxes that many of his Strip competitors offered to the average visitor. "We are unique because we built a high-end hotel that's not pretentious," Unwin told the *Las Vegas Review-Journal* a few days before the opening. "This is a type of hotel you'll find in Los Angeles, San Francisco, Paris or London. It's what makes us different."

Unwin told the *Sun* that his target audience is the "curious class": sophisticated people who are "creative, independent, broad-minded and love foreign food and travel." In short, people who don't decide to take a trip to Las Vegas because they've earned enough loyalty club points for a cheap room and free buffet. His Las Vegas competitors, Unwin said, were not going after this lucrative market, and if they tried, they would fail because they could not deliver what the "curious class" is seeking.

Strong words, but Las Vegans had heard such ambitious rhetoric before. After all, Las Vegas is a city built on braggadocio. Jaded by the two dozen resort openings of the past two decades, few expected the Cosmo to stand out from the crowd on a street where everybody is striving to do just that. But the Cosmo's smart style and innovative amenities immediately attracted local customers. Its restaurants, nightclubs, pools and music venues filled with residents who rarely get excited about the Strip's other resorts.

On opening night, the Cosmo drew widespread raves, including from Strip competitors and politicos. "I was very impressed with the décor, very impressed with the crowd and very impressed with the martini they made me," Las Vegas Mayor Oscar Goodman told the *Review-Journal.* Wynn Resorts owner Steve Wynn added, "I thought the place was fun and exciting. I had great sushi."

Mike Prevatt, longtime arts and entertainment editor of *Las Vegas CityLife* and a frequent critic of the Strip's corporate facades, was among the Cosmo's early cheerleaders. "It's all in the property's name," Prevatt explained in an interview. "The post-Rat Pack Strip really hasn't had what you could call a true 'cosmopolitan' spot. Its properties have been fancy, frugal, family-friendly—but they have not been fashionable. The Cosmo has a sensibility that makes it simultaneously trendy and alternative. It's unapologetically urbane. If New York City could build and operate a casino-hotel, it would be the Cosmo."

Prevatt took notice of how the Cosmo actively turned Las Vegas conventional wisdom on its head. "Modern-era casino management always seems to be saying that the marketing must be this way, the music piped into the casino must be this familiar, the entertainment must appeal to this wide an audience and the offerings must always be the same for every property. But the Cosmo goes and commissions bizarro TV commercials, has the promoter for Lollapalooza book the lounge acts, 'hides' the best pizza joint on the boulevard, doesn't bother with a headliner showroom or production, and broadcasts its sold-out concerts to the rest of the Strip on its sixty-foot marquee."

The Cosmo appealed to a younger, hipper clientele turned off by the cheesy antics of other resorts. "When I look at the Cosmo, sometimes I see a fifty-story-tall middle finger," Prevatt said. "I then look at its neighboring properties, and I indulge in some schadenfreude: If the rest of the Strip can't suss out why people aren't talking about other casinos like they are the Cosmo, they're blind to their own militant corporatism and stubborn conformity."

One key to the Cosmo's hipster appeal was its booking of indie pop and rock acts in its Book and Stage lounge. The price: free. Acts such as Best Coast, Foster the People, Black Rebel Motorcycle Club and Mumford & Sons performed there at a time when no other Strip property would have given them a second thought.

The *Sun*'s Patrick Coolican identified the Cosmo's appeal by listing some of the things it does not have. "No Cirque nor magicians nor impressionists nor past-their-prime rockers nor country nor pop stars. And no Prada. And no chefs who phone it in from some other resort. You know why? ... Those things are no longer cool, if they ever were."

The Cosmo figured out how to appeal not only to hip young tourists but to locals of the same stripe. "I've never run into friends or acquaintances at CityCenter, and I rarely do anywhere else on the Strip, for that matter," Prevatt said. "And yet, I'm just as likely to see people I know at the Cosmopolitan as I am at the downtown bars I frequent. That's saying something."

The resort also drew attention for its lively and inventive restaurant scene. Among the fans was veteran Las Vegas food critic John Curtas. "The Cosmo has reset the paradigm for Vegas restaurants by becoming more 'foodie-focused' instead of relying on celebrity chefs as the main draw," Curtas said in an interview. "Name chefs are still a big draw, but the younger, hipper crowd looks more to what's on the plate than whose name is on the door."

Curtas cited Jose Andrés's China Poblano as the "ultimate example" of this food-first philosophy. His view was echoed in the summer of 2011 by *The Atlantic* magazine, which identified a "second-wave restaurant renaissance" in Las Vegas, led by the Cosmo.

"Even glimpsed through the crowd, China Poblano is arresting," wrote *The Atlantic*'s Corby Kummer. "There are neon-signed takeout windows for Chinese food on one side and for Mexican food on the other, and a sculpted Chinese-filigree doorway. At one bar, you can watch Chinese chefs roll out noodles and fold dumplings; at another, Mexican chefs make tacos and carnitas."

Andres is also responsible for Jaleo, a classic Spanish restaurant in the Cosmo. "There I had the best paella I've had in this country," Kummer wrote.

Meanwhile, another national magazine, *Esquire*, took notice of the Cosmo's Chandelier bar, naming it one of the country's best new watering holes in 2011. "While many casino bars feel like sad, removed, half-empty after-thoughts lined with hookers tapping at video poker machines, the brand new Cosmopolitan has erected its entire structure around the bar. The three-level Chandelier bar serves as the hotel's beating heart—or like the glimmering, power-generating chest device that keeps Iron Man alive. Set literally inside a gigantic chandelier composed of two million crystals, it's not like any bar you go to back home, and that's the point."

The travel publication *Fodor's* named the Cosmo one of its world's 100 best hotels in 2011. "Design innovation is at the center of the Cosmopolitan, the sleekest new hotel on the Vegas Strip," according to the editors.

The Cosmo kept the innovations coming. In February 2012, the resort debuted its Pop-Up Wedding Chapel, offering faux weddings in a chapel visible to pedestrians on the Strip. The wedding rings were dispensed from a gumball machine. The weddings called for a twenty-four-hour commitment—for those impulsive visitors who want to try out the marriage thing without the complications of making it official. A month later, the EA Sports Bar opened, offering visitors access to PlayStation 3 consoles to play sports-oriented video games or watch live games on seventy-inch TVs.

While the Cosmo generated a great deal of buzz for itself—and by extension for Las Vegas—it still somehow lost money, $58.5 million, in the third quarter of 2011. This incongruity reflected the paradox of recession-era Las Vegas: A packed restaurant or nightclub or casino floor does not necessarily translate into big profits.

In his examination of this conundrum, Coolican's research identified the Cosmo's problem. Just like any other casino, it needs gamblers. It needs its hip clientele to sit down at the tables and slot machines and lose money, which may not be a favorite pastime for many of them. The frumpy visitors whom the Cosmo wants to ignore are the ones who tend to blow their budgets at other casinos.

And while its competitors design their properties to put slot machines and table games in the path of customers wherever they go, the Cosmo's coolest areas are essentially gambling-free zones. "We like the Cosmopolitan because it's so easy to ignore gambling," Coolican wrote. "The genius of Rockwell's design is also its very real weakness as a casino."

Still, those looking for signs of where Las Vegas is going in the future need look no further than the Cosmopolitan. "If [the Cosmo] succeeds, it will have broken the mold and brought us something new," Coolican wrote. "It would be a piece of Las Vegas a little less focused on manipulating customers to lose their money and more on encouraging guests—for a steep price—to soak up the energy of this great moment to be alive."

### Looking ahead

The Strip remains unique—it's still the place gamblers must go to experience the real thing. But resort executives were well aware that to maintain that dominant position, they needed to offer newer and bolder attractions. Competition was growing—regionally, nationally and internationally. Almost every state now had some form of casino gambling, In California, the Indian casinos were no longer tin barns in remote areas. Many were near or in cities. They were run professionally, and physically they compared favorably with Las Vegas's smaller properties. Meanwhile, states such as Pennsylvania, Wisconsin and Iowa were dotted with casinos.

The hottest growth area in the 2000s was Asia, especially tiny Macau, where thirty-five casinos drew Chinese gamblers with a penchant for marathon sessions at the tables. Macau generated far more gambling revenue than Las Vegas. Macau earnings helped some Las Vegas casino companies to weather the recession.

But gaming companies also sought opportunities in Europe and South America. In 2012, Sheldon Adelson, owner of the Venetian and Palazzo resorts on the Strip, as well as casinos in Macau and Singapore, proposed the first-ever Las Vegas-style resort in Spain. Adelson wanted to invest $22 billion in "Eurovegas," a complex of six casinos, eleven hotels, a convention center and three golf courses in either Madrid or Barcelona. Seemingly no part of the globe—except maybe North Korea or Iran—was off limits in the fertile minds of the gaming industry.

With the exceptions of CityCenter and the Cosmopolitan, the recession put an array of Las Vegas resort projects on hold, if not canceled altogether. The $3 billion Fontainebleau would have been a major new resort on the north Strip, but construction was suspended in 2009. Investor Carl Icahn acquired the property out of bankruptcy in 2010 but by 2012 he had announced no plans to resume construction. Boyd Gaming's Echelon Place project was halted amid recession fears, with no signs that construction would resume anytime soon. The Elad Group's Plaza Hotel, planned to replace the Frontier, never got off the ground. Caesars discussed elaborate plans for $500 million in new development on the east side of the Strip—including a giant Ferris wheel—but by 2012 it had not submitted any formal plans.

Surprisingly, only one major resort closed amid the economic nosedive. The Sahara, which had undergone a modest renovation, could not survive

*Sun, Sin & Suburbia: The History of Modern Las Vegas*

the ravages of the recession and closed in 2011. But in 2012, the owner, SBE Entertainment, announced plans to redevelop the property and reopen it in 2014 as SLS Vegas, a luxury hotel brand.

With a glut of hotel rooms in Las Vegas—150,000—the thought of adding more amid a sluggish economic recovery was impossible for resort operators to contemplate. Besides, even if they wanted to build a new resort, many of them were saddled with so much debt that they couldn't afford to do so. For the foreseeable future, the primary line of thinking would be to upgrade what was already in place: adapt, improve, innovate.

That said, skeptics have been proved wrong so many times that it would be foolish to feel overly confident about predictions pertaining to the Strip. Every time somebody thinks he has it figured out, along comes another Mirage or Cosmopolitan to shift the paradigm.

## CHAPTER 4

# Howard Hughes: The Game Changer

Howard Hughes was one of the most fascinating and bizarre men of the twentieth century. He is remembered as a movie mogul, record-setting pilot, aviation innovator, entrepreneurial businessman, playboy who dated Hollywood starlets and a behind-the-scenes political manipulator who had an indirect role in the Watergate scandal that brought down President Richard Nixon. He was often described as the richest man in the world.

But while Hughes no doubt would have preferred to be remembered for his aviation achievements, he is best known for his reclusiveness and eccentric habits later in life, for his intense phobias about people and germs, for his drug addictions and for the tragic story of how he died in 1976. His deteriorating mental and physical health, kept secret by his inner circle of lieutenants, lawyers and nursemaids, began to leak into the public arena during his four-year residence on the ninth floor of the Desert Inn Hotel in Las Vegas from 1966-70.

It is this relatively brief period of Hughes's very full life that has most fascinated journalists, biographers and the public. The intense secrecy surrounding Hughes during this time, the mystery, accounts for much of this. But it's also because Hughes, though in declining health and confined to the penthouse floor of a hotel, was extremely active in business and political affairs during this period. Using the telephone and handwritten memos, Hughes commanded his empire, paying particular attention to the new fiefdom he was building in Las Vegas.

Hughes added another title to his biography: casino owner. He went on a buying spree, picking up casinos, airports, ranches, mining claims and choice land parcels in Las Vegas and across Nevada, revealing to his close associates that he intended to take over this burgeoning city in the desert. Robert Maheu, who was Hughes's chief aide during most of the time he stayed in Las Vegas, wrote, "He wanted to become King of the Strip." Hughes was well on his way to becoming just that when, with his anxieties getting the best of him, he abruptly left Las Vegas in 1970.

While Hughes continued to own and operate his Las Vegas holdings for the next six years until his death, making decisions from his new far-flung lodgings in the Bahamas, Vancouver and London, he gave up his grand dreams for Las Vegas. He had described extensive plans for the city, sometimes privately to his aides, sometimes publicly. At the height of his Las Vegas machinations, he explained in a memo to Maheu what he envisioned for the city. Recalling the high-rolling Hollywood glamour of Las Vegas when he was a frequent visitor and part-time resident in the late '40s and early '50s, Hughes wanted to give the city a new touch of class, as well as an environment conducive to his personal obsessions.

"We can make a really super environmental 'city of the future' here—no smog, no contamination, efficient local government, where the taxpayers pay as little as possible, and get something for their money," Hughes wrote.

Hughes announced plans for a $150 million "new super Sands" that would be the world's largest resort with 4,000 rooms. He envisioned one floor dedicated entirely to shops open twenty-four hours, another floor full of family recreation, including a bowling alley, billiards room, ice skating rink and rooms dedicated to games such as chess, bridge and table tennis. The resort would have a state-of-the-art movie theater showing first-run films. "A resort so carefully planned and magnificently designed that any guest will simply have to make a supreme effort if he wants to be bored," Hughes wrote.

Hughes also announced plans to build a giant airport in Las Vegas to accommodate the new supersonic jets. Rather than filtering his ideas through his lieutenants, Hughes took pen in hand and drafted his announcement to the public. He saw Las Vegas becoming the new hub for air travel in the

Southwest, with high-speed trains running to Los Angeles, Phoenix and other cities. The idea received mixed reviews. While local officials praised the proposed $200 million investment, federal aviation officials considered it a bit pie-in-the-sky. They suggested that McCarran Field (now McCarran International Airport) was a perfectly suitable airport for Las Vegas.

Hughes responded angrily with another personally crafted press release. Defending his vision of a regional airport, he made a prophetic statement: "I do not believe Las Vegas will remain dormant without future growth. There is no reason in the world why this city should not, in a reasonable number of years, be as large as, say, Houston, Texas, is today. If this sort of growth should take place, the present location of McCarran Field would be approximately comparable to having the airport for Los Angeles located on Wilshire Boulevard at Miracle Mile."

Hughes never followed through on his ideas. Some of them were implausible, and he rejected others. More significantly, his physical and mental health deteriorated rapidly in his final years. He bought hotel-casinos, airports and numerous tracts of land in and around the city, but he did not develop them much, if at all, after he acquired them. What's more, his vision for Las Vegas did not resemble the development that would become his greatest legacy.

It's ironic that Hughes's largest contribution to Las Vegas—the Summerlin master-planned community—did not take shape until a decade after he died. And a master-planned community never came up on his radar. While he talked of building airports and casinos, it's unlikely he would have entertained the mundane task of building neighborhoods, parks and shopping centers.

And yet, although Hughes's direct involvement with Las Vegas was relatively brief, he left a huge imprint on the community, one that continues to be felt in a variety of forms to this day.

### Weird tales

Hughes's strange behavior during his Las Vegas residency is well-documented—from the urine-filled mason jars to marathon sessions on the commode—and much of it appears to actually have been true. A few of the best stories aren't as well-known.

A year after buying the Desert Inn, Hughes canceled the resort's annual Easter egg hunt. The prospect of hundreds of tiny, snot-nosed vandals rampaging through his property was too much to bear. Hughes sent a six-page memo to Maheu explaining his paranoia. "I am not eager to have a repetition, in the Desert Inn, of what happened at Juvenile Hall when the ever-lovin' little darlings tore the place apart," he wrote.

In *Howard Hughes: The Hidden Years*, James Phelan related the infamous Baskin-Robbins saga. Hughes's favorite ice cream was Baskin-Robbins banana nut. For months, he ate two scoops of it with every meal. His assistants kept large containers of it available at all times. When the supply ran low one time, aide Mell Stewart was sent to get more. "He came back with bleak news," Phelan reported. "The ice cream chain, which adds new varieties periodically and drops others, had discontinued the Hughes favorite. No more banana nut. The aides went into a panic."

With the supply running out, the aides called the Baskin-Robbins corporate offices and asked the company to make some more. Company execs said it could be done, but the minimum order would be 350 gallons. Fearing Hughes's reaction to an announcement of no more banana nut, the aides agreed to the large order. The ice cream was made in Los Angeles and trucked overnight to Las Vegas, where it was stored in the Desert Inn's kitchen freezer.

According to Phelan, after the banana nut was served to Hughes the next day, he decided it was time for a change to French vanilla. "It took the Desert Inn almost a year to get rid of the stockpile of ice cream," Phelan wrote. Stewart became known in the community for his generosity in giving away ice cream.

Hughes's "Palace Guard," the handful of attendants with whom he interacted while in Las Vegas, as well as the administrators he entrusted with his most secretive assignments, were almost all Mormons. Although few of them had much business experience, Hughes trusted them above the executives who ran the day-to-day activities at his various companies. The extensive Mormon network was largely the handiwork of Hughes's top administrator, Bill Gay, who often advertised job openings on the Mormon Church's bulletin boards.

In his memoir *Fly on the Wall*, longtime Las Vegas publicist Dick Odessky related a story he was told about Hughes in the early '50s. Hughes, who in

*Sun, Sin & Suburbia: The History of Modern Las Vegas*

those days stayed for long periods at the Flamingo and eventually, with his staffers, occupied an entire wing, called the hotel's publicist, Abe Schiller, to his room. "Schiller found him in the sitting room holding a large pink blanket, one of the standard linens the Flamingo used on its beds," Odessky reported. Hughes asked Schiller to help him drape the blanket over the picture window in the suite's bedroom.

"Hughes stepped back and admired his work," Odessky wrote. "He then sat on the bed, turned on the lamp, picked up a book, and turned it in various directions to test the light for reading. Finally he gave the makeshift curtain his approval. "That's absolutely perfect, Abe. Now, I want the exact same blankets placed over every window in my rooms." It turned out there were seventy-eight windows in the rooms Hughes had rented, all of which he expected to be covered exactly the same way.

Hughes bought KLAS-TV Channel 8 mainly so he could control the late-night movie lineup. He tinkered with other aspects of the station's programming as well, but the late-night movies were his passion. Hughes often stayed up late in his Desert Inn penthouse, and he wanted to see movies all through the night and only the ones he liked, typically adventure flicks such as the submarine thriller *Ice Station Zebra*. Channel 8's late-night movie show was called the "Swinging Shift," and Hughes picked the movies, sometimes at the last minute, often rendering the TV guide useless.

Bob Stoldal, a Channel 8 reporter and anchor in the late '60s, did not recall Hughes doing much meddling with the local newscasts. "What he did do was, we'd get calls after the newscast at night, and someone would say that Mr. Hughes was watching and would like you to get more information on such and such a story. So we'd go get more information and read it into a reel-to-reel tape recorder. The idea that you were reporting directly to Hughes was fascinating."

One time, Stoldal recalled, an executive who reported directly to Hughes advised the fledgling newsman to smile more on the air. "Mr. Hughes thinks you frown too much," he said. Despite his too-serious countenance, Stoldal eventually was promoted to news director and a top executive at Channel 8. Stoldal later became the news director at KSNV-TV Channel 3.

On a more serious note, Hughes could be a blatant racist. As Michael Drosnin related in *Citizen Hughes*, at one point during the Las Vegas period Hughes wanted to buy the ABC television network. But he abruptly changed his mind after watching back-to-back episodes of *The Dating Game* and *The Newlywed Game*—both Chuck Barris-produced game shows. In a memo to Maheu, Hughes wrote: "I think all this attention directed toward violence on TV dramatic shows is certainly misplaced. These two game shows represent the largest single collection of poor taste I have ever seen."

But Hughes wasn't merely commenting on the quality of the shows. He was incensed that a *Dating Game* episode featured interracial contestants. In an ironic twist, Hughes did not realize that a white woman selected to go on a date with a black man actually was a light-skinned African-American.

The rioting that broke out in many cities in the wake of the assassination of Martin Luther King Jr. only steeled Hughes's racist resolve. In another memo to Maheu, he wrote: "I can summarize my attitude about employing more negroes very simply—I think it is a wonderful idea for somebody else, somewhere else. I know this is not a very praiseworthy point of view, but I feel the negroes have already made enough progress to last the next 100 years, and there is such a thing as overdoing it."

### Casino buying spree

After Hughes settled into the Desert Inn's penthouse suite, he embarked on a Las Vegas buying spree that was the talk of the city. He had a lot of money to spend, having recently sold his stock in TWA for $546,549,771. He received a check believed at the time to be the largest ever written.

Hughes started with the hotel-casino in which he was living. Just a few weeks after he and his staff commandeered the entire eighth and ninth floors, Desert Inn officials complained that they wanted the rooms back for high-rolling guests scheduled to come to town for the New Year's holiday. But Hughes wouldn't budge. The only solution was to buy the place. An intense negotiation ensued, with Hughes questioning every dollar. The final purchase price was $13.25 million, and the deal closed on April 1, 1967.

Maheu, Hughes's right-hand man and public face during his Las Vegas years, soon learned that the Desert Inn purchase was a huge tax benefit for

*Sun, Sin & Suburbia: The History of Modern Las Vegas*

the billionaire. In his memoir *Next to Hughes*, Maheu says Hughes quickly decided he wanted to expand his burgeoning Las Vegas empire. "Howard wanted every casino in town," Maheu wrote.

Licensing turned out to be no problem. Hughes normally would have been required to appear in person before the Nevada Gaming Commission in order to receive permission to operate a casino. But Nevada officials were so eager to have Hughes on their team—offering the state an economic boost and a degree of respectability to counter its mob reputation—that they awarded him licenses sight unseen.

"He was not fingerprinted, interviewed or investigated," wrote Omar Garrison in *Howard Hughes in Las Vegas*. "Also waived was the usual requirement that a photograph taken within the past two years accompany the application form. ... Answers to questions contained in the applications were also few and far between. The only personal information given was what everybody already knew: Howard Hughes was 61; height, 6 feet 2 inches; weight, 150 pounds; eyes, brown; occupation: self-employed."

One of Hughes's biggest backers at that time was Hank Greenspun, crusading publisher of the *Las Vegas Sun*. Greenspun had known Hughes from the billionaire's late '40s/early '50s forays into Las Vegas, and he became a go-to guy for Hughes subordinates. But Greenspun's primary value for Hughes was as a public relations vessel. Through his front-page column, Greenspun urged Las Vegans not to bother the reclusive Hughes. Later, he championed Hughes's effect in improving the city's image.

Next on Hughes's agenda was the Sands, which he bought on August 1, 1967, for $14.6 million. The purchase particularly embittered the crooner Frank Sinatra, who had been the uncrowned king of the Sands for years and had once owned a piece of the hotel. He and Hughes had a history of enmity dating to when Sinatra starred in several movies for Hughes's RKO Pictures, and Hughes set out to put the singer in his place. After learning that his credit line at the casino had been suspended, an angry and drunk Sinatra drove a golf cart through a plate-glass window at the D.I.

As Garrison told it, "In a frenzy of frustration and anger, the manic troubadour shouted more curses and gutter phrases in the presence of lady patrons, threw chips in the face of a casino employee, and defied hotel security officers who tried to quiet him. He staggered into the Garden Room, the Sands' 24-hour restaurant. There he found [casino manager] Carl Cohen at his customary front table. Spluttering curses, Sinatra grasped Cohen's table and overturned it onto the casino manager."

This was a mistake: Cohen was a large man of about 275 pounds. "With a single, well-aimed blow to the mouth, he sent the singer reeling backward onto the floor," Garrison wrote. "When Sinatra picked himself up, he had a bloody nose and two missing front teeth."

Don Digilio, covering the incident for the *Las Vegas Review-Journal*, came up with a memorable lead on his story: "Singer Tony Bennett left his heart in San Francisco and Frank Sinatra left his teeth—at least two of them—in Las Vegas."

Sinatra promptly took his show to Caesars Palace.

Hughes's next conquest was the Frontier, which he purchased on September 22, 1967, for $14 million. Once again, Hughes took over a casino that had a reputation for mob influence. Soon after, he purchased the smaller Castaways for $3 million. Then he snapped up another small property, the Silver Slipper, for $5.3 million.

The spending spree would have continued with Hughes's purchase of the Stardust, but before that could happen the U.S. Justice Department's Antitrust Division stepped in, raising concerns that Hughes's ownership of Las Vegas casinos was on the verge of monopoly. Rather than tangling with the feds, who conceivably could subpoena him to testify, Hughes decided to back out of the Stardust deal.

### Landmark fiasco

But Hughes wasn't quite done. While the Justice Department nixed the Stardust deal, it was more amenable to Hughes's plan to purchase the bankrupt Landmark. Construction had begun on the hotel back in 1961 but it had never been finished. Hughes picked up the thirty-one-story hotel, patterned after the Space Needle in Seattle, for $17.3 million. It appealed to him in part because it was just down the street from Kirk Kerkorian's International Hotel, which was under construction and promised to be the biggest, best resort in Las Vegas. Not to be outdone, Hughes proceeded to spend millions to finish the Landmark and prepare for an opening around the same time as Kerkorian's in the summer of 1969.

Hughes's obsessiveness about details led to verbal warfare with Maheu, who was in charge of making the Landmark opening party memorable. First, the two clashed over the timing of the opening. Hughes did not want to commit to a date, refusing to make a decision until just days before the actual opening. In a memo to Maheu, Hughes explained: "I would hate to see the Landmark open on the first of July and then watch the International open a few days later and make the Landmark opening look like small potatoes by comparison." Hughes's indecision put Maheu in an impossible situation in terms of planning a party and inviting guests.

But it got worse. Hughes also wanted to approve the guest list, which was fine with Maheu as long as he actually agreed to put some people on the list. Instead, Hughes got bogged down in the philosophical underpinnings of why certain people should be invited and not others. Just days before the opening, he had approved just three people to be invited. What's more, Hughes refused to allow Maheu to order food for the party. In a memo to Hughes, Maheu expressed his dire frustration: "Howard, I really don't know what you are trying to do to me, but if your desire is to place me in a state of complete depression, you are succeeding."

Maheu's tirade backfired on him. Rather than convincing Hughes of the urgency of making vital decisions about the opening party, it prompted him to take a step back from the subject. "I am sorry," Hughes wrote, "but I cannot give a go-ahead on the Landmark until the situation of disaccord which has developed between us is put in better condition."

Hughes's absurd party planning continued even on July 1, the day he finally approved for the opening. With just hours to go, Hughes had signed off on only forty-four invitees. Maheu, however, had surreptitiously invited 400 other people. At five p.m., two hours before the party, Hughes at last gave Maheu permission to order the food.

In *Next to Hughes*, Maheu says the opening of the Landmark represented the peak of Hughes's power in Las Vegas. "He not only owned more hotel rooms and casinos than any other single individual in the history of the gambling mecca, he was also the state's largest employer, revered as the Pied Piper who had brought Las Vegas back to economic life."

## Behind the façade

While Hughes was the most powerful individual in Nevada, his casinos weren't making him richer. In fact, they were losing money. Hughes's Nevada operations lost $700,000 in 1967, $3.2 million in 1968, $8.4 million in 1969 and $13 million in 1970. Different reasons have been cited for this poor record. Local observers noted that when Hughes bought a casino, he tended to hire people with no gaming experience to run it. Hughes blamed Maheu, whom he came to believe was stealing from him. Maheu blamed Hughes for buying properties "to boost his ego, rather than as sound business investments. He acted on impulse, rather than recommendation." Sergio Lalli, writing of Hughes in *The Players: The Men Who Made Las Vegas*, suggested that Hughes's casino purchases did not rid them of mob influence as conventional wisdom suggests.

"Popular lore gives Hughes credit for chasing the mobsters out of town and for ushering in the era of corporations," Lalli wrote. "He supposedly pioneered the way for reputable corporations by showing Wall Street that it was safe to run a legitimate casino business in Las Vegas. None of this is true, except by happenstance ... While Hughes did bring an image of legitimacy to the gambling industry, it was only that, an image."

Lalli wrote that "it is too much to say that Hughes chased the mob out of town. Mobsters, as well as everyone else in Las Vegas, tried to take advantage of Hughes ... Hughes had often boasted that he could buy any man or destroy any man, but Hughes was just as often exploited by those around him."

The Desert Inn and the Sands "probably were plundered" by mob interests, Lalli contended. "Overnight they went from being two of the Strip's money-making jewels to fading has-beens ... While the inexperienced Hughes executives wallowed in their big offices, the casino employees who had been there from the early days may have helped themselves to what they could. It must have been a free-for-all."

*Sun, Sin & Suburbia: The History of Modern Las Vegas*

Maheu, who died in 2008, disputed that the mob continued to meddle in the casinos Hughes acquired, and he had a different explanation for why they were not strong performers. After Hughes acquired the casinos, he did very little to improve them. "He was a buyer, not a builder," Maheu said.

Burton Cohen, who ran the Desert Inn for Hughes, credited the billionaire with helping to push the "old guard"—aka the mob—out of Las Vegas. "When you buy the Sands, the Frontier, the Desert Inn and the Castaways, which were four hotels owned by the old guard, you gotta say you accelerated that departure."

After Hughes died in 1976, his heirs eventually sold the gaming properties. Today, not one of his six Strip casinos is still operating. The Sands was imploded in 1996 and the Venetian was built in its place. The Landmark was imploded in 1995 and the property became an overflow parking lot for the Las Vegas Convention Center. The Silver Slipper was torn down in 1988 to make room for a parking lot. The Castaways was closed in 1987 and demolished to clear a space for Steve Wynn's Mirage Hotel. The Desert Inn closed in 2000 and was demolished to make way for Wynn's Wynn Las Vegas resort. The Frontier was imploded in 2007, with plans to build a $5 billion resort there inspired by the Plaza in New York City. That project stalled when the national recession hit, and it was canceled outright in 2011.

While Hughes did not kick the mob out of Las Vegas entirely, he did help usher in a new era of corporate ownership of casinos, and his presence gave the city a degree of legitimacy it did not enjoy before. In 1967 and 1969, the Nevada Legislature revised state laws to allow corporations to be licensed to operate casinos without having to conduct background checks on each and every shareholder. At the time, Governor Paul Laxalt said Hughes's investment in Las Vegas had given the city the "Good Housekeeping seal of approval." Despite what was happening behind closed doors, there was an element of truth to the sound bite. "Hughes's arrival brought respectability to a city overrun by organized crime," Maheu wrote.

## Germs and nuclear testing

Years before his seclusion at the Desert Inn, Hughes had developed an irrational fear of germs. But his phobias went haywire during the four years he lived on the hotel's ninth floor.

But while Hughes demanded that his aides follow detailed written procedures to prevent exposing him to germs, his own actions contradicted the basics of cleanliness. "[Hughes] was surrounded only by filth and disorder," wrote Michael Drosnin in *Citizen Hughes*. "Mountains of old newspapers, brittle with age, spread in an ever-widening semicircle on the floor around his bed, creeped under the furniture, and spilled into the corners of his cramped fifteen-by-seventeen-foot room, mixed together haphazardly with other debris—rolls of blueprints, maps, *TV Guides*, aviation magazines, and various unidentifiable objects.

"A narrow path had been cleared from his bed to the bathroom, then lined with paper towels, but the tide of trash overran even that, topped off by numberless wads of used Kleenex the billionaire wielded to wipe off everything within reach, then casually cast upon the accumulated rubbish. It was all united in a common thick layer of dust that settled in permanently over the years. The room was never cleaned."

Hughes's obsession with contamination prompted a passionate campaign against nuclear testing. Hughes was a major defense contractor and supporter of nuclear power and nuclear weapons, not to mention a patriotic American and staunch anti-communist. But the proximity of the nuclear tests to Las Vegas, where he was investing $200 million, made him anxious and determined to use his influence to stop them.

"The Atomic Energy Commission nuclear tests in Nevada infuriated and frightened him," wrote Phelan in *Howard Hughes: The Hidden Years*. "He saw them as a threatening two-edged sword. The tests would scare off tourists from his gambling resorts and ... they would pollute the air he breathed and seep their radioactivity through underground strata and poison the earth and water beneath Las Vegas."

Hughes's campaign against nuclear testing reached its apex when the AEC announced plans to explode the largest atomic bomb in history—a

1.2-megaton hydrogen bomb code-named Boxcar—on April 26, 1968. Upon learning of the plan about two weeks before the scheduled test, Hughes dispatched Maheu to Washington to lobby for a postponement.

"It became his greatest obsession," Drosnin wrote. "He would carry his battle through every level of government and finally into the White House, offering bribes to presidents and presidential candidates, trying, in fact, to buy the government of the United States, all in a desperate effort to stave off nuclear devastation."

The hyperbolic language Hughes used to describe the devastation caused by the underground blasts could have come right out of a post-apocalyptic science fiction movie.

"If the gigantic nuclear explosion is detonated," Hughes wrote, "then in the fraction of a second following the pressing of that fateful button, thousands and thousands, and hundreds of thousands of cubic yards of good potentially fertile Nevada soil and underlying water and minerals and other substances are forever poisoned beyond the most ghastly nightmare. A gigantic abyss too horrible to imagine filled with poisonous gases and debris will have been created just beneath the surface in terrain that may one day be the site of a city like Las Vegas."

Maheu lined up allies from the fields of politics and science to join Hughes's fight against the bomb but the AEC was unimpressed, insisting the show must go on in the interest of national defense. Even Nevada political leaders ultimately abandoned Hughes, preferring not to sacrifice the high-paying jobs the test site provided.

With just hours remaining before the scheduled test, Hughes took his case to President Lyndon Johnson. He wrote a four-page letter to the president, seeking a ninety-day postponement—enough time, he said, to make his case for moving the test somewhere else. "I think Nevada has become a fully accredited state now and should no longer be treated like a barren wasteland that is only useful as a dumping place for poisonous, contaminated nuclear waste material," he wrote.

Although Hughes worried endlessly that Johnson would not get the letter in time, the president did, in fact, read it and took Hughes's eleventh-hour plea seriously. Johnson went so far as to withhold approval of the test while he consulted his advisers. But when they unanimously supported proceeding with the test, Johnson gave the go-ahead.

His failure to stop Boxcar did not deter Hughes. Rather, it convinced him that taking the high road did not work; politicians needed to be paid off to do what he wanted. When presidential candidate Hubert Humphrey agreed to fight nuclear testing, he received $100,000 in campaign contributions from Hughes. After Nixon won the presidency, Hughes sought to pay him $1 million to stop another large blast. Alas, nuclear testing continued in Nevada until 1992, when President George H.W. Bush declared a moratorium.

## Early years in Las Vegas

Hughes had a long association with Las Vegas that dated more than twenty years before he sequestered himself at the Desert Inn. Possibly his earliest visit to the city occurred in 1942 when he landed one of his experimental airplanes at the newly opened Sky Haven Airport (now North Las Vegas Airport).

Florence Murphy, who, with her husband, Red, opened the airport on the fateful day December 7, 1941, recalled Hughes's first landing: "The first time he came in he called us from Los Angeles and told us he was coming in. He said he might come in after dark and so we should be sure to have some lights on the runway. We didn't have lights, so we got some automobiles parked at the terminal building and got them out beside the runway [with their lights shining on the runway]. He came in and landed."

Hughes frequently landed there over the next few years, Murphy said, including one landing in which he ground-looped, damaging the wingtip. "He came into the office and said, 'Now, none of you saw that,'" she remembered.

Murphy described Hughes as a "very nice fellow, very soft-spoken." She said he invited her and her husband to the old El Rancho Vegas for dinner a few times. "He'd invite a whole bunch of us, and he'd have a table ready for twelve or fifteen of us. He'd come in and say you can have anything you want. He never did sit down to eat with us. He always had some business to take care of."

Hughes had mechanics from Los Angeles at the Sky Haven Airport working on his plane around Christmastime, Murphy said. "They hadn't heard anything from him for a week, so we told the crew to go home for Christmas. They didn't want to because Mr. Hughes would be very mad if they did. They finally left and wouldn't you know it, he came in. He found them gone and fired them all. I told him it was my fault and he put them all back to work."

In 1943, Hughes came to Southern Nevada to fly his beloved Sikorsky S-43 amphibious airplane. Hughes spent his nights in Las Vegas, taking in the burgeoning scene, and during the days he tested the Sikorsky at Lake Mead. "For hours at a stretch, he taxied the plane while speedboats loaded with cameramen trailed alongside shooting hundreds of feet of film of the Sikorsky's hull as it glided through the water," according to Donald Barlett and James Steele in *Empire*.

Hughes planned to sell the plane to the Army Corps of Engineers for use in transporting its employees to remote parts of the globe. But before the transaction could take place, the Civil Aeronautics Administration sent Charles Von Rosenberg to check out the aircraft. Hughes, who insisted on being involved in the process, brought him to Lake Mead. With Hughes at the controls, Von Rosenberg in the co-pilot's seat and three other men in the cabin, the plane took off from a small airstrip near Boulder City and soon was rumbling over the lake. As Hughes sought to land on the water, the plane started acting up.

"The Sikorsky started settling in, displacing water and picking up drag," according to *Empire*. "It pitched forward slightly and became a little unstable, but that was normal during the first few seconds. It started to go left, but Hughes straightened it out. Then, without warning, the Sikorsky lunged forward on its nose and veered sharply right. Before Hughes could react, the plane turned in the water and began skipping sideways on the lake."

As the airplane rocked and crashed at eighty miles per hour across the water, various pieces of the craft were ripped off. When the Sikorsky finally stopped, it began taking on water and the passengers scrambled to get out. Hughes and Von Rosenberg managed to escape the cockpit and climb into a rubber life raft. But one of the men in the cabin, William M. Cline, died in the accident, and Richard Felt died two days later.

Hughes paid the medical bills for all the crash survivors. He also had the plane raised out of Lake Mead at a cost of $100,000, hauled it back to California and rebuilt it at a cost of $500,000. He ended up flying it again.

A frequent visitor to Las Vegas in the late '40s, Hughes filmed parts of a movie called *Jet Pilot* there in 1949. He stayed for long periods in Strip hotels in the early '50s. "He liked the glamour and gaudiness of the town," according to Barlett and Steele. "He enjoyed prowling the city at night, cruising the casinos and hotels in search of attractive young women available for an evening's dalliance."

In 1953, Hughes leased a five-room house near the Desert Inn, the so-called "Green House" (because it was painted green). Hughes hired people to come in and seal the windows and doors to prevent germs from contaminating the interior. After about a year in Las Vegas, Hughes returned to California, but he insisted on keeping the house just as he had left it. He never returned to it.

After he died in 1976, Hughes's aides opened the airtight house and found it just as he had left it in 1954. "The Green House contained an electric Westinghouse refrigerator—still running—two newspapers dated October 13, 1953, and April 4, 1954, keys to Room 186 at the Flamingo and Room 401 at the Hotel Miramar ... some Sahara casino gambling chips" and other odds and ends of his previous existence there, Barlett and Steele wrote.

The Green House still stands. KLAS Channel 8, which is next door, used it as meeting and office space and for various special projects. Bob Stoldal worked at KLAS when Hughes owned it and when the house was opened after his death. He remembered that the Hughes people came in and burned all the clothes. "The closets were stuffed with clothes," Stoldal recalled. "Suit after suit after suit."

After the Hughes people cleared out the house, some other curious folks entered to pick through the remaining bits of the billionaire's belongings. Clothes hangers, a toilet seat and other items have become prized pieces of memorabilia, Stoldal said.

Stoldal, a history buff, turned the Green House into something of a memorial to Hughes, with posters from his movies and other memorabilia on the walls and tables. Stoldal had several layers of paint scraped from the house's exterior to reveal the original green color.

Incidentally, Stoldal swore that he once saw Hughes in Channel 8's offices. "It was a Saturday morning, and I'm walking down the hallway from the newsroom past the executive suites to the studio. This guy came around the corner in a dark blue, double-breasted suit, with his hair pulled back, and I was kind of startled and said, 'Can I help you?' He said no and kept on walking through. He had sort of a bum look to him." Stoldal realized "there is not one shred of evidence that it was Howard Hughes." Most believe Hughes never left his Desert Inn penthouse while he stayed in Las Vegas. "The logic just doesn't fit—except that I believe it was him," Stoldal said. Stoldal was hardly alone among Las Vegans who believed they had crossed paths with Hughes in the late '60s but evidence was hard to come by.

### Properties Hughes touched

Hughes and the executives who took over his estate are linked to a wide array of developments in Las Vegas beyond his casino empire. Hughes himself actually built little except the final phases of the Landmark Hotel and the Channel 8 building, but he bought vast tracts of land and properties that were or later became well-known landmarks.

• Hughes bought the North Las Vegas Airport and the fixed-base aviation terminal at McCarran International Airport. Both are county-run facilities today.

• His company later developed Hughes Center, the 100-acre professional office park on Paradise Road, on land he owned. The Rouse Company, the Maryland-based firm that bought Howard Hughes Corporation in 1997, sold the Hughes Center in 2003 for $233 million. The new owner, Crescent Real Estate Equities, received thirteen undeveloped acres in the deal. The Hughes Center celebrated its twenty-fifth anniversary in 2012.

• Hughes Airport Center, an office and industrial park along Sunset Road, is perhaps best known as the site of the U.S. Regional Post Office. Rouse sold it in 2000.

• Summa, the name of his Las Vegas umbrella corporation for many years, developed industrial park facilities along Cheyenne Avenue north of the North Las Vegas Airport on Hughes land. Rouse sold them in 2000.

• The Fashion Show Mall on the Strip was built on Hughes land. The Rouse Company invested $1 billion in the early 2000s to renovate and expand the mall. Today, the Fashion Show is owned and operated by General Growth Properties Inc. It is one of the country's largest and busiest shopping malls.

• The Wet 'n Wild water park was built on Hughes land in 1985. The water park closed in 2004 and was torn down. Since then, there has been talk of building a resort on the prime Strip real estate but the recession squelched those plans.

• The Excalibur, Mirage and Treasure Island megaresorts were built on Hughes land.

• Spring Mountain Ranch State Park, a popular attraction in Red Rock Canyon, once was a private ranch that Hughes owned. He bought the property from German actress Vera Krupp to serve as a home for his wife, actress Jean Peters. Peters never moved to the ranch.

• The Paradise Valley Country Club, located within what is now the Green Valley master-planned community in Henderson, was a Hughes property. It later was renamed the Showboat Country Club and today it is the Wildhorse Golf Club, owned by the city of Henderson.

• Hughes owned several houses in the exclusive Rancho Circle neighborhood on Rancho Drive north of Alta Drive.

Perhaps more intriguing are the local properties that Hughes coveted but never managed to acquire. One of his great frustrations was his inability to buy everything he wanted in Nevada. For example, he failed in a bid to buy the *Las Vegas Review-Journal* newspaper as part of a larger scheme to create a print and electronic media network crisscrossing the state. He also failed to buy the Stardust Hotel on the Strip, the Silver Nugget in North Las Vegas and Harrah's in Reno. Hughes had come to Nevada to escape higher taxes in California and to enjoy the benefits of being a big fish in a small pond. But to his everlasting frustration, even he could not take over an entire state.

## The Hughes estate

When Howard Hughes died on April 5, 1976, on an airplane en route from Acapulco, Mexico, to Houston, Texas, his financial affairs were not in order. He did not leave a will.

Or did he? Alleged wills started popping up all over the place, with people holding the flimsiest of connections to Hughes, or none whatsoever, claiming a piece of the giant pie. The controversy over the $360 million estate marked another long and contentious chapter in the Hughes saga that lasted a dozen years after his death.

One thing was immediately apparent: The estate needed an executor. The task fell to Hughes's cousin, Houston lawyer William Lummis, who had met Hughes only briefly as a child.

"When Hughes died, it was like a safe dropping on my head," Lummis told a *Review-Journal* reporter in 1988. "My mother was his aunt and his closest heir and so I knew that when he died I was in trouble."

Lummis, who became chairman of the board of Summa Corporation (later Howard Hughes Corporation), went to work untangling the Hughes empire, which stretched across twenty-five operating companies and numerous states. "When Hughes died, I think everybody assumed he had a will," Lummis told the *Review-Journal*. "Most people of that substance leave a will. It was apparent to me early on that Hughes had not left a will."

It was less clear to the courts, which were bombarded with sixty-five lawsuits involving people laying claim to a share of the estate. In addition, Lummis had to deal with the Internal Revenue Service, since Hughes had not filed an income tax return in the nine years before he died.

Hughes's heirs saw no money until 1983. Long before that, however, the battle for his money became a media circus, with the spotlight shining for a while on a bizarre story told by a man whom it seemed impossible for Hughes to have known. Melvin Dummar, a working-class stiff living in tiny Willard, Utah, and Gabbs, Nevada, claimed he had given Hughes a ride to Las Vegas in December 1967 when he happened upon the billionaire, bleeding and dehydrated, in a remote patch of desert off the highway between Beatty and

Tonopah. Dummar said he picked up Hughes, drove him to Las Vegas and dropped him off behind the Sands Hotel.

Then, a few weeks after Hughes's death, Dummar said he was working at a gas station in Willard when a well-dressed man approached him and left an envelope directing him to take its contents to the Clark County Courthouse in Las Vegas. Dummar took the envelope to the Mormon Church's headquarters in Salt Lake City instead.

The envelope contained a three-page handwritten will that, conveniently in the eyes of skeptics, left one-sixteenth of the Hughes estate to Dummar. Dummar became a celebrity, appearing on numerous television programs, but a seven-month trial resulted in the so-called Mormon Will being deemed a forgery. In hindsight, it's a wonder it took that long to throw it out. The hand-scrawled document contained numerous spelling errors that the meticulous Hughes was unlikely to have made, such as misspelling cousin Lummis's name, and it left money to causes in which Hughes had showed little interest. Furthermore, it mentioned giving his "Spruce Goose" airplane to the city of Long Beach, California, although Hughes detested that nickname for the aircraft he dubbed Hercules.

Although Dummar's story seems highly improbable, people across the country stubbornly continue to believe he was unfairly denied his rightful payday. Lawsuits seeking to validate his claims, based on new tidbits of evidence, continued to filter through state and federal courts as late as 2008. For his part, Dummar had mixed feelings about the whole thing. While sticking to his story, in a 2007 interview he said that he probably would have been better off in his life if Hughes "had never remembered me."

Other alleged wills suffered the same fate as Dummar's Mormon Will, and in 1981 a probate judge in Houston ruled that Hughes had not left a valid will.

Lummis actually took on two big jobs: handling the estate for the heirs and running Summa Corporation. The latter task required a complete revamping of the complex organization and selling numerous companies and properties. Lummis transformed the company from a money loser into a profitable and logical modern corporation. During the '80s, Lummis converted Summa from a potpourri of casino, aircraft, mining and media interests into a real estate development company—one that would become among the largest and most influential players in the impending Las Vegas population boom.

## His greatest legacy

For all the business ventures Hughes was involved in during the '60s and '70s, his greatest legacy in Nevada is the result of a land deal he executed in the early '50s. Hughes wanted to expand the research facilities for his growing aircraft company, based in Culver City, California, and decided he would do so outside Las Vegas. His top executives strongly objected to the plan because they didn't want to separate the company's operations, but Hughes pressed ahead, in part because he would pay lower taxes in Nevada.

He managed to obtain 25,000 acres of federal land west of Las Vegas in exchange for 73,000 acres he owned scattered across Northern Nevada. It wasn't easy, though. The Interior Department initially opposed the land trade, arguing that it was lopsided in Hughes's favor. Hughes then hired attorney Clark Clifford, who had been an aide to President Harry Truman, to lobby for the swap. He also convinced the Air Force to support the deal, in the interest of national security. Under pressure, the Interior Department approved the trade in 1952.

Hughes never built any aircraft research facilities on the land, primarily because his executives so adamantly opposed his plans. The research laboratory eventually was built in Culver City, and "Husite," as the Southern Nevada acreage was known, lay dormant for more than thirty years.

Several years after Hughes's death, Summa executives came up with an idea for the giant parcel: a master-planned community. They later dubbed it Summerlin, which was Hughes's grandmother's maiden name. More than a decade later, Summerlin was heralded as one of the nation's largest and most attractive planned communities, winning awards for high sales and quality planning.

Summerlin is Hughes's greatest contribution to Las Vegas, and yet, amid all his varied interests, he never was known to express a desire to develop subdivisions or shopping centers. Unlike other rich men, Hughes did not pour his money into mansions, usually preferring a darkened hotel room to a personal palace. The only reason he ever bothered with home buying was to please a woman. He designed and built numerous cutting-edge airplanes, but houses were of little interest.

When Summerlin is finally completed, its population will exceed 150,000—almost as many people as lived in the entire Las Vegas Valley when Hughes was perched atop the Desert Inn in the '60s. Although Hughes was one of only a few who predicted Las Vegas would grow into the metropolis it is today, he never imagined the role he ultimately would play in making it happen.

# CHAPTER 5

# Summerlin: Taking the Edge Off Desert Living

onjure an image of a typical neighborhood park and it will have little in common with Pueblo Park in Summerlin. Pueblo Park is the oldest of the master-planned community's "village trails," most of which are located in natural arroyos coursing through the community.

Actually, when you park your car and get out at Pueblo Park, near Buffalo Drive and Lake Mead Boulevard, it does look like a typical park. There are leafy trees, playground equipment and a wide expanse of grass, perhaps with a children's soccer team practicing on the green. But venture a hundred yards west and you leave the Midwest-style oasis behind. A trail winds through a deep wash that, for the most part, remains in its natural state, a preserved piece of Mojave Desert snaking through suburbia.

Pueblo Park is lightly populated by joggers, rollerbladers, dog-walkers and bicyclists. But they are invasive species. The natives also are in abundance: playful ground squirrels, curious rabbits and chattering birds, all highly visible as you traverse the undulating trail, bordered a few hundred yards away on each side by houses and apartment complexes. Shade-giving mesquite trees have been planted all along the paved trail, with occasional benches for those in need of a breather, yet the feeling remains that this is largely wild desert, similar to what you would find on a hike in nearby Red Rock Canyon. Half a mile along the trail, the traffic noise evident back in the green area is gone, replaced with a degree of silence almost unheard of anywhere else in the metropolitan area.

137

This is Summerlin at its best—an homage to the desert rather than a rebuke. Pueblo Park and other large open spaces in Summerlin are what separate this planned community from so many others in Las Vegas that aim to fill every acre with a house, a store or some other revenue-producing unit.

Still, organic is the last word one might hear to describe Summerlin, Southern Nevada's largest master-planned community. Almost everything in Summerlin is carefully planned. The roads, the neighborhoods, the parks, the shopping centers, the community events—they are all part of a grand scheme. Nary a nail gets hammered nor a bush planted without a sign-off from somebody in the Summerlin hierarchy.

Some dismiss Summerlin as the epitome of the soulless suburb, and for those who thrive on the Dickensian clutter and anarchy of urban life, the command and control of Summerlin's development certainly can be off-putting. That was the sentiment voiced by Alex Beam, a *Boston Globe* columnist, when he visited Summerlin. Beam returned home to pen a column that oozed vitriol (not to mention East Coast snobbery) about the community's lack of "authenticity."

"It all feels fake to me; every store a franchise, every place to shop a quadrilateral mall," he wrote. "The maps handed out to prospective homeowners show a network of 'street-side trails,' which residents can exploit for fitness purposes. Back East, we call these sidewalks."

Beam's quick-draw critique may sell papers in Beantown, but it lacks a certain level of perspective. Summerlin was barely ten years old when Beam dropped in; Boston, settled in the early seventeenth century, was one of the first five cities in America. One suspects that Englanders who got their first look at Boston in 1630 weren't all that impressed either.

Of course, Summerlinites probably aren't too concerned about what a Boston newspaper columnist thinks. Most people moving to Las Vegas aren't looking for the same things they might find in history-laden population centers along the Eastern Seaboard. Summerlin is nirvana for those who appreciate the benefits of community-minded, modern urban planning.

Simply put, Summerlin is the hardest-working community in the development business. Howard Hughes Corporation found financial success by offering the breadth of amenities that families are looking for, from neighborhood parks and nearby schools to convenient and comfortable shopping centers. While most developers in Las Vegas throw up houses as fast as they can and don't stake out land for parks, schools or other nonprofit-making facilities, Summerlin builders discovered they could charge more for the same houses if the neighborhood was attractive to the buyer. At the same time, home buyers quickly realized a house in Summerlin was more likely to increase in value than one wedged into a nameless subdivision.

In addition to paying attention to the quality of the built environment, Summerlin has organized a variety of community events, from arts festivals and concerts to ice cream socials, to enhance the quality of life. And while these events are well-attended by Summerlin residents, they also are flooded with people who live elsewhere but crave the sense of community that it offers.

That doesn't mean Summerlin is free of strife or controversy. It's had its share of battles, from neighbors warring over whether they can leave their portable basketball hoops on the street overnight to residents protesting zoning plans. It's even had a few high-profile crimes in its midst. But by and large, Summerlin's rigorous planning and constant oversight have played a large role in reducing such conflicts compared with the rest of Las Vegas.

Summerlin's progressive, environmentally friendly approach to development has had a tremendous impact on the Las Vegas area generally. Its advocacy of desert landscaping spurred its growing acceptance throughout the community. Its extensive roadside landscaping has been copied across the valley. Its commitment to neighborhood parks and school sites has convinced other builders to set aside space that otherwise would have been used to squeeze in a few more crackerboxes.

Of course, those plaudits don't take all aspects of urban life into consideration. For example, racial and ethnic diversity is not Summerlin's strong suit. Census Bureau statistics show that Summerlin is seventy-eight percent white, nine percent Asian, six percent Hispanic and five percent African-American, while Clark County as a whole is forty-eight percent white, twenty-nine percent Hispanic, ten percent African-American and six percent Asian. In

Summerlin's defense, however, its diversity far outstrips some of the suburbs around, say, Boston, which are close to 100 percent white.

What's more, Summerlin offers little in the way of affordable housing. It did proceed with apartment projects in the late '90s, but its pricey fees for special improvement districts and homeowners associations deter some first-time home buyers. That said, Summerlin has always reflected an inclusive, friendly ethic. Surely Summerlinites are paragons of tolerance—unless, of course, you want to paint your house purple. It's about as close to modern middle-class America as you can get.

## Origins

Executives with Summa Corporation (later renamed Howard Hughes Corporation) started talking with city officials about developing their 25,000-acre "Husite" property in 1981, but their plans did not become public knowledge until a few years later. An October 1984 *Las Vegas Review-Journal* article detailed the potential effects on Red Rock Canyon if the Husite property were to be developed. Bureau of Land Management officials and local environmentalists expressed concerns that the development—which could reach just 200 feet from the Red Rock visitor center—would bring more vandals, shooters and dirt bike riders into the canyon, and they called for creation of a buffer zone to protect Red Rock from the onslaught. As early as 1982, the BLM and Summa had discussed a land swap in which a large chunk of Husite would be traded to the government in exchange for other land in the Las Vegas area, but no agreement was reached.

In the fall of 1984, Summa officials declined to provide details about their plans for Husite. But according to the article, "government officials familiar with the initial proposals say the company is considering development of a massive 'master-planned' residential community with a self-contained employment base, possibly a high-tech park or light industrial facility." The community, they said, could one day have a population of 200,000 to 400,000.

Las Vegas City Councilman Ron Lurie (who later became mayor) said he envisioned "beautiful, expensive homes … that overlook the valley," predicting the area will be "one of the most popular places to live in the next fifteen to twenty years." Lurie was right about that, though a lot would happen in the meantime.

The article explained just how much infrastructure still needed to be put in for the Husite development to be viable. Lurie, representing the city on the Regional Transportation Commission, pushed for an extension of the U.S. 95 expressway to link to the Husite property, and the city was in the process of extending major sewer lines west along Lake Mead Boulevard and Vegas Drive that "eventually will bring sewer service within a mile of the Husite property." Lurie and others also discussed building a beltway through Husite to link up with the expressway extension.

Discussions about a land trade to protect Red Rock Canyon continued in 1985, with Summa officials talking about relinquishing 5,000 acres adjacent to Red Rock and Sierra Club officials wanting 9,000 acres. Interestingly, one popular idea at the time was for the U.S. Air Force to pay for the land deal to compensate for its illegal seizure of nearly 90,000 acres at Groom Lake, 100 miles north of Las Vegas, for a top-secret air base—Area 51. The Air Force, of course, summarily rejected the proposal.

Environmentalists worried about Summa's plan to build "the Scottsdale of Las Vegas" in the foothills next to the canyon. For their part, Summa officials remained mum on the details of their development. "We're still in the process of master-planning the area," said company president John Goolsby, generally considered the father of Summerlin. But Goolsby, reflecting the company's early commitment to Red Rock, added, "We understand the necessity of preserving Red Rock and we're open to discussion."

A few weeks later, Summa outlined its long-term development plan for city and county officials and others in closed-door meetings at the Frontier Hotel. The plan called for 18,000 acres of residential development, 2,000 acres of office space and 2,600 acres for recreational purposes. The entire project, company officials said, could take fifty years to complete and probably wouldn't start for several years. The meetings were unusual in that Summa officials welcomed input on what they should do with the property. This was such a new concept in Las Vegas that some participants questioned whether it was a legitimate act of good-faith planning. "They essentially held a meeting for all kinds of people in the community to come to an open house and express their concerns," recalled Jeff van Ee, a longtime Las Vegas environmental activist who attended the meeting. "I thought, wow, this is pretty amazing. From that moment early on, I could sense that the Hughes corporation was a different kind of development corporation."

## Early development

The first development identified as being part of Summerlin was the Meadows School, a private college preparatory school that opened on forty Hughes-donated acres in 1988. To this day, Meadows is the premier secondary school in Southern Nevada. The Meadows stood a lonely vigil in the far western valley until development took shape several months later at Del Webb Corporation's Sun City retirement community. The project, announced in August 1987, started with the purchase of 1,050 acres of Husite land between Lake Mead Boulevard and Cheyenne Avenue. Del Webb officials chose the site for the community, patterned on similar communities it had built near Phoenix and Tucson, over sites in Boulder City and Green Valley. With an eighteen-hole golf course already under construction, ground was broken on the first Sun City house in March 1988.

That same month Summa officials finally announced plans for their newly named master-planned community—Summerlin, the maiden name of Howard Hughes's grandmother. The announcement followed three years of brainstorming and market research during which a team of Summa officials, led by vice president Dick Bonar and marketing director Mark Paris, came up with several hundred possible names, including "Summaville" and "Hugheston." (Later, Bonar became a Clark County planning commissioner and Paris the longtime CEO of the Fremont Street Experience Limited Liability Company. Paris moved on to become CEO of the LandWell Company, a Henderson-area developer.)

"It had to be easy to spell and easy to pronounce," Paris told the *Review-Journal*. "I had a couple of books on Howard Hughes and the name Summerlin, which was his grandmother's maiden name, kept coming to mind."

Though still talking in generalities, company officials noted at the press conference that construction of Summerlin Parkway, a four-lane extension of the U.S. 95 expressway through the property, had begun the week before and that a land swap protecting Red Rock Canyon was nearly completed. Several months later, in September 1988, the complicated land trade, brokered by The Nature Conservancy, was finally completed. Using funds obtained by Nevada's congressional delegation two years earlier, the Bureau of Land Management paid $2.8 million to Summa for 439 acres near the Red Rock Canyon visitor center. Also, Summa gave the BLM 4,863 acres east of Red Rock in exchange for 3,767 acres south of the Summerlin property.

Environmentalists were ecstatic about the final deal. "This has been a monumental effort, but it has been worth it all the way," John Hiatt of the Audubon Society told the *Las Vegas Sun*. "[It] represents one of the most important conservation achievements in the history of Southern Nevada." Van Ee said pulling back the development boundary made all the difference for the protection of Red Rock Canyon, which later became a national conservation area. "If you're standing at the visitor center there will never be block walls or back yards or golf courses within a couple hundred feet," he said.

What was gratifying to van Ee is that Summa didn't have to agree to the land swap. "In response to public concerns, they listened and they were proactive," he said. "They recognized that Red Rock is an asset for Summerlin and for the rest of the Las Vegas Valley, and they had a responsibility and a duty to protect it."

With the land swap completed and infrastructure work well under way, Summerlin geared up in 1989 for its entry into the real estate marketplace. Construction began on an eighteen-hole Tournament Players Club golf course as well as a six-acre park.

Also that year, the Las Vegas City Council approved its first-ever special improvement district for a developer. Most SIDs are imposed on individual property owners to make infrastructure improvements in established neighborhoods. Under Summerlin SID 404, a city-sponsored bond sale would reimburse Summa Corporation for $68 million worth of public improvements. Then, future homeowners in Summerlin would repay the bonds through annual assessments. This agreement allowed Summa to make the public improvements before the homes were built, not as the need arose. It was the first of numerous SIDs that have helped fund Summerlin's development.

Sun City Summerlin held its grand opening in January 1989, with the first residents moving into their homes the following month. The project was an immediate success. Del Webb received more than 6,000 inquiries from prospective home buyers in the ten months before the grand opening and 250 sight-unseen home sales.

Summerlin proper started later, partly because the federal government placed the desert tortoise on the endangered species list in 1989. The designation froze construction at Summerlin and other area developments until a regional habitat preservation plan was put in place to protect the tortoise. But the project bogged down for other reasons as well. "Summerlin was having trouble getting their community off the ground," said Mark Fine, the successful Green Valley builder. "They just kept stumbling." The company's corporate mentality and lack of land development experience turned off many home builders. Fine approached Goolsby about a joint venture with American Nevada Corporation, of which he was president. "I said, 'We do this every day. Let's do a joint venture.' Goolsby responded by saying, 'What if I hire *you* to do this?' That's how it started."

Fine took the job in 1990 and immediately started meeting with home builders interested in doing business in Summerlin. "I knew how to do business with the builders," Fine said. "They trust me. They know I'm going to deliver. It wasn't corporate." When he arrived, Fine said, the company's building contract was seventy pages long with hundreds of pages of exhibits. "Builders were putting it on the bottom of the pile," he recalled. "I took forty pages off the contract, and made it look like a Green Valley contract. Builders liked the builder-friendly contract. They liked the access to somebody if they had a problem. We were working out of a trailer, not the Hughes Center. We were creating a sense of community from day one." Fine put together a stable of the best builders in town. "We started getting some momentum," he said. "You get houses built and you build momentum."

Home building began in Summerlin in late 1990, with Coleman Homes, Signature Homes, Lewis Homes, Watt Nevada and Woodside Homes getting in on the first phase of the first village, The Hills, just south of Sun City. The first home was sold in 1991. The Hills, running along the south side of Lake Mead Boulevard, may be the best-recognized portion of Summerlin. It's home to the TPC golf course, sprawling Hills Park and the Summerlin Library and Performing Arts Center.

The Hills village was followed by The Pueblo (home of the Meadows School), then The Trails and The Crossing (home of Summerlin Hospital) in a steady march south and west. The Canyons followed with another TPC golf course as well as the JW Marriott Hotel. (The Suncoast hotel-casino is next to but not in Summerlin.)

Like the Sun City community before it, Summerlin was an immediate financial success. In 1992, just a year after the first house was completed, Summerlin was ranked No. 1 nationally in new home sales. From 1991 through 2001, more than 18,000 homes were sold in Summerlin, half of those after 1999. The acceleration of development meant the fifty-year building plan for Summerlin was cut to twenty-five years.

Howard Hughes Corporation solidified its reputation as an environmentally sensitive company in 2002 when it agreed to a second land swap with the federal government to further protect Red Rock Canyon. Hughes traded 1,071 acres in the foothills of the canyon for 998 acres at the flatter south end of its community. Hughes could have built mansions in those foothills featuring inspiring views of the Las Vegas Valley, but it elected to preserve the natural beauty of Red Rock instead. "It was land that they could have used for very high-end homes because of the elevation," said Charles Kubat, vice president of planning and design for Summerlin from 1995 to 2003. "Up that high [4,000-4,500 feet], the views are incredible."

## Other players

While Summerlin's development moved slowly at first, the valley's west side did not suffer from inactivity. It was becoming a hot real estate market without Summa's direct involvement. The Lakes, encompassing 1,300 acres, was the first master-planned community on the far west side. Developed by Collins Brothers starting in 1984, the community surrounding a large man-made lake is synonymous with the residential area along Sahara Avenue west of Buffalo Drive and encompassing the giant Citibank credit card processing center. Next came Desert Shores, a 1,000-acre planned community just north and east of Summerlin that features four large lakes and sandy beach areas for residents. Developed by R.A. Homes, Desert Shores started in 1987. Finally, the 700-acre Peccole Ranch runs between Charleston Boulevard and Sahara. Its best-known assets are the Sahara West Library and the giant Boca Park Marketplace.

Interestingly, while these developments are not part of Summerlin, two of them could have been. Much of the land on which The Lakes sits and all of the Desert Shores property originally belonged to Howard Hughes, but the company sold it off in the mid-'80s to help finance the Summerlin project. "This was a mechanism to generate capital, which paid for a large portion of the initial infrastructure costs," said Tom Warden, spokesman for Howard Hughes Corporation. "Other master-planned communities have struggled with the financial disadvantage of those initial huge infrastructure costs. This early sale of land is one of the reasons that Summerlin was a successful master-planned community almost from the get-go."

Peccole Ranch's history bears a striking similarity to Summerlin's. Under the Taylor Grazing Act, developer Bill Peccole exchanged 15,000 acres he had acquired in Northern Nevada for 3,000 acres of federal land west of Las Vegas. He executed the exchange in 1949—just a couple of years before Howard Hughes made a similar deal to get the 25,000 acres that eventually became Summerlin. Peccole's 3,000 acres later were divvied among the Peccole Ranch, Canyon Gate and Queensridge communities.

### Master planning

From its inception, Summerlin, encompassing thirty-six square miles, was envisioned as a series of "villages." Villages range from 300 to 1,000 acres and feature an array of neighborhoods, each constructed by a different builder. Neighborhoods range from apartment complexes to starter homes to guard-gated golf course mansions. Regardless of income level, each village has a core of community facilities, such as schools, parks, ballfields, libraries and churches.

A more than 150-mile trail system connects the villages, with most trails embracing the desert environment rather than trying to emulate the leafy Midwest or California coast. Summerlin, in fact, can take credit for popularizing desert landscaping in Las Vegas. Major thoroughfares in Summerlin are bordered by extensive landscaping that uses minimal water yet, after a few years of growth, feels nearly as lush as the Vermont countryside.

One of the more controversial aspects of Summerlin is the use of roundabouts to guide vehicle traffic. Rather than the four-way stops common across the valley, Summerlin has numerous roundabout intersections, or traffic circles, designed to maintain traffic flow, increase safety and reduce pollution from idling cars. They also eliminate the need to install expensive and unsightly traffic signals. Roundabouts are common in England and on the East Coast, but rare in the West. Motorists unfamiliar with this intersection style often are confounded by the traffic patterns. Practice makes perfect, however, and many Summerlin residents have become big supporters of roundabouts. Studies show that roundabouts are safer than conventional intersections, with fewer accidents and, more tellingly, fewer accidents causing serious injuries. Nevertheless, in 2003 the Howard Hughes Corporation modified two of its busier roundabouts to make them easier for motorists to navigate. A narrow island was installed to force motorists in the outside right lane to turn right, while street markings better defined lane boundaries and traffic flow.

Kubat said the community's strongest attribute is its overall appearance. "What stands out is the public realm landscaping and open spaces," he said. "The landscape that we've done in Summerlin immediately creates an image of the place as you drive in that is separate from everything that surrounds it." While walls are a given in Las Vegas, Summerlin has made efforts to keep them to a minimum. "Not everything is totally walled off," Kubat said. "We have eliminated walls wherever possible. That's different from a lot of places in town."

Kubat's one regret is that Summerlin has not insisted the various home builders in the community display more creativity in their architecture. Many Summerlin neighborhoods, after all, aren't much different from less expensive subdivisions built by the same companies elsewhere in the valley. "I wish that we could earlier on have gotten the builders to be more flexible in offering more variety of product," he said. "The builder wants to generally build what he knows will be successful. He's got a lot of money invested. But, on the other hand, I wish we could have been stronger in sharing the risk with the builder or finding some way of making sure each time we did a new neighborhood we were putting something new on the table, not simply repeating other neighborhoods."

Kubat's *piece de resistance* is the 1,400-acre Summerlin Centre, situated between Sahara Avenue on the south, Charleston Boulevard on the north and Hualapai Way on the east, and extending west of the I-215 beltway. "It is the mixed-use heart of Summerlin," he explained. "It is the central gathering place, the central workplace and the most urban-like place that you will find in Summerlin."

Summerlin Centre is best known today for the Red Rock, a Station Casinos resort. A large shopping mall next to the casino, under construction for just a few months when the recession hit, has been idle ever since. The Shops at Summerlin Centre had promised more than one million square feet of shopping, including high-end retailers such as Nordstrom and Macy's.

But the mall is only part of the picture.

Some neighborhoods in Summerlin Centre are more creatively designed than the typical Southwest subdivision, emphasizing the village's urban vibe. Perhaps the best example is Westwood, by Westmark Homes. Unlike houses in most other subdivisions in the valley, garage doors are not the focal point in Westwood. Garages are tucked at the back of the houses, accessible through a wide driveway shared by four homeowners. Four homes also share a landscaped courtyard, designed for friendly interaction among neighbors. Officials say future developments in Summerlin Centre will feature even more progressive models, with, for example, residential lofts over business enterprises.

On the commercial side, Summerlin Centre planners made an immediate statement with the design for Center Pointe Plaza, which is your basic supermarket-anchored shopping center but with several aesthetic twists. First, the buildings feature extensive ledgestone facades, giving the center a distinguished feel. Even the center's fast food restaurants are part of the scheme.

This has to be the only place in the valley that makes eating at McDonald's feel like an elegant experience. Second, the center is extensively landscaped with trees and bushes, giving it a shady, garden feel you won't find in most strip malls in town. At the Chevron station on the corner, the gasoline pumps are located behind the building rather than in front, hiding them from the streetscape. A cluster of towering palm trees is the gas station's focal point rather than a sea of pavement.

These were just the first manifestations of what Summerlin Centre planners promise to be an almost revolutionary way of living in Las Vegas. While the village may fall short of the ideals that fall under the heading "New Urbanism," a city design movement focused on de-emphasizing automobile travel and rebuilding the sense of community, it's about as close as you're going to get in car-centric Las Vegas.

Acceptance of the urban nature of Summerlin Centre was tested in 2003 when residents learned that Station Casinos wanted to build a 300-foot tower at its planned Red Rock resort. The proposal met vocal opposition from some residents who complained that the imposing tower would ruin their views of Red Rock Canyon. Opponents said they knew when they bought their homes that a casino was planned for the site, but they were unaware it would be so large, since the existing zoning allowed for a maximum height of 100 feet. In addition to the 300-foot tower, Station proposed to build 1,500 hotel rooms and two more tall timeshare towers—in short, a resort significantly larger than the valley's other neighborhood casinos and rivaling the stature of Strip resorts.

Angry residents organized as the Summerlin Residents for Responsible Growth, and the Sierra Club and the Culinary Union joined their campaign against the 300-foot tower. The Culinary got involved primarily to give Station a hard time. Although union officials publicly professed an aesthetic opposition to the tower height, their primary interest was to unionize Station workers, using a variety of tactics to reach that goal. In any case, the Culinary's organizing skill and large numbers boosted the cause.

The tower issue vexed the Clark County Commission, which was slated to address the matter in December 2003 but delayed a decision for a month, hoping the residents and casino executives could reach a compromise. The commissioners' strategy worked. Two days before their next meeting in January, Station officials and Summerlin Residents for Responsible Growth struck a deal under which the tower would top out at 198 feet. Station also scrapped the timeshare towers and reduced the number of hotel rooms to 1,000. Furthermore, the Howard Hughes Corporation eased another fear of critics when it announced it would adhere to the strict 100-foot height limit on three other casino-zoned parcels on the western edge of Summerlin.

The compromise didn't please all the residents, some of whom insisted the commission should maintain the 100-foot maximum height limit. But those residents active in the negotiations saw the compromise as a victory. In Las Vegas, the conventional wisdom isn't, "You can't fight City Hall," it's, "You can't fight the casino industry." In this case, a well-organized and articulate group of citizens was able to bring a large casino company to the negotiating table. The fairly major concessions that Station agreed to represent a rare case in Las Vegas history: The dominant industry was forced to adopt a conciliatory position on a zoning issue. It's no surprise that this unusual event occurred in Summerlin, where urban planning matters are placed on a higher pedestal than anywhere else in Southern Nevada.

### Commercial hub

Summerlin today is the focal point for the entire west side of the Las Vegas Valley. It's the largest residential enclave, of course, but it's also the primary location for name-brand shopping, restaurants, medical care and community events. It boasts twenty-four schools, nine golf courses, more than 100 parks and more than 150 miles of trails. Major private schools have campuses in Summerlin, including the Meadows, Bishop Gorman, Faith Lutheran, Alexander Dawson and the Adelson Educational Campus. Bishop Gorman, which had been located for many years on Maryland Parkway in the central city, moved to its extravagant new campus in 2007. Large employers have settled in Summerlin, providing residents with the ability to work close to home. The community has an employment base of more than 22,000. This will only become more pronounced as the Summerlin Centre evolves and the community nears buildout.

*Sun, Sin & Suburbia: The History of Modern Las Vegas*

And whatever Summerlin does not offer, it's likely to be available on the periphery. When Summerlin started in the early '90s, residential development came first, creating shopping and service needs for its residents. Enterprising commercial developers built shopping centers, restaurants and the like just outside Summerlin's borders, lining up along West Lake Mead Boulevard to capitalize on the well-heeled population. Perhaps the most visible example of this is the Best in the West shopping center at Lake Mead and Rainbow Boulevard. The thirty-five-acre complex, featuring major tenants such as Best Buy, Office Depot, PetSmart and Old Navy, was a shopping mecca for Summerlin until comparable centers opened within the planned community. Another prime example is the Boca Park Marketplace at Charleston and Rampart. Boca Park is home to Target and Vons stores as well as dozens of other major retail tenants and restaurants. Today, hundreds of businesses that advertise a Summerlin location are not, in fact, in Summerlin and may be as many as two or three miles outside the community's borders.

In the '90s, Las Vegas reached a population level that drew the interest of franchise companies the world over. Every restaurant chain and service company of any size wanted to take advantage of Las Vegas's growth. The most common business plan was—and basically still is—to open your first two stores in or near Summerlin and Green Valley. Most firms see these two planned communities as offering the best return and least risk for a new brand.

## Quality of life

What truly sets Summerlin apart is its involvement in matters beyond the strictly commercial realm. The Summerlin Council, the nonprofit arm of the Summerlin homeowners associations, has established a range of programs and activities, largely for children. For example, the Gardens Community Center is the setting for hands-on science lessons, where kids conduct experiments and make things like rockets. At the Willows Community Center, the council holds a sleepover party for kids, including pizza, games, movies and a nighttime swim. The council aims to provide the social infrastructure to complement the physical. The quasi-governmental council has assumed the traditional job of the city parks and recreation department, coordinating programs and events that government agencies handle in other parts of the valley.

Robert Fielden, a longtime Las Vegas architect, said Summerlin was the first master-planned community in Southern Nevada to move beyond the fundamental task of selling plots of land in an organized way. Neither Spring Valley, built in the '70s, nor Green Valley, built primarily in the '80s, engaged so deeply in master planning. "Summerlin brought a whole new model into play and that was creating an environment," Fielden said. "It was the environment that created the market and demand for the land. The landscaping, pathways and open space created an environment for living."

On the down side, Fielden contended that planned communities like Summerlin have taken much of the variety out of life in Las Vegas. "Everybody living in the same house, the same yard, the same trees, is boring," he said. "It sets a pattern for everything else to occur around it. As a result, once they set standards for one, they think those are the standards everyone else should follow."

Still, Fielden has a soft spot for one landmark in Summerlin—the Summerlin Library and Performing Arts Center, which he designed. He's proud the building was adapted to fit its sloping site rather than manipulating the site to fit the building. The library also was one of the first "green" buildings in Las Vegas, maximizing energy efficiency through design and materials. "It's designed around the sun and the way it tracks across the building," he explained. "This keeps energy use down and artificial lighting to a minimum. It uses twenty-five percent less than most other libraries in energy costs." The library also was built to last. "It's a 200-year structure," Fielden said. "Its life cycle is much longer than other libraries."

Jim Veltman, Summerlin's chief planner from 1989-1995, summed up the community this way: "What Summerlin did was show the rest of Las Vegas that quality development works. It raised the bar." Mark Fine went a step farther: "You'll have a hard time finding anything comparable to Summerlin in the country."

By 2012, Summerlin's population had exceeded 100,000 scattered among nineteen villages. Growth slowed dramatically during the recession, and the bankruptcy of owner General Growth Properties in 2009 put the whole enterprise on hold temporarily. But Summerlin did not fold its cards. Plans have

*Sun, Sin & Suburbia: The History of Modern Las Vegas*

proceeded to eventually build thirty-one villages housing more than 200,000 people, and officials indicated that construction eventually would resume on the mall. But with the unlikelihood that Las Vegas will ever resume its rapid growth rates of the '90s and early 2000s, it may end up taking fifty years to complete Summerlin after all.

# CHAPTER 6

# Henderson: The Master-Planned City

No other Southern Nevada city has undergone as profound a transformation as Henderson. Its industrial origins during World War II gained it a reputation as a grimy, polluted outpost undesirable for civilized living. The "Henderson Cloud," the result of emissions from its industrial plants, was the city's dismal calling card. Public housing, trailer parks and hulking industrial plants dominated the community's landscape.

Today, remnants of Henderson's industrial heritage survive. But the city of 265,000 also offers some of the most desirable neighborhoods in the state, if not the entire Southwest. It is home to the upscale planned communities of Green Valley, Green Valley Ranch, Seven Hills, Macdonald Ranch, Anthem and Lake Las Vegas. It hosts four large hotel-casinos, Sunset Station, Green Valley Ranch, Fiesta Henderson and the M Resort, as well as a regional shopping mall, the Galleria at Sunset. Over its more than fifty-year history, Henderson has grown from thirteen square miles to 105 square miles. And thanks to progressive city policies, Henderson has the most extensive network of parks and recreation facilities in the region. The transformation of this blue-collar company town into a sea of upscale master-planned communities and panoramic open spaces is one of the most dramatic developments of the modern era in Southern Nevada.

Henderson celebrated its fiftieth birthday in 2003, suggesting its origins date to 1953. Actually, this was merely when the town formally incorporated as a city. But the earliest habitation of what is now Henderson occurred

155

decades before. In 1910, James Miller homesteaded land in the Pittman area of present-day Henderson—east of Boulder Highway and north of Lake Mead Drive. Miller's Jericho Ranch was acquired three years later by B.R. Jefferson, who in the early '20s sold a piece of his land to T. Alanzo Wells, who thus became the area's second property owner. In the late '20s, the Jericho Ranch began to be subdivided as "Jericho Heights" and developed into a small community known as Midway City.

The start of construction of Hoover Dam in 1931 attracted many dam workers to Midway City. Some dam workers lived in Boulder City, which the government built specifically for them. But those who couldn't get jobs at the dam or couldn't afford to live in Boulder City settled in Midway, so named because it was halfway between Las Vegas and Boulder City. The residents of Midway—later renamed Pittman—lived in tents and shacks. Midway was essentially a "Hooverville," one of several Depression-era settlements in the Las Vegas area (and many other cities of the time) populated by jobless families surviving primarily on charity. The completion of Hoover Dam in 1936 left Midway City largely deserted—until the start of World War II, when what we now know as Henderson was born.

Pittman was—and in some ways still is—a wrong-side-of-the-tracks kind of place. It remains a neglected hodgepodge of trailer parks and raggedy neighborhoods, auto repair shops and daily-weekly motels. The stretch of Boulder Highway streaking through Pittman is not exactly that lengthy thoroughfare's pride and joy. The city was still working to pave the roads in Pittman in the late '70s. Nevertheless, Pittman represents the first significant settlement in Henderson.

The second, much larger settlement started in 1941, when plans were developed to build a giant magnesium plant on what became known as the Basic Townsite. Magnesium, the so-called miracle metal, was light and strong, with an array of military uses. Several years earlier, geologists for Basic Refractories Incorporated of Cleveland, Ohio, had discovered large deposits of magnesite and brucite—the key elements of magnesium—near Gabbs, a small mining camp in central Nevada. Howard Eells, president of Basic Refractories, entered into a partnership with British magnesium manufacturer C.J.P.

*Sun, Sin & Suburbia: The History of Modern Las Vegas*

Ball to establish Basic Magnesium Incorporated in 1940. With help from Nevada's eager congressional delegation, they obtained a loan from the federal Reconstruction Finance Corporation, chaired by Charles B. Henderson, a former U.S. senator who came from Elko. The $70 million project included a magnesite refinery in Gabbs and, thanks to the area's access to ample power and water, a magnesium factory in what is now Henderson. Hoover Dam provided the power, and Lake Mead supplied the water.

Ground was broken for the massive BMI plant in September 1941. The facility was to be two miles long and one mile wide. Extensive power transmission lines and fourteen miles of water pipeline were constructed to bring those vital resources to the plant.

Finding thousands of workers to construct the plant was no small feat: Just as construction began, the Japanese bombed Pearl Harbor and many potential workers went into the armed forces. BMI recruited replacements from small Southern towns such as in Fordyce, Arkansas, and Tallulah, Louisiana. At the height of construction, more than 13,000 men worked feverishly to complete the plant, many of them living in tents with no running water, toilets or electricity.

Initially, BMI officials had no plans to house workers near the plant. The government didn't want to bear the expense. Las Vegas officials, hoping to stabilize their boom-and-bust economy, wanted the workers to live there, while Eells sought to have the workers reside in Boulder City. The federal Bureau of Reclamation, which ran Boulder City at that time, rejected the latter idea, while Las Vegas lacked the infrastructure to handle an influx of more than 10,000 people.

The government initiated plans for a temporary town adjacent to the plant, retaining the McNeil Construction Company of Los Angeles to build 1,000 "temporary" houses at the Basic Townsite in 1942. Most of the houses turned out to be less temporary than originally thought—hundreds of the small, redwood-paneled homes remain standing today. This area is now considered downtown Henderson, home to City Hall, the Henderson Library and other government offices.

Apartment buildings also were constructed to house BMI workers. Victory Village, a 519-unit complex, housed white workers starting in 1942, while 324-unit Carver Park, primarily for African-Americans and named for the famed slave-turned-scientist George Washington Carver, followed in 1943. Since Victory Village and Carver Park were built during the war, construction materials were scarce, so they were constructed with whatever was available. They were intended to last five years, but just as the townsite houses have stood much longer, the apartment complexes survived for many years afterward. The Clark County Housing Authority was created to operate the apartment complexes, and they housed low-income tenants into the '50s and '60s. Bill Cottrell recalled that when he took over as housing authority director in 1968, the buildings were in bad shape. Half the units were so bad they could no longer be rented out.

While the housing authority operated Victory Village and Carver Park, the land beneath them still belonged to the BMI plants. The housing authority believed it had the right of first refusal to purchase the land, but this was not included in the lease. In 1968, the housing authority sued BMI, and an out-of-court settlement sealed the fates of both complexes. The housing authority agreed to give up the Victory Village land, about fifty acres, on the condition that BMI demolish the complex. BMI agreed to turn over the Carver Park land, about thirty acres, to the housing authority. Victory Village was demolished in 1973 and later the land south of Lake Mead Drive east of Boulder Highway became the home of a Walmart-anchored shopping center. Carver Park continued to provide low-income housing, primarily to black individuals and families, into the mid-'70s, but efforts to rehabilitate the buildings failed to bring them up to code. The substandard wartime materials just weren't fit to last. The city eventually condemned the complex and sold it to a developer, who demolished the buildings. However, the developer left the concrete slabs and underground utilities, some of which were still visible for many years north of Lake Mead east of Boulder Highway. In a confusing twist, a housing complex called Victory Village was later built on part of the Carver Park site.

BMI was already producing magnesium ingots before the plant was finished, but the final units of the plant were completed in 1943, making it the world's largest magnesium plant. Yet almost as soon as the BMI facility was completed and a sense of community was developing in what soon became known as Henderson—named for the Reconstruction Finance Corporation official who was instrumental in making the plant happen—demand for magnesium halted. Production stopped on November 15, 1944. The government had a surplus supply and, besides, the end of World War II was in sight. During the plant's 807 days of operation, it produced 166.3 million pounds of magnesium.

Henderson emptied out. Following the war, more than half the homes went vacant, while school enrollment dropped by two-thirds. The federal government, however, began to lease portions of the BMI plant to private industry, and airmen stationed at the Las Vegas Army Airfield (now Nellis Air Force Base) used Victory Village and Carver Park.

In 1946, the government decided to sell off the BMI facilities, including the townsite, to the highest bidder. It distributed sales brochures throughout the country and overseas. Excluded from the sale was the Basic Magnesium Hospital, which was given to the Adrian Dominican Sisterhood for $1. Thus was born St. Rose de Lima Hospital, later known as St. Rose Dominican.

City leaders hatched a plan in 1947 for the state of Nevada to take over the BMI complex. More than forty state lawmakers toured the facilities that March 8, and about a week later they passed Assembly Bill 162, authorizing the state's Colorado River Commission to negotiate with the federal government to purchase the facilities. The following year, the federal government approved the sale of the plant to the state for $24 million. The state made a $1 down payment and paid the balance from its profits over the next twenty years.

Two primary issues occupied Henderson after the war: 1) finding companies to use the BMI plant and 2) seeking private ownership of the Basic Townsite homes and businesses. The onset of the Korean War prompted companies to begin operations at BMI. And after years of handwringing, state officials decided in May 1951 to begin selling the commercial and residential properties. "By the end of the month, the department store had been sold for $59,000, the drug store for $20,000, the barber shop for $4,500, and the recreation center for $50,000," wrote Matt Lay in his *Narrative History of the City of Henderson.*

The houses weren't sold yet because the companies leasing at BMI wanted housing available for their employees. The companies went so far as to move to evict residents who were not employed at the plants. But Henderson residents resisted.

Finally, in 1952, the state sold the BMI facilities, including the townsite, to a consortium of industrial tenants for $18 million. The agreement included a provision for the sale of the townsite homes, with plant employees getting the first option to buy. Privatization of the housing triggered efforts by the Henderson Chamber of Commerce to form a city. But there was a roadblock: Henderson did not have enough property owners to qualify. To solve that problem, Henderson leaders convinced the residents of nearby Pittman to join the city, and a May 1953 election produced the city's first mayor, Dr. James French, and four other city council members.

Lou LaPorta was one of those original council members. LaPorta was stationed at the Las Vegas Army Air Field during World War II. When the war ended, he and his wife decided to stay in the West, settling into a Basic Townsite house. LaPorta started an insurance business on Water Street and became involved in efforts to incorporate Henderson. "After the war, the issue was either sell the [BMI] project or dismantle it," LaPorta recalled. "We would not accept dismantling." Henderson had a small-town atmosphere that LaPorta and others wanted to preserve and build upon. "It was a lifestyle where everyone knew each other and we helped each other," he said. "It was just such a good feeling to know these people. It was one good, wholesome kind of town."

The first city council created a municipal government from whole cloth. "We were involved with taking care of public safety, health and welfare," LaPorta said. "We started a town with $80,000 in cash. Our first budget was around $350,000. We had to conduct government within the confines of our budget. We [council members] accepted no funds for the first few years, except for a few expenses."

City budgeting was a tough business in those early years. As historian Lay wrote: "The operating costs for the fire department were roughly $120,000 annually, while the operating costs for the police department were roughly $60,000 annually. The annual cost of water and sewage facilities was approximately $45,000. Together, these three departments expended more than $225,000, leaving only $65,000 in the budget for other miscellaneous expenditures in 1954, including the payroll for city employees."

But Henderson started growing, and municipal budget issues soon ceased to be a front-burner issue. As the BMI plants prospered, obtaining land to grow became the city's top priority. In 1957, Congress authorized the federal Bureau of Land Management to sell 7,000 acres to Henderson, which bought the land for about $70 per acre. The city, in turn, parceled it out to developers at a profit. In 1959, the city obtained another 3,000 acres from the BLM.

The '60s were a period of growth and maturation for Henderson. The city's population doubled from 12,525 in 1960 to 23,376 in 1970. The old BMI facilities expanded. The city resolved persistent water delivery problems by building a large reservoir. The federal government sold another 15,000 acres to the city in 1963, doubling the city's geographic size. A $300,000 city hall facility opened in that same year. City officials annexed more than 2,000 acres that later became the Lake Las Vegas resort.

But problems also arose in the '60s. The city's growth led to new municipal budget crises, but no issue loomed larger than pollution from the industrial plants. The community faced a classic dilemma: The plants were the city's economic lifeblood, yet their emissions were damaging the quality of life (and perhaps the health) of residents. An accidental emission of chlorine gas from the Titanium Metals plant in 1966 caused trees in nearby neighborhoods to lose their leaves. An explosion at the Stauffer Chemical plant in 1967 caused three injuries. By and large, though, Henderson residents saw the plants as a necessary evil in their midst.

Lorna Kesterson was among those who did not raise alarms over the plants' emissions. She moved to Henderson in 1955, when she and her husband bought a house in the burgeoning "Valley View" area east of Boulder Highway and south of Lake Mead Drive. "We were among the first to move into the neighborhood," she recalled. "Nobody had a lawn or sidewalks. The LDS church put in some of the sidewalks, and other people contracted to have theirs put in."

Kesterson worked as a freelance reporter for the *Las Vegas Review-Journal* and *Las Vegas Sun* before accepting a full-time position with the *Henderson Home News*, where she worked for thirty years, eventually as the editor. She served on the city council from 1977-81 and was elected mayor in 1985, serving through 1993. Until her death in 2012, Kesterson still lived in the modest house that she and her late husband bought almost fifty years before. The one-story home has a carport and large palm trees in the front yard. Some of her neighbors had been there as long as Kesterson. It's the same house where, years ago, when she would put her laundry on the line, she would come back out to take it down and find the clothes had a different smell.

"They were here first," Kesterson said of the city's industrial nucleus. "I've always defended the plants. We've tried to work with them. They are the reason we're here."

Henderson continued to grow and mature in the '70s, though at a slower pace than before. The BMI plants expanded production facilities. Levi Strauss Company opened a distribution center in Henderson in 1978. Clark County Community College (now College of Southern Nevada) approved plans for a permanent campus in Henderson, which finally occurred in 1980. But it was during the '80s that Henderson began to take on a whole new look.

### The father of Green Valley

Green Valley changed everything for Henderson. It was the catalyst for a profound reinvention of the city, converting the small industry-dependent town into the valley's premier bedroom community. For a time, Green Valley actually overshadowed the name Henderson, with proud (or arrogant) residents of the master-planned community printing "Green Valley, Nevada" on their correspondence rather than "Henderson, Nevada." The white-collar suburbanites identified more closely with Green Valley than with distinctly blue-collar Henderson. While this separatist movement caused some social strife, it was a relatively minor issue for city leaders, who knew the brash new community would provide enormous benefits for the city as a whole. They were right.

Green Valley didn't happen overnight. Hank Greenspun, crusading publisher of the *Las Vegas Sun*, began buying land south of McCarran International Airport in the mid-'50s. At bargain prices, he picked up 100 acres here and 500 acres there over a twenty-year period. Greenspun originally partnered with Wilbur Clark, operator of the Desert Inn Hotel, on the purchases. When Clark died, Greenspun assumed full control of the 3,500 or so acres they had assembled, which, at the time, was not part of Henderson.

Greenspun was a legendary figure long before he put together a history-altering community in the hinterlands of Henderson. A New York lawyer, Greenspun first ventured to Las Vegas in 1946 with friend Joe Smoot, who dreamed of building a racetrack in the emerging desert paradise. "I guess it was love at first sight," Greenspun said of Las Vegas in his 1966 memoir, *Where I Stand: The Record of a Reckless Man.* Greenspun described the city that attracted him so greatly: "Las Vegas was still a small town with more dirt roads than sidewalks, replete with swinging-door saloons, blanketed Indians, bearded prospectors and burros." But Greenspun saw great potential in a "six-million-dollar concrete-and-steel fantasy" rising on the Los Angeles Highway south of town. This fantasy, the Flamingo Hotel, was being built by Benjamin "Bugsy" Siegel, and Greenspun soon went to work as the notorious mobster's publicity man, staying on until just after Siegel was gunned down in Beverly Hills, California, in 1947.

Greenspun moved on to invest in and handle publicity for Clark's Desert Inn Hotel, as well as become a partner in a new Las Vegas radio station, KRAM 1340-AM. But none of these ventures could compare with Greenspun's bold move in 1950 to take over a struggling thrice-weekly newspaper, the *Las Vegas Free Press*, and convert it into a a crusading daily that eventually attained national renown for taking on some of the biggest names in local, state and national politics.

The International Typographical Union had founded the *Free Press* after its printers were locked out of the *Review-Journal.* Greenspun picked up the financially struggling paper for $104,000, which was the amount the union had invested in equipment, but his down payment was just $1,000. Greenspun had already had run-ins with the *Review-Journal*, and he saw the *Free Press* as a way to provide some healthy press competition in Las Vegas. His open letter to the "citizens of Clark County" in the June 21, 1950, edition, summed up his approach:

"I have purchased this newspaper ... in the belief that the southern part of Nevada is desperately in need of another newspaper. There can only be a free press when a competitive spirit prevails." Greenspun vowed to "always fight for progress and reform; never tolerate injustice or corruption; never lack sympathy with the underprivileged; always remain devoted to the public welfare; never be merely satisfied with merely printing news; always be drastically independent."

Whether Greenspun lived up to that credo over the years has been a topic of considerable debate, but nobody could question Greenspun's passion, especially in his early years as editor and publisher of the *Free Press*, which he soon renamed the *Sun*. Greenspun put his column, "Where I Stand," on the front page, and blasted the powers that be in Nevada, particularly U.S. Senator Pat McCarran, the state's most powerful man and a person with a reputation for pulling strings at the rival *Review-Journal*. Greenspun also took on red-baiting Senator Joseph McCarthy of Wisconsin at a time when most Americans feared McCarthy's wrath. Greenspun fired away at his foes, using colorful language and occasionally making unsubstantiated claims. But more often than not in those early years, his aim was true, and Las Vegas readers and advertisers responded, turning the *Sun* into a profitable operation.

McCarran, however, became determined to bring Greenspun down to size, so he engineered a boycott of the *Sun* in 1952. Most Las Vegas casinos pulled their advertising from the paper. Despite pleas from his friends in the casino industry to "lay off the Old Man," Greenspun persisted in his attacks. When the boycott took effect, Greenspun exposed it in his column. Soon after, he filed a lawsuit against McCarran and several dozen hotel-casino executives, accusing them of a conspiracy to ruin the *Sun*.

Greenspun won a settlement in the boycott case in 1953 and gained supporters across the country who were alarmed at McCarran's efforts to stifle

*Sun, Sin & Suburbia: The History of Modern Las Vegas*

freedom of the press. In the meantime, Greenspun attracted national attention with a series of scathing columns about McCarthy, a McCarran ally who built a rabid following in the early '50s by investigating and punishing those he accused of involvement with the Communist Party. McCarthy and Greenspun even squared off at a Republican campaign rally in Las Vegas. After McCarthy railed against Greenspun, Greenspun rushed to the microphone and railed back as McCarthy retreated from the auditorium.

Greenspun's brashest assault on McCarthy came on October 25, 1952, when, in his Where I Stand column, he accused the senator of being a homosexual. Although Greenspun cited some vague incidents and coincidences that suggested homosexual proclivities, he descended into mud-spewing rhetoric that would make the *National Enquirer* blanch. "It is common talk among homosexuals in Milwaukee who rendezvous at the White Horse Inn that Senator Joe McCarthy has often engaged in homosexual activities," Greenspun wrote. "The persons in Nevada who listened to McCarthy's radio talk thought he had the queerest laugh. He has. He is."

Greenspun felt safe in attacking McCarthy because, if the senator sued, Greenspun would sue him back for being labeled an "ex-Communist" at the Las Vegas rally. As he said, he was fighting fire with fire. Greenspun continued to lambaste McCarthy, in 1954 printing a series of columns, each headlined, "Is Senator McCarthy a Secret Communist?" A February 4, 1954, column in the *Denver Post* described the confrontation:

"Far from ceasing his fire—which began in 1952—Editor Greenspun is preparing additional high explosive. He is using his newspaper as the launching ground of charges new and old, including repetition of accusations so shocking that no one else has dared utter them in print, or, in fact, above a whisper."

For his part, McCarthy, usually a loudmouth, was silent in the face of the Greenspun barrage. But he got back at Greenspun another way: by moving to revoke his second-class mailing permit, an important privilege in the newspaper business. Further, Greenspun was indicted, ostensibly for mailing obscene material—a vitriolic column about McCarthy in which Greenspun predicted the senator's demise. It was a classic First Amendment case, with federal prosecutors accusing Greenspun of attempting to "incite murder" and Greenspun's attorney defending him on constitutional grounds. Greenspun was acquitted in 1955.

While Greenspun crusaded in his newspaper, he pursued other investment opportunities in Las Vegas. He co-founded the valley's first television station, KLAS Channel 8. His first development venture on the south valley acreage was the Paradise Valley Country Club, in partnership with Clark. The plan was to build custom homes along the golf course, but financial difficulties prevented the installation of a sewer line to what was then a remote location. Three houses eventually were built, with the owners taking domestic water from the golf course's country club.

Greenspun sold the Paradise Valley Country Club to reclusive billionaire Howard Hughes in 1968, but the newspaperman's desire to develop his vast acreage did not diminish. Greenspun began talking with his new son-in-law, Mark Fine, in the late '60s about his idea for a community there someday. "Whether he understood what a large-scale master-planned community was about, I don't know, but he intuitively knew what he wanted," Fine recalled. "He was a visionary. He saw something."

In 1971, Greenspun more than doubled his acreage. The city of Henderson advertised to sell 4,720 acres just south of his land holdings. City leaders weren't just trying to make a few bucks, however. They had specific thoughts about what should happen with the land. They wanted to find a deep-pocketed developer who would build a master-planned community that met the city's standards. They rejected Greenspun's first two bids for the city land in 1970.

Greenspun did not necessarily have deep pockets, and he did not see himself as a developer. But putting the two land parcels together was appealing. He originally planned to partner with the Great Southwest Company, a subsidiary of Penn Central, a huge corporation, but they never signed the contract—luckily, as Penn Central went bankrupt soon afterward. Then Greenspun hooked up with industrial giant D.K. Ludwig, who had experience with planned communities in California and Hawaii. Together with Ludwig, Greenspun wined and dined Henderson officials and flew them to see Ludwig's other finished developments. As a final sweetener, they agreed to allow the city to annex Greenspun's 3,500 acres.

Everything looked good. The city was ready to make the deal, but suddenly Ludwig changed his mind. Fine recalled: "Ludwig said, 'I don't like Las Vegas. I don't want to do this deal. I don't think the market is there. I'm not sure what the future of Las Vegas is.' He was taking a hike. But in the meantime Hank had developed relationships with some of Ludwig's key people on the development side. They said they would leave Ludwig and come work for him. They brought management expertise but not Ludwig's money, and Hank didn't have Ludwig money. These guys felt they could use Hank's land to leverage and borrow against and use that to try to cover the front-end cost of the development."

The city was sold on the plan, and Greenspun got the land for about $280 per acre. But it soon became clear that the newly created American Nevada Corporation's lack of deep pockets was a problem. For one thing, Las Vegas in the '70s wasn't exactly a dynamic market. It wasn't growing nearly as fast as it had in the '50s or would in the '90s. "The best you could hope for was 200 homes a year, which was ten percent of the market at that time," Fine said. "From a financial point of view, that was not enough to support the cost of the front-end infrastructure to do a master-planned community."

The first builder in what became Green Valley went bust after building about twenty houses. Meanwhile, only a modest amount of infrastructure had been installed, and the debt was building up. Enter Mark Fine. Fine moved to Las Vegas in 1973 and soon was installed as acting president of American Nevada. He could see that he had to act or the whole project could fall on its face.

His strategy was to sell pieces of raw land at the south end of the acreage to generate much-needed cash flow for the company. "We basically went out and sold 2,000 acres at $2,500 per acre in ten-acre parcels," he said. While his plan succeeded in getting Green Valley off the ground, in hindsight Fine wishes he had been able to re-acquire those parcels as his project became more viable. What he sold for $2,500 per acre in 1975—on Eastern Avenue on the way to the Anthem planned community—later was valued at $500,000 to $1 million per acre.

In the meantime, Fine was on the road a lot, looking at planned communities in other parts of the country to pick up ideas for Green Valley and learn from others' mistakes. He was impressed with the Irvine Ranch in Southern California, as well as the Woodlands development in Houston. One constant thread, he noticed, was that many large-scale developments struggled because they had invested too much money upfront and lacked the income to compensate. The formula for Las Vegas, he decided, was to build Green Valley piece by piece out of available cash flow. In other words, to let the market decide how fast Green Valley would grow.

The first major subdivision in Green Valley was built by Pardee Construction Company in 1976-77. Pardee had built Spring Valley, Las Vegas's first large-scale planned development, and later would be the major catalyst for suburban growth in North Las Vegas with its Eldorado planned community. Pardee took 100 acres and eventually built 500 homes on the site. The second builder to commit to Green Valley, the Collins Brothers, would go on to build The Lakes planned community on the valley's west side. Two other builders, U.S. Home and Metropolitan Homes, got in on the first wave of Green Valley development in the late '70s.

In those early days, Fine said, the "Green Valley master-planned community" was as much an image as it was a reality. "At that time we were four subdivisions with a brochure that said we were Green Valley," he said. "In the beginning it was all about public relations and image. It was all very elementary, ABCs at the beginning."

Green Valley was starting to take off in the late '70s—Fine remembered how elated he was when the 200th home was built—but the momentum halted with the recession of 1980-81. "Everything slowed down," Fine said. "But because we were financing everything out of cash flow, we had enough to keep ourselves going. We had patience at that point to ride out that difficult time, and we were well-positioned for when the market came back."

Which it eventually did, and Green Valley during the '80s took on more of the characteristics of a master-planned community. Major turning points were the opening of the 120,000-square-foot Green Valley Athletic Club in 1988 and the development of the upscale Quail Ridge and Fountains neighborhoods about the same time. "We now had a full complement of products," Fine said. "We had schools, parks, athletic facilities, shopping centers. We had a group of people who believed they lived in something special."

"Social engineering" was part of Fine's formula from the start. Creating a strong sense of place and identity involved holding Fourth of July parties and other events that brought Green Valley residents together. "Green Valley always had heart," he said. "People saw a chance to get away from the boomtown of Las Vegas and into a suburb that they could feel a part of. People there had a tremendous pride of ownership."

Fine admitted some families had a less-publicized incentive to settle in Green Valley in those days. "Henderson was exempt from busing," he said. "None of the kids in Green Valley had to take a bus to any other place. Nor were any kids bused into their schools. We didn't promote it, we didn't advertise it, but people knew about it. It was one of the things that helped us."

Green Valley built momentum in the late '80s as Las Vegas grew and transformed into a more corporate city attracting young professionals seeking the types of neighborhoods they knew back home. It attracted the city's best and brightest, which helped to give the community's public schools a reputation for academic excellence.

Fine's involvement with Green Valley ended in 1990. His marriage to Hank Greenspun's daughter had dissolved and it was time to move on, which he did in a big way by signing on with Howard Hughes Corporation to develop Summerlin. Looking back, Fine is proud of what he and other American Nevada executives accomplished with Green Valley. On the design side, he said: "I like the parks, I like the variety of housing, from entry level to custom housing. I like the design of the neighborhoods so the schools are most accessible for students. I like the trail system, the athletic club. It's still one of the nicest clubs in the country."

Fine was primarily responsible for one of the unique aspects of Green Valley: its lifelike public sculptures by J. Seward Johnson. In the mid-'80s, Fine attended an Urban Land Institute conference in San Antonio and noticed sculptures by Johnson around the Four Seasons Hotel. "I was fascinated by people who would walk by, stop, touch and communicate with these sculptures," he said. "Here was a way for people to communicate with art. People in the art community are sometimes a little bit snobby about something that's so realistic. But it's a medium in which people can get introduced to art." Fine struck a deal with Johnson to create seven sculptures for Green Valley, and they were spread out in the community. "The response was overwhelming," Fine recalled. "We had tours. When you drive down the street, you think they're real people. Today people drive out there and take pictures with the sculptures."

But aside from the physical landscape, Fine is gratified that people enjoy living there. "The thing I'm most proud of is I've seen people move to Green Valley in the last ten years who were raised in Green Valley and want to raise their kids there. We created an image of a lifestyle that these young people felt so good about that they wanted to raise their own children in that environment."

Green Valley set a new standard for large-scale development in the Las Vegas Valley. "It became the standard by which all other communities had to gauge themselves if they wanted to be successful," Fine said. "When Howard Hughes Corporation came to me to help them with Summerlin, they said we want Green Valley as our standard. It wasn't that we were the most beautiful community in the world, but it had all the programs. They wanted to create the same sense of place."

As Fine suggested, Southern Nevada's master-planned communities have improved on the Green Valley model. "It was the beginning of master plan-itis," he said. "They just kept getting better and better." Green Valley Ranch, which is really a repackaging of the final piece of Green Valley, ups the ante, as do Summerlin in Las Vegas, Seven Hills and Anthem in Henderson and Aliante in North Las Vegas. It's no coincidence that American Nevada Corporation is also responsible for Seven Hills and Aliante, while Fine played a large role in Summerlin's success.

Fine remembered fondly when Hank Greenspun, struggling with cancer, would come to his office in the late '80s. "He was overwhelmed by what had happened. He never expected it to happen in his lifetime. He wanted to leave a legacy that Las Vegas would be a better place because of that land he acquired all those years ago. He wanted to take it to the next level, and Green Valley was an outlet for him to do that. Developers get a bad rap sometimes, but we were a developer that gave something back. We developed a better quality of life."

## Green Valley critics

Of course, not everybody saw Green Valley as an ideal living environment. One of its harshest critics unloaded in an article for *Harper's* magazine in 1992. David Guterson, who would go on to write novels, including the popular *Snow Falling on Cedars*, wandered around Green Valley. Its ubiquitous walls, the sameness of the homes and the lack of people in its "forlorn-looking" public places horrified him. "Green Valley is neither green nor a valley—it's brown and flat," Guterson reported.

But try as he might, Guterson had to work hard to find fault with the community. His descriptions, which, to his way of thinking, attack the worst of corporate development, sound fairly pleasant and normal to the average reader. And he was forced to admit repeatedly that people who live in Green Valley seemed to like it. "It did not seem strange to anyone I spoke with that a corporation should have final say about their mailboxes," he wrote.

Guterson found the walls particularly offensive. "Walls are everywhere in Green Valley," he wrote. "They're the first thing a visitor notices." Well, maybe a visitor from Mars, but anyone who has spent more than an afternoon in the American Southwest takes for granted that walls surround most residential property. Guterson, however, saw a deeper meaning: "Their message is subliminal and at the same time explicit; controlled access is as much metaphor as reality." He was equally offended by the codes and restrictions typically found in a planned community managed by a homeowners association. While this is another common practice in newer communities across the West, Guterson saw ugly motives, saying these restrictions are aimed at ensuring "the absence of individuality and suppressing the natural mess of humanity."

Homeowners associations do sometimes inhibit individuality—horror stories abound—but it's equally true that nobody is forced to live in a neighborhood overseen by a homeowners association. People generally live under these restrictions because they want to. They fear that their neighbor's individuality might include hoisting an old car up on blocks in the front yard or splashing purple paint on the garage door.

In a final, astounding bit of illogic, Guterson ventured into a desert wash winding through Green Valley, where he found young kids chasing lizards and teenagers, apparently finding refuge from "the manicured squares of park grass provided for them by the master planners" to "drink beer and write graffiti." Guterson's perspective suggests that in public parks elsewhere in America, teenage drinking and graffiti are condoned.

Strangely enough, Guterson never even mentioned Green Valley's key drawbacks in the early '90s: airplane noise and lack of highway access.

Master-planned communities draw their share of critics, largely because they are intensely controlling in nature. But Americans vote with their feet. If they were turned off by the corporate oversight of planned communities, they would not buy homes in them. By contrast, planned communities are the most popular form of residential living available today in the Las Vegas area. The malevolent motives attributed to them by Guterson rarely keep residents up at night.

Fine said he was familiar with what Guterson desired in an urban environment, but he didn't think it was practical. For example, he would love for Las Vegas to have more pedestrian-oriented communities, where walking supplants driving to get to the store, to school or to work. But, he said, the harsh climate makes this lifestyle difficult to reproduce in Las Vegas. People just aren't inclined to opt for a vigorous walk when it's 110 degrees. Also, Fine said: "Las Vegas is an automobile-driven community, and it's very difficult to get people to do what you want them to do. What you have to do is provide the best experience you can under those circumstances."

For his money, Fine thinks master-planned communities are far superior to the Las Vegas alternative: the endless sprawl of subdivisions that, in aggregate, fail to be accountable for public needs such as schools, parks and adequate road systems.

## Tragedy and triumph

The transformation of Henderson that began to accelerate in the late '80s was almost stopped in its tracks. Shortly before noon on May 4, 1988, the Pacific Engineering & Production Company plant, a relatively late addition to the BMI industrial complex, caught fire and then exploded with a thundering sound that could be heard across the Las Vegas Valley.

"It happened at 11:48 a.m., and time stood still," *Las Vegas Sun* reporter Erik Kirschbaum wrote a few weeks after the tragedy. "Virtually everyone in Southern Nevada remembers where he was when PEPCON exploded. Three earthquake-like explosions followed, sending out shock waves that overturned cars, crumpled railroad freight cars like empty beer cans, blasted gaping holes in buildings more than a mile away, shattered thousands of windows throughout a five-mile radius, jolted a passenger jet flying above and knocked out power to 15,000 homes. The concussion from the hellish blast, which measured 3.5 on the Richter scale, was felt in downtown Las Vegas, twelve miles northeast, and in Boulder City, twelve miles in the opposite direction. A candy factory 200 yards away … was engulfed by the explosion and burned to its foundation."

The PEPCON explosions left Henderson stunned as a toxic plume rose from the burning plant. Panicked parents rushed to their children's schools to make sure they were all right. Eleven schools were damaged by the blasts, and three children were treated for minor injuries. Police and firefighters scurried to the scene, closing off roads in their wake. Many PEPCON workers were injured, as were motorists passing nearby when the explosions occurred. Some were injured by flying debris resulting from wind gusts caused by the explosions. Amazingly, just two of PEPCON's 135 employees were killed, and none of the Kidd & Company marshmallow factory employees suffered fatal injuries. About 4,000 buildings in Henderson—homes and businesses—were damaged, the cost to repair the wreckage later estimated at more than $70 million. National Guard troops were called in to prevent looting.

Many called it a miracle that more people weren't killed. The two PEPCON workers who died, Bruce Halker and Roy Westerfield, were executives who helped other employees get out of the burning plant. Lorna Kesterson, who was mayor at the time, flew over the scene in a helicopter the day after the explosions. "It was pretty terrible," she recalled. "And it was terrible for weeks after." Kesterson most vividly remembered the stories of "people who weren't where they were supposed to be" when the explosions occurred, meaning they were out of harm's way. The human toll was lower than it might have been because the explosions occurred on payday for PEPCON and Kidd workers, many of whom had left the plants to deposit their checks. Another positive: High winds kept the toxic cloud aloft, preventing the chemicals from settling in the valley.

The PEPCON plant's location was a mixed blessing. On one hand, the plant, which opened in 1958, was relatively isolated on the west side of U.S. 95 north of Lake Mead Drive—just west of where the south end of the Valley Auto Mall is today. With the exception of the marshmallow factory, PEPCON had no immediate neighbors. If PEPCON had been located in the heart of the BMI complex, east of U.S. 95, the death toll surely would have been higher. On the other hand, the plant's location west of U.S. 95 put it much closer to Green Valley, where damage to the city's newest subdivisions was substantial.

Miracles aside, Henderson was a mess. In the ensuing weeks and months, as the city cleaned up, made repairs and restored order, tough questions were raised about how and why the PEPCON plant had exploded. PEPCON manufactured ammonium perchlorate, an ingredient used in rocket fuel for the space shuttle and Titan missiles. Volatile stuff, to be sure, but the Clark County Fire Department, which had jurisdiction, had done a lackadaisical job of inspecting the plant, and warnings about hazardous conditions at the facility were ignored. (Since the industrial plants technically reside on unincorporated county land, Henderson officials were not involved.)

In addition, the cause of the accident was in dispute. Fire investigators determined that a welder's torch ignited the stored ammonium perchlorate and caused the explosion. But PEPCON executives insisted a ruptured natural gas line had caused the fire, and so Southwest Gas Corporation was to blame. PEPCON officials also claimed early on that ammonium perchlorate was not a flammable or explosive chemical. The strategy was clear enough:

174        *Sun, Sin & Suburbia: The History of Modern Las Vegas*

PEPCON had a meager $1 million insurance policy, so it needed someone to help pay the mounting bills resulting from the explosions. A giant court battle ensued, with more than fifty law firms involved and tens of millions of dollars in legal fees. A $71 million global settlement finally was reached in 1992. PEPCON's scenario for the cause of the accident was largely discounted.

In the meantime, the explosions outraged residents of Green Valley, some contending they didn't know the dangerous plant was operating nearby. Residents' ignorance of their own community aside, the explosions were unprecedented in Henderson, and local, county and state officials were committed to seeing that it didn't happen again. While PEPCON executives announced they would rebuild their plant in rural Utah, residents demanded that other BMI plants move out of Henderson as well. They noted that Kerr-McGee Corporation continued to manufacture ammonium perchlorate just a mile away. A state blue-ribbon commission concluded that the plants should move to Apex, an industrial site fifteen miles north of Las Vegas. Kerr-McGee did eventually move its ammonium perchlorate storage to Apex, but none of the other plants relocated.

The PEPCON disaster could have dealt a harsh blow to Henderson's rising hopes of capitalizing on the impending Southern Nevada growth boom. But to the city's credit, determined residents, business leaders and politicians hung together and recovered quickly from the deadly accident. If anything, the explosions served as a catalyst—however coincidental—for Henderson's emergence as a leading player in the growth and development of the Las Vegas Valley in the '90s.

The city population increased from 67,000 in 1990 to 186,000 in 2000. The massive expansion of the Las Vegas Strip, starting with the opening of the Mirage in 1989, created a suburban construction spree, nowhere more so than Henderson. Green Valley accelerated its development pace during this period. In addition, dozens of subdivisions sprouted around Green Valley, including the Whitney Ranch planned community, all benefiting from their proximity to the most desirable address in the valley. Sunset Road, running through the northern part of Green Valley and east to U.S. 95, became the commercial hub of the southeast valley, with the Galleria at Sunset Mall opening in 1996 and the Sunset Station hotel-casino debuting across the street a year later. The Valley Auto Mall also opened in 1996, offering eighty acres of new car dealerships in one location. Today, the Sunset-Stephanie area also is home to Walmart, Target, Home Depot, Costco and a host of other major retail outlets.

In the late '90s, Henderson's focus shifted farther south. A major impetus was the completion of the Interstate 215 beltway connecting Interstate 15 to the west of Green Valley with U.S. 95 to the east. The Seven Hills, Macdonald Ranch, Green Valley Ranch and Anthem planned communities all were being developed along the Lake Mead Drive corridor. (Part of that thoroughfare eventually became the I-215 beltway.) The centerpiece of Green Valley Ranch is the Green Valley Ranch hotel-casino, as well as The District, an urban village-style development featuring upscale stores, restaurants and lofts. Close by is the city's forty-acre cultural complex, Liberty Pointe, which includes the Paseo Verde Library, a recreation center and pool and a 7,000-capacity outdoor performing arts amphitheatre. The focal points of Macdonald Ranch and Anthem are their Del Webb senior citizen communities. The I-215 corridor rapidly filled up with retail centers (RC Willey in 2002, Kohl's in 2003) and office parks.

While Henderson's uncharted areas west of U.S. 95 enjoyed rapid growth in the '80s and '90s, its older areas remained largely stagnant, with the exception of new and expanded municipal government facilities on Water Street. But there were significant signs of life in "old Henderson" east and south of the Basic Townsite area. In the '90s, dozens of new subdivisions were built south along U.S. 95 as it winds toward Boulder City and in areas east of long-established areas bordering Boulder Highway. This new growth helped "old Henderson" to retain its seat as a player in city politics, not to mention providing benefits such as new schools and parks accessible to older neighborhoods.

Another plus for old Henderson was the election of Jim Gibson as mayor in 1997. Gibson's family was inextricably linked with the city's industrial heritage, so the new mayor was determined to make sure old Henderson was not neglected. During Gibson's tenure, the city accelerated a downtown

176          *Sun, Sin & Suburbia: The History of Modern Las Vegas*

redevelopment program in hopes of rehabilitating the Basic Townsite area and giving it new cachet as a cultural district.

Even more significantly, Gibson successfully lobbied the Nevada Legislature in 2001 to open a state college in Henderson. The college was controversial from the outset. The state's universities and community colleges were financially strapped, yet Henderson officials pushed for creation of a new four-year college that, critics feared, would drain funds from existing campuses. Critics said the state would be more prudent to invest additional money in the community college's Henderson campus instead. But Gibson, along with state Assembly Speaker Richard Perkins, succeeded in establishing Nevada State College, which opened in temporary quarters, an old vitamin factory, off Boulder Highway in 2002. The city set aside more than 500 acres for the campus.

The college started slowly in 2002. The college's first president, Richard Moore, was an abrasive figure who had been embroiled in numerous controversies while running the College of Southern Nevada, and that baggage damaged his effectiveness in getting Nevada State off the ground. In its first year of operation the college enrolled just 200 students. Nevada State began growing quickly, however, and ambitious plans, under the guidance of its second president, Kerry Romesburg, held the promise of making Henderson a major player in Southern Nevada higher education.

By 2012, Nevada State College had a student population of 3,200 taught by seventy full-time professors.

## City of parks

Henderson has built a reputation for a lot of good things, but perhaps the most appreciated element of its recent development is the plethora of excellent parks and recreation facilities. The city leaped ahead of other local jurisdictions in the '90s in providing parks, ballfields, swimming pools and the like for its residents. The genesis of this was a modest $4 million parks and recreation bond issue that city voters approved in 1988.

Bond issues are the primary way that local governments raise money for public improvements in Southern Nevada. Property taxes go up slightly for each individual but the burden is spread over the entire community. Bond questions have had mixed success over the years. Area voters have supported school construction bonds, for example, but not library bond questions. Phil Speight, who served as Henderson city manager for nineteen years, said the 1988 parks and rec bond passed because it was designed to benefit everyone in the community. "They made sure that no matter where you lived in this community you were going to benefit from this bond," Speight said. "We were going through some times when there was a split in the community between Henderson and Green Valley. In those years there was the older part of town vs. the new part of town."

So the bond passed, creating a nice chunk of change to build parks and other facilities. But city officials did not realize at the time the gold mine they were sitting on. As the city's growth accelerated in the early '90s, the assessed value of its property increased dramatically along with it. As a result, the city was able to ask voters twice more, in 1993 and 1997, to approve parks and rec bond issues without their taxes having to increase at all. Voters readily complied. The same property tax assessment that raised $4 million in 1988 brought in $54 million in 1997. "We happened to be lucky, frankly," Speight said. "I don't think any of us at the time strategically thought it would generate those kinds of dollars. We never thought residents would be as receptive as they have been."

Speight credited the city council with making parks and recreation a priority in the late '80s. "They decided that quality of life was an important issue for residents," he said. "It was becoming obvious that as the population numbers started to increase, we were dealing with young families coming into the community."

The city also benefited from much of its growth occurring within master-planned communities. When a developer came to the city seeking approval for a 500- or 1,000-acre master plan, city officials were in a good position to make demands, such as reserving space for parks, schools and fire stations. By contrast, if a builder applied, say, to build fifty houses on ten acres, it would be difficult to make such demands. Speight added that large developers could use these public amenities to their advantage, incorporating them into their marketing programs.

*Sun, Sin & Suburbia: The History of Modern Las Vegas*

A classic example of this dynamic was the 2003 opening of Anthem Hills Park. The developer, Del Webb Corporation, spent $7.5 million to construct the fifty-five-acre park (per city specifications) and then turned it over to the city to maintain. Anthem Hills has a diverse array of features, including a skate park, volleyball and basketball courts, baseball and soccer fields, playgrounds, walking trails and a regulation roller hockey rink. Although the developer paid for construction, it didn't complain: The expenditure was viewed as money well spent. While the city added a great park to its system, the developer got to use it as a selling tool.

## Lake Las Vegas

The crown jewel of Henderson is Lake Las Vegas, an upscale community sprawling over 2,245 acres of rolling hills smack in the middle of the Las Vegas Wash, through which the valley's excess water drains into Lake Mead. The focal point is a 320-acre man-made lake that is, depending on your perspective, an amazing feat of design and engineering or an environmental abomination.

Construction of the engineering facilities that made Lake Las Vegas possible began in 1989, but the idea germinated thirty years earlier in the mind of an actor and casino executive named J. Carlton Adair. Adair belongs to that small group of visionaries responsible for most of the major community developments in the valley. In 1960, Adair owned sixty-seven acres of shoreline property on Lake Mead and intended to build a resort. But the National Park Service opposed the plan, and a few years later Adair traded his modest holdings at Lake Mead to the Park Service for 2,175 acres in the Las Vegas Wash. From the beginning he envisioned a man-made lake—to be called Lake Adair—with luxury resorts and housing along its vast shoreline. Seven years later, Adair's company, Port Holiday Authority, announced plans for a community surrounding a giant lake. At the time, Adair's acreage was not in Henderson. He offered to allow Henderson to annex his property if the city would agree to change its name to Lake Adair. As an added inducement, a new city hall would be built on the lake's shore.

The city, seeing dollar signs in the form of construction jobs and tax revenue, tentatively agreed to Adair's scheme, and the state Legislature passed a bill to allow it to happen. Everything was in place, it seemed, with construction slated to start in 1968. But nothing happened. Adair blamed his developer, Boise Cascade Home and Land Company, for reneging on its financing. Lawsuits ensued. Adair kept announcing start dates and timelines, but he could not get the project off the ground, eventually filing for bankruptcy in 1972. Port Holiday Authority, now called Lake Adair Corporation, owed more than $1 million and had assets of about $200. Henderson, needless to say, did not change its name.

But the idea of building a man-made lake on the wash property did not die with Adair's failure to make it happen. On the contrary, throughout the '70s and early '80s, a string of fast-talking investor types paraded through Southern Nevada, vowing to revive the project. "Every six months or so, somebody would fly in with a suitcase full of plans for a project and that would be the last we saw of them," recalled Bob Campbell, the Henderson city manager from 1977-81, who later went to work on Lake Las Vegas.

The *Las Vegas Review-Journal* reported one example of the disparate ideas for Lake Adair in 1977. A group called Nevada Venture received approval from the Henderson Planning Commission for a 1,600-acre development called Monte Vista that was to be a "horse owners' haven." The plan called for the subdivision of "300 large lots speckled throughout the rugged property" with riding trails connecting the separate "mini-communities." The plan also called for a riding stable and several clubhouses. There was no talk of a man-made lake in the Nevada Venture proposal. Neither "Monte Vista" nor several other proposals panned out.

What we now know as Lake Las Vegas began to take shape in November 1984 when the Army Corps of Engineers gave approval to Pacific Malibu Development Corporation to build a dam across the Las Vegas Wash to create what was then called "The Lake at Las Vegas." The federal agency endorsed the plan despite opposition from the Clark County Commission and state Colorado River Commission. The river commission opposed the project on grounds that it would be a "frivolous" use of Nevada's finite allocation of water from the Colorado River. But Pacific Malibu President Barry Silverton argued that, thanks to conservation measures, the development actually would use less water with the lake than without it.

Pacific Malibu, formed in 1982 in Los Angeles specifically for the $3 billion lake project, had partnered with New York City's venerable George A. Fuller Construction Company, builder of the Lincoln Memorial, U.S. Supreme Court building and Metropolitan Opera House, to co-develop The Lake at Las Vegas. But solid financing remained elusive, and Henderson city officials were skeptical that Pacific Malibu could get it done. "I think the project is a good one and would be beautiful to have in the city," then-Mayor LeRoy Zike told the *Review-Journal*. "But right now it's a promotion and that's all it is."

In March 1985, the state Board of Finance approved a $100 million bond issue to pay for the dam, as well as streets, sewer systems and other public facilities within the development. But a few months later, a state investigation into the background of Pacific Malibu executive Silverton came to light, revealing that he had been a defendant in thirty lawsuits between 1965 and 1976 and that his driver's license listed his home address as the UCLA Medical Center. That probe did not derail the project, but still it only inched forward. In October 1986, Pacific Malibu unveiled more specific plans, outlining a resort featuring six hotel-casinos, eight golf courses and 5,000 housing units surrounding the man-made lake.

In 1987, with the project still stagnating, things looked bleak. Pacific Malibu had scheduled an auction of some of its land within the project in order to pay a $300,000 debt to James Montgomery Engineers for planning services. But a year later, the tide seemed about to turn. Pacific Malibu sold out to Transcontinental Properties of Scottsdale, Arizona. Transcontinental, financed by billionaire Texas developers Lee and Sid Bass, finally moved the project forward, securing several key government approvals, including a sign-off from the state engineer. One major obstacle remained: the Clark County Regional Flood Control District board, which was asked for an exemption from regulations because the project would be in a flood plain.

At the time, the project still had many critics, including the Flood Control District staff and the city of Las Vegas, which objected fundamentally to the idea of putting a 4,800-foot-long, 150-foot-high dam in the primary drainage channel for the Las Vegas Valley. Some Clark County commissioners also remained skeptical, asking numerous questions about the project. In addition, Colorado River Commission director Jack Stonehocker continued his campaign against the lake, telling the *Review-Journal* in December 1988 that "lakes in the desert are an inappropriate use of water."

In January 1989, after four hours of testimony, the Flood Control District board voted 5-3 against a variance that would have allowed Transcontinental to break ground. One board member, County Commissioner Paul Christensen, said he voted against the project on simple grounds: "I just don't want to put a plug in the bathtub."

But Henderson city officials and Transcontinental executives did not give up. They obtained a rehearing, and in March the Flood Control District board voted 7-1, with only Christensen dissenting, to approve the variance. What changed? Not the project itself. Two board members, Chris Christensen of Boulder City and Theron Goynes of North Las Vegas, said that in the time after they had rejected the variance in January, all of their questions about the project had been satisfactorily answered.

Within a week of Flood Control District approval, the developer started grading operations at Lake at Las Vegas, and two weeks later the Army Corps of Engineers renewed its permit to allow the dam to be constructed. Soon thereafter, work began on the wastewater bypass system: two seven-foot-diameter pipes laid seventeen feet beneath the lake and through the dam. Work on the dam began before year's end.

In 1990, Lake at Las Vegas was officially rechristened Lake Las Vegas, and the developer estimated that the now $4 billion project would be completed by 1998. The dam was finished in the spring of 1990, and water started flowing at a rate of 5,600 gallons per minute to fill the lake, a process that was completed in 1993. That year the developer began building its first golf course and selling custom home lots.

Things moved slowly, at least by Southern Nevada standards, in part because of the massive infrastructure demands to prepare the property for development. The first Jack Nicklaus-designed golf course did not open until December 1995. The first residents, Jeffrey and Marie Schepps, moved into their 6,400-square-foot home on the lake's south shore in early '96. And the first hotel-casino on the commercial northern shore, the Hyatt Regency, opened in 1999. Lake Las Vegas slowly attracted millionaire home buyers, a process that gained momentum in 2002 when pop star Celine Dion bought a house there in conjunction with a long-term performance contract at Caesars Palace.

By the mid-2000s, a typical visit to Lake Las Vegas started at MonteLago Village, a pedestrian-oriented center designed to look like an Italian fishing village. The lakeside commercial area featured spaces for thirty upscale shops, restaurants and art galleries, and it hosted regular public events such as musical performances, vintage movie nights and holiday gatherings. Two large yachts were docked at the village, available for dinner and wedding cruises. MonteLago Village was bordered on the south and east sides by the MonteLago condo hotel and Casino MonteLago, and on the west side by the posh Ritz-Carlton Hotel. The Hyatt Regency was a short drive to the north. The rest of Lake Las Vegas consists of exclusive neighborhoods and lush golf courses, all contoured around the massive lake. Noticeably absent from the landscape: gasoline stations, grocery stores, fast-food restaurants and other necessities. Those kinds of amenities are found several miles away down Lake Mead Drive.

Forty years after J. Carlton Adair dreamed of a man-made lake and resort at the site, Lake Las Vegas had finally become the premier community that so many envisioned and promised for so long. It terms of sheer beauty and opulence, it was the crème de la crème of Southern Nevada—a rich man's paradise, and a dramatic contrast to the blue-collar origins of the city in which it resides.

Lake Las Vegas was hardly immune from the real estate collapse in 2007 and national economic crisis of 2008. Lake at Las Vegas Joint Venture LLC filed for Chapter 11 bankruptcy protection in 2008, with debts of more than $500 million. The Ritz-Carlton hotel and Casino MonteLago both closed in 2010. All three of the community's three golf courses were foreclosed. But these were temporary setbacks. Lake as Las Vegas Joint Venture emerged from bankruptcy in 2011. That same year, the hotel and casino both reopened, with the Ritz-Carlton now called Ravella. By 2012, one of the golf courses had reopened.

### Redevelopment

Henderson is most commonly identified with its upscale master-planned communities. But the original city—old Henderson—remains the heart and soul of the community, even if it is showing its age. Hundreds of the 1,000 "temporary" houses built in the Basic Townsite during World War II, many of them expanded and improved over the years but retaining much of their quaint charm, still dominate the area. Water Street, the commercial hub of old Henderson, is no longer a consumer destination, but its long-term relevance is assured by the presence of the Henderson City Hall, Henderson Police Department, Henderson courthouse, James I. Gibson Library and Henderson Convention Center.

Buoyed by the success of its suburban developments, Henderson officials decided in 1995 to launch a downtown redevelopment program to reinvigorate Water Street and adjoining streets, as well as create new businesses and cultural amenities in the area. "There's a feeling here that we have a community of 225,000 now and have no buildings over two stories high, no downtown," City Manager Phil Speight said in 2004. "We don't want to forsake our downtown. Creating the redevelopment agency was a step in that direction."

The redevelopment project started slowly. Although the city moved into a new City Hall complex in 1989, ensuring its long-term residence on Water Street, some promising commercial development proposals came and went. But the city did not give up. Redevelopment often is about timing, and the time for downtown Henderson to blossom had not yet come. In the meantime, the city spent several years planning exactly what it wanted to do with Water Street, a process that culminated in 2002 with the completion of a "downtown investment strategy," a detailed plan outlined in an inch-thick full-color binder.

The strategy warned upfront that Henderson's downtown would not be transformed overnight, but through an incremental process of trial and error. But it also touted the downtown area's strengths, particularly its ample employment base of 8,000, including 2,500 workers at City Hall and other

*Sun, Sin & Suburbia: The History of Modern Las Vegas*

city facilities, 1,000 at St. Rose Dominican Hospital and 400-500 at the Titanium Metals Corporation plant. The trick was to find ways to get these people to shop and eat downtown, and perhaps even to live there.

The strategy envisioned converting Water Street into a classic "Main Street" experience, a mixed-use thoroughfare with wide and attractive sidewalks, trees, good lighting, outdoor cafes and creatively designed storefront windows—all intended to entice pedestrian activity. The basic ingredients for this environment were already in place. The key to success, however, was expanding the times of day and week when Water Street attracted those pedestrians. With such a large employment base nearby, it's not difficult to get workers to spend their lunch break in a Water Street café and maybe browse in area stores. But how do you get them to stay after work or come down on weekends?

The answer was new housing opportunities. Certain segments of the population would, in theory, jump at the opportunity to live near where they work and within walking distance of a vibrant downtown corridor. Plans were in the works to develop condos and other types of housing downtown on properties the city owned. "I think it will be primarily young urban professionals and empty-nesters who are looking for a more urban lifestyle," said Robert Ryan, the city's redevelopment manager. California developer Jack Webb announced plans for a loft-style condominium project in early 2004. The forty-eight-unit Parkline Lofts, on city land at Basic Road and Pacific Avenue, would be within easy walking distance of Water Street. Nine houses would be torn down to build the lofts.

Meanwhile, another element of the city's downtown game plan showed promise: arts and culture. In late 2003, four art galleries operated on or near Water Street. The city subsidized the rent for one gallery and helped form an artist co-op to run another. "We'd like to get a few more galleries going and ultimately some performing arts kind of space," Ryan said. The commitment to the arts was evident in the vast murals the city commissioned to be painted throughout the downtown area. The first one, 45 feet wide by 22 feet tall, was on the side of the Sprint building at Water Street and Pacific Avenue. The creation of Henderson artist Robert Beckmann, the mural depicted the city's World War II origins. Up to ten murals were planned downtown.

The city also wanted to bring more boutiques and restaurants downtown, as well as services such as doctor's offices. "It's really been picking up momentum over the last six or eight months," Ryan said in late 2003. "The market is helping us. Developers who traditionally haven't done redevelopment projects are taking a look at it."

What started to happen in 2003 was that many developers were having trouble finding suburban land to buy. In addition to the dwindling amount of available land in the valley, the skyrocketing prices left many of them out of contention. As a result, developers started looking inward, seeking fresh opportunities within the urban core. Henderson's Water Street area was likely to benefit from this trend, just as Las Vegas hoped to with its downtown redevelopment efforts. "It's a painstakingly slow process to convince people they should live downtown," Speight said. "It's going to take some time, but I think it will come together."

Ryan said patience pays off in redevelopment. He pointed to San Diego, where downtown redevelopment was in its third decade. "In ten years downtown Henderson will be substantially different," he predicted. "I think once we get a couple of projects coming out of the ground, it will build on itself."

By 2012, Henderson's downtown had been rebranded as the "Water Street District," achieving much of what the city originally envisioned. A diverse mix of businesses created an inviting atmosphere for those seeking an alternative to the sensory overload of the Strip.

## Inspirada

During the early 2000s, Henderson eyed expansion to the west as the key to its long-term future. In 2003, the city annexed 6,700 acres of mostly federal land west of its Anthem community stretching all the way to Las Vegas Boulevard. The land was to be auctioned off in chunks, the first of which—1,940 acres—was sold in 2004. Developers had balked at the $250 million minimum price and city requirements, so there were no bidders at a 2003 auction. But when the Bureau of Land Management put the property up for bid again in the spring of 2004, with a relaxing of the city's requirements for affordable housing and other amenities, it sold to Focus Property Group for $557 million. At $287,000 per acre, this was the most any developer had ever paid for raw public land in the Las Vegas area.

Focus created a planned community called Inspirada, and it brought together a consortium of eight major home builders to develop seven villages eventually housing more than 25,000 people. Inspirada gained national attention for its adherence to the principles of New Urbanism, a movement to build high-density, mixed-use neighborhoods that encourage walking and community pride. But Inspirada was a classic case of rotten timing. It got under way just before the real estate crash, after which home buying practically stopped in the Las Vegas Valley.

Although several hundred homes had been sold and built in Inspirada, this was a tiny fraction of the more than 11,000 units planned for the development, and the ambitious New Urbanist visions were far from realized. Inspirada was forced into bankruptcy in 2010, but a reorganization plan was approved a year later, with four of the original eight home builders, led by KB Home, moving forward with the project. Homes continued to be sold in Inspirada, but at a drastically slower pace than anticipated.

The western annexation brought Henderson's physical size to 105 square miles, dwarfing the meager thirteen square miles the city started with more than fifty years ago and coming close to Las Vegas's 114 square miles. Change is a constant in the Las Vegas Valley, but it has been most evident in the transformation of Henderson from industrial company town to the state's second-largest city.

**FUTURE RECLUSE:** *Howard Hughes speaks July 21, 1938, at the National Press Club in Washington, D.C. Earlier that month, Hughes had completed a record-setting flight around the world. Hughes later would leave aviation behind to invest in Las Vegas.*
Library of Congress, Harris & Ewing Collection

**STRIP PIONEER:** *Moe Dalitz, a bootlegger and organized crime boss from the Midwest, became a revered casino operator and civic leader in Las Vegas. In this picture he is ready to march in the Helldorado Parade.*
Courtesy of the Mob Museum

**HUGHES'S MAN:** *Bob Maheu, pictured in front of his opulent Desert Inn Estates home, executed all of Howard Hughes's plans while the billionaire was sequestered in the Desert Inn Hotel's penthouse suite in the 1960s.* Las Vegas Review-Journal

**THE MASTERMIND:** *Clay Lynch, city manager of North Las Vegas in the 1960s and '70s, was a renowned dealmaker who was instrumental in bringing the small city into the modern era.* Wolf Wergin/*Las Vegas Review-Journal*

**TRAGEDY:** *The MGM Grand fire on November 21, 1980, was Las Vegas's worst tragedy, with eighty-five fatalities, and put a temporary damper on Kirk Kerkorian's Strip game plans. The resort reopened and later became Bally's.* Las Vegas Review-Journal

**OPENING DAY:** *A massive crowd turned out for the opening of the Mirage in November 1989. The Sands, later demolished to make way for the Venetian, is visible at top left.*

Las Vegas Review-Journal

**KABOOM:** *The Dunes Hotel was imploded in 1995. The Bellagio opened in its place in 1998.*

Wayne Kodey/Las Vegas Review-Journa

**BMOC:** *Kirk Kerkorian, center, has been a major player on the Strip for six decades. Today, he's the majority shareholder of MGM Resorts, owner of the MGM Grand, Bellagio, Mirage, New York–New York, CityCenter and several other resorts. To his right is former MGM CEO Terry Lanni.* Las Vegas Review-Journal

**THE SHOWMAN:** *It is no exaggeration to say that Steve Wynn invented modern Las Vegas, starting with the Mirage, upping the ante with Bellagio and continuing to push the boundaries with Wynn Las Vegas. He is pictured here at the Bellagio opening in 1998.*
Las Vegas Review-Journal

**WHERE I BUILD:** *Hank Greenspun is best known as the crusading editor of the* Las Vegas Sun, *but his lasting legacy may be development of the Green Valley master-planned community.* Gary Thompson/*Las Vegas Review-Journal*

**SNOW JOB:** *Florida developer Bob Snow built the opulent Main Street Station in downtown Las Vegas, in part with city redevelopment funds, only to see it close after just a few months. The failed hotel-casino was later purchased by Boyd Gaming and reopened to handle the overflow from the company's other downtown properties.*
Jim Laurie/*Las Vegas Review-Journal*

**INDUSTRIAL DISASTER:** *On May 4, 1988, a series of explosions and a huge fire at the PEPCON rocket fuel plant in Henderson killed four people, injured hundreds and caused more than $70 million in property damage. The plant was later relocated to an isolated valley in southern Utah.* Jeff Scheid/*Las Vegas Review-Journal*

**PUBLIC ART:** *Green Valley is home to an array of bronze statues by J. Seward Johnson depicting scenes from everyday life.* Lynnette Curtis/*Las Vegas Mercury*

195

**TRANSIT TITAN:** *Clark County Commissioner Bruce Woodbury was instrumental in the development of the Las Vegas Beltway and the Citizens Area Transit bus system.*
Gary Thompson/*Las Vegas Review-Journal*

**CIRCUS BOSS:** *William Bennett revamped Circus Circus in the 1970s and made it successful, then built the Excalibur and Luxor megaresorts in the early '90s. He died in 2002.*

**MADAM MAYOR:** *Jan Jones was the Las Vegas mayor from 1991-1999 — a period of rapid growth and downtown redevelopment. After leaving office, she became a vice president of Harrah's.*

**MOUNTAIN OF TROUBLE:** *Yucca Mountain, ninety miles northwest of Las Vegas, is the focus of a twenty-year battle between the state of Nevada and the federal government over whether the nation's high-level nuclear waste will be dumped there.*

**BREAK A LEG:** *When the award-winning Broadway musical* Chicago *debuted at Mandalay Bay in 1999 and ran for about a year, it spawned a wave of high-quality stage productions on the Strip. Pictured: Jasmine Guy and Charlotte d' Amboise*

**LIGHT BRIGADE:** *The Fremont Street Experience lighted canopy, which debuted in 1995, is credited with saving the downtown casino district. The cooperation among the downtown casino operators needed to make it happen was unprecedented.*

**ROCK OF AGES:** *Congress designated Red Rock Canyon a national conservation area in the early '90s, providing additional federal funding to protect its natural wonders.* F. Andrew Taylor/*Las Vegas Mercury*

**ROAD TO NOWHERE:** *Before there was Summerlin there was the Summerlin Parkway, which is in the early stages of construction in this undated photo.* Jeff Scheid/*Las Vegas Review-Journal*

**SUBURBAN GURU:** *Mark Fine, center, was responsible for the success of Green Valley, after which he was hired to bring the same magic to Summerlin. Also in this 1991 photo, from left: Mark Schofield, Brian Cram, Ron Lurie and Bill Noonan.*

**DESERT LANDSCAPE:** *Pueblo Park was the first natural walking park in Summerlin, which now has several of them snaking through its neighborhoods.* Newt Briggs/*Las Vegas Mercury*

200

**WATER'S EDGE:** *MonteLago Village is the commercial hub of Lake Las Vegas, an upscale planned community in Henderson surrounding a large man-made lake.*
F. Andrew Taylor/*Las Vegas Mercury*

**LIVING HIGH:** *The Turnberry Place luxury condominiums are an imposing presence at the north end of the Strip. The success of this project triggered a short-lived high-rise condo boom in Las Vegas starting in the late '90s.* Newt Briggs/*Las Vegas Mercury*

**Two for one:** *Steve Wynn acquired the historic Desert Inn in 2000. He tore it down a year later and built two resorts in its place. The Wynn opened in 2005, and the Encore opened in 2008.* K.M. Cannon/*Las Vegas Review-Journal*

**Mob rules:** *A historic federal building in downtown Las Vegas was transformed into the Mob Museum, the National Museum of Organized Crime and Law Enforcement.* Geoff Schumacher

**TOURIST TRAIN:** *The $650 million Las Vegas Monorail began carrying passengers along the Strip in July 2004. But ridership numbers never came close to meeting projections, and the transportation system was beset with financial deficits.* Newt Briggs/*Las Vegas Mercury*

**QUEST FOR A CURE:** *Designed by famed architect Frank Gehry, the Cleveland Clinic Lou Ruvo Center for Brain Health, opened in 2009, is the most distinctive building in Las Vegas. It's also home to treatment and cutting-edge research into the causes of Alzheimer's, Parkinson's and other cognitive disorders.* Martin S. Fuentes/*Las Vegas Review-Journal*

**ENTER STAGE LEFT:** *After years of planning and fund-raising, the Smith Center for the Performing Arts debuted in the spring of 2012, filling a gaping hole in Las Vegas's cultural landscape.* David Becker/*Las Vegas Review-Journal*

**DIGITAL DOWNTOWN:** *Tony Hsieh, CEO of the shoe retailer Zappos.com, moved his corporate headquarters from suburban Henderson to the old Las Vegas city hall, furthering the revival of downtown.* Jeff Scheid/*Las Vegas Review-Journal*

**THE STRIP GETS HIP:** *As the recession took hold and Las Vegas casino companies put their ambitions on hold, the Cosmopolitan forged ahead, bringing innovations and a hip new mindset to the Strip.*

Jessica Ebelhar/*Las Vegas Review-Journal*

**GOING BIG:** *CityCenter, a massive $8.5 billion complex of hotels and casinos developed by MGM Resorts, opened in the depths of the recession.* Jason Bean/*Las Vegas Review-Journal*

**LEAVING LAS VEGAS:** *The back of the famous "Welcome to Las Vegas" sign on Las Vegas Boulevard South is rarely photographed.* F. Andrew Taylor/*View Newspapers*

# CHAPTER 7

# North Las Vegas: Two Cities in One

Mike Dyal was a management services coordinator for Clark County when he came up with an idea to jumpstart the city of North Las Vegas. Studying maps of the valley, Dyal noticed a large "regional park" north of Craig Road, which was then "the middle of nowhere." Dyal's idea was to acquire the 1,080 acres, owned by the federal government, and use it for development.

When North Las Vegas hired Dyal as city manager in 1982, he immediately went to work to acquire the park property, which was desert except for a paved landing strip used by remote-control airplane enthusiasts. "I knew that if we could turn that land into development, we could turn the corner," he recalled. At first, Dyal's plan was for North Las Vegas to purchase the land, but the perennially cash-strapped city couldn't find the money, even with the great price it was getting from the feds ($5,000 per acre).

The city was in a constant fiscal bind for a variety of reasons, but primarily because state sales tax revenues were distributed to local governments using a formula that favored growing cities. North Las Vegas wasn't growing much at that time, so it received less tax revenue than other cities. When Dyal started as city manager, just one residential development—Palomino Estates—was under construction in the city. "When they finished that, there were none," he said. "North Las Vegas was like a rock in the river and all the water went around it."

207

North Las Vegas wasn't growing for several reasons, but none more so than its reputation for a high crime rate. Many North Las Vegas officials insist to this day that the reputation was undeserved—that the city was blamed for a lot of crime that actually occurred in neighborhoods across the border in Las Vegas. But the city's abundance of low-income housing and its high minority populations also fueled the perception. "I always felt it was a city on the wrong side of the tracks," said Dyal, who went on to become the city manager of Medford, Oregon. "People were afraid to come to North Las Vegas. I once had a woman who was middle class, educated, who said she was afraid to come to City Hall to meet with me."

After several frustrating years of being unable to buy the federal park land, the city changed its strategy. It invited major home builders to bid on the opportunity to buy the property and develop it as a master-planned community. "We asked them to make presentations to the City Council as to why they should be given sole rights to acquire the land from the city," Dyal said.

In 1988, the city received responses from three developers: Pardee Construction, Lewis Homes and Northern Meadows Development Corporation. Dyal recalled that Lewis, a respected local home builder, put together an impressive presentation but Pardee got the nod because of its extensive local track record, including the planned community of Spring Valley. "Pardee at that time was the largest home builder in Southern Nevada, and the council felt confident in its ability to perform," he said. It didn't hurt that Pardee had made its first mark in the valley in 1952 with College Park, a forty-acre neighborhood it built in North Las Vegas. Dyal said the city was confident Pardee was big enough and smart enough to make the project work despite the city's image issues. "They were a market leader, not a follower," he said. "They would make the market. Once we had a development agreement, we never doubted our future anymore. We knew once they got going, it would happen."

Of course, the cheap land that North Las Vegas offered attracted developers. But the project probably wouldn't have been practical without some public improvements that came before it. Although the northern valley, situated between the valley's two main highways, Interstate 15 and U.S. 95, was

208          *Sun, Sin & Suburbia: The History of Modern Las Vegas*

ideally positioned for development, it simply wasn't ready. The major road-ways, Craig Road and Cheyenne Avenue, needed to be improved and widened, which they eventually were after intense city lobbying of the county's Regional Transportation Commission.

Meantime, the city borrowed $9 million to extend sewer and water lines to its northern frontiers. Dyal described the move as an "educated gamble." At the time it borrowed the money, the city didn't have sufficient funds to pay the debt service. "We had just $50,000 in our sewer fund," Dyal recalled. "That was the nadir." Years later, after the city joined the valley's growth boom, the sewer fund had a $3.5 million surplus, Dyal said.

A new attitude also was required for North Las Vegas to succeed, Dyal said. The city had a negative image that it considered undeserved. According to Mary Kincaid-Chauncey, a North Las Vegas councilwoman for seventeen years and later a Clark County commissioner, some gang and drug crimes occurred in Las Vegas, but the media reported them as having happened in North Las Vegas. "North Las Vegas got a lot of undeserved bad press," she said.

Perhaps the nastiest bit of press North Las Vegas ever received came from gonzo journalist Hunter S. Thompson, who described the city in his 1971 book, *Fear and Loathing in Las Vegas*:

"North Vegas is where you go when you've fucked up once too often on the Strip, and when you're not even welcome in the cut-rate downtown places around Casino Center. This is Nevada's answer to East St. Louis—a slum and a graveyard, last stop before permanent exile to Ely or Winnemucca. North Vegas is where you go if you're a hooker turning forty and the syndicate men on the Strip decide you're no longer much good for business out there with the high rollers. ..."

The truth is, Thompson, whose drug-soaked "journalistic" style featured heavy doses of fiction and hyperbole, probably never spent more than five minutes in North Las Vegas. But clearly he had picked up on the city's reputation as the wrong side of the tracks.

But rather than constantly whining about the city's image, Dyal urged the City Council members not to let "negative reference points" come out of their mouths. The word "image" was not to be uttered.

### Finding Eldorado

When you drive through the Eldorado master-planned community today, you might be hard-pressed to understand how this low-key suburban neighborhood north of Ann Road could have had such an enormous impact on North Las Vegas. Eldorado displays some of the basic features of master-planned communities, such as a foliage-lined main thoroughfare, well-groomed homes and large, rolling parks. But compared with Summerlin or Green Valley, it's not very big, and it incorporates no commercial development into its plan. As a result, supermarkets, gasoline stations, video rental shops and the like have crowded in on the community's fringes in a decidedly un-master-planned way.

Nevertheless, Eldorado's effect on North Las Vegas was profound. In the late '80s, when Las Vegas and Henderson started growing rapidly, North Las Vegas did not follow suit. Real estate agents shunned the city. It was not a difficult decision for home buyers to steer clear of North Las Vegas when making the biggest investments of their lives. There were just too many other options.

As a result, some believed Pardee was embarking on a risky proposition. But the company found the opportunity worth the risk for several reasons. First, it obtained the land cheaply—$5,000 per acre. "They made it very lucrative to buy that property," recalled Ray Landry, Pardee's assistant vice president. Second, Pardee believed most buyers would not link the land north of Ann Road—far removed from the North Las Vegas urban core—with the city's reputation. "That area had no typecasting at all," Landry said. (Even today, with development occurring all around Eldorado, it still feels removed from the bustle of the city.) Third, Pardee believed, like all wise builders, that it could see the future. The valley was starting to boom, and the developer correctly saw the northern part of the valley as the next suburban frontier. Finally, to ensure Eldorado's success, Pardee invested $27 million in the project before it sold a house. It built 5 1/2 miles of streets, 9.2 miles of sidewalk, nine miles of sewer and water lines and 142 streetlights. It planted 748 trees and finished a nine-acre park. "We stuck our neck out and put money into that community like you can't believe," Landry said. The company wanted to make sure its gamble would pay off.

Even with all that preparation, however, Pardee did not foresee the public response when it opened its sales office on April 6, 1990. "We sold everything that first weekend," Landry said, referring to seventy-four houses in the development's initial phases. Landry himself used a walkie-talkie to help direct traffic. Eldorado attracted people from all over the valley who were looking for new, affordable housing. It offered the comforts and securities of Green Valley and Summerlin without the extra cost. "It put North Las Vegas back on the map," Landry said. By August, Pardee had sold 250 homes in Eldorado.

Price was a major factor. Small homes in the early phases could be purchased for less than $80,000, with larger homes barely inching past the $100,000 mark. Eldorado's high-end "Estates" neighborhood offered homes from 1,917 to 3,082 square feet, with prices ranging from $126,900 to $165,350. Those prices in the late '90s and early 2000s couldn't get you a new one-bedroom condo in the Las Vegas Valley. Landry said the prices of the upscale homes were kept low to attract professionals to the neighborhood, from police officers and city officials to active and retired Air Force officers. The thinking was that if those people were willing to invest in Eldorado, others would follow.

The scheme worked, as the top echelon flocked to Eldorado. In addition to the affordable prices, buyers were attracted to its remote location (reflecting the persistent psychology in Las Vegas and elsewhere that farther out is always better, safer). At the time, Eldorado was several miles from the nearest store and accessible by just one two-lane road, but this no doubt struck many as a positive rather than a negative. Also, the builder's proven reputation instilled confidence that the homes would be well built and the neighborhood would maintain its high quality.

It didn't hurt that Eldorado's master plan called for two large parks, one of which was finished before the model homes opened. The other, James Seastrand Park, named for the city's late longtime mayor, opened in 1999. Today, most new-home neighborhoods of any size have park space built into the plan, but that wasn't common in 1990.

Eldorado's immediate success sparked a building boom in North Las Vegas, at least in the region north of Cheyenne Avenue that realtors started calling "the Golden Triangle." Where maybe half a dozen developments were under construction when Eldorado started, soon there were thirty. "Eldorado encouraged other builders to be more adventurous," Landry said. Some of those opportunists failed in their haste to tap this emerging market. But the die had been cast: North Las Vegas joined the Southern Nevada growth boom. It would be as much a part of the action as Las Vegas or Henderson.

Eldorado and the residential developments that followed also spurred creation of one of the largest commercial hubs in the valley. In the late '90s, the intersection of Craig Road and Martin Luther King Boulevard became the northern valley's retail center, home to two major discount retailers (Walmart and Target), three supermarkets (Albertson's, Vons and Walmart), a home-improvement store (Home Depot), an office supply store (Office Max), drugstores and a range of restaurants (Applebee's, Outback), shops and banks. The corner also had the only Starbucks coffee shop within a several-mile radius.

## BLM bonanza

As Eldorado was getting under way, North Las Vegas leaders were eager to secure another large chunk of BLM land for a planned community. The process, however, proceeded more slowly than they hoped. Dyal recalled that efforts to secure 7,500 acres at the northern reaches of the city limits actually began before the Eldorado project, but the process bogged down repeatedly in disputes and bureaucracy. The city formally applied to acquire the twelve square miles in 1988. It assembled a group of developers to develop the 7,500 acres all at once, but the negotiations ultimately fell apart, according to Jacque Risner, North Las Vegas's community development director.

Then, in the mid-'90s, the BLM changed its mind, saying it wanted to break up the 7,500 acres into smaller parcels of one to five acres and sell them individually for maximum profitability. The city strongly opposed this idea, rightly arguing that a master developer was needed to put in infrastructure and to make sure the development proceeded smoothly and logically.

Passage in 1998 of the Southern Nevada Public Lands Management Act changed the nature of the discussions between the city and BLM. The act

*Sun, Sin & Suburbia: The History of Modern Las Vegas*

required the BLM to auction federal lands in the valley rather than put together controversial land swaps. The law also stipulated that the BLM get a local government's approval before it could sell any land within that entity's borders. This gave North Las Vegas a new advantage regarding the 7,500 acres. Consultants were hired to do a market study, and they recommended dividing the giant parcel into villages of 500-600 acres each and dedicating at least twenty-eight percent of the land for recreational facilities and open space. The city's efforts finally came to fruition in 2001 with an auction of 1,905 of the 7,500 acres, or two 600-acre villages plus twenty-eight percent for recreation and open space. Under the moniker North Valley Enterprises, two partners made the high bid of $47.2 million for the parcel, or about $25,000 per acre. The partners were American Nevada Corporation, developer of Green Valley, and Del Webb Corporation, developer of the Sun City retirement communities.

City officials could not have been happier with how things turned out. Two of the most respected developers in Southern Nevada had won the bid and promised to build an upscale community patterned after Summerlin and Green Valley. Called Aliante, the community, bisected by the northern stretch of the Las Vegas Beltway, was planned for 7,500 homes (about 20,000 people), with more than 420 acres set aside for parks, trails, recreational centers, schools, a library and an eighteen-hole golf course. Aliante includes a Sun City 55-and-older community, as well as the first truly high-end homes in North Las Vegas. Aliante, which broke ground in 2003, represented a big step forward from Pardee's Eldorado project, echoing and improving upon the mixed-use designs and strict standards of modern master-planned communities. Public interest in Aliante was immediate, just as it was with Eldorado. The community logged its 1,000th home sale in September 2003, just six months after getting started. That fateful sale occurred, appropriately enough, in a neighborhood being built by Pardee Development.

While North Las Vegas leaders eyed the tax revenues that Aliante would generate, they saw another benefit. The new community offered something the city had long lacked: housing options for young residents who eventually can afford to buy a bigger house. "One of the problems we have is that people move out of North Las Vegas when they have a little success," Mayor Mike Montandon told reporters after Aliante's groundbreaking.

Just as a key landmark in Summerlin is the Red Rock hotel-casino, Aliante's centerpiece is the Aliante Station hotel-casino, which opened in 2008. Although smaller, Aliante borrowed some elegant design elements from the Red Rock.

Aliante was the next, though hardly final, frontier for North Las Vegas, less than half of which has been developed. Plans to auction and develop the other 5,600 acres of BLM land were waylayed by the recession. The easternmost portion of the acreage—near Interstate 15—has been tentatively reserved for a university campus.

Risner said the delays in developing the 7,500 acres probably were prudent, intended or not. When the process started in 1988, the beltway was just a bright idea on traffic planners' wish lists. "It was probably premature," she said of the city's early efforts.

## Downtown

From the start, North Las Vegas officials hoped development in the northern part of the city, and the revenue that comes with it, would serve as a catalyst for redevelopment of older neighborhoods. To an extent, older parts of the city have benefited through some much-needed street improvements and funding to beautify commercial areas and update facades. But for the most part, old North Las Vegas looks much the same today as it did when the first shovel of dirt was turned for Eldorado.

Driving north on Las Vegas Boulevard, the first landmark upon entering the city is Jerry's Nugget, a small casino known for good food and an active bingo parlor. Jerry's Nugget, however, is a small diamond in the rough, as the thoroughfare is dominated by '60s-era motels, crusty auto repair shops, topless nightclubs, trailer parks and pawn shops. North Las Vegas once had a large African-American population, but today Latinos dominate older parts of the city. Cruising up Las Vegas Boulevard, Spanish-language signs are common, from a Latino record store to La Bonita Market to Amigo Auto Sales. The city's eastern end, at Pecos Road, is home to the Broadacres Swap Meet, a weekend swirl of cheap goods. Fast-food restaurants, convenience stores and

North Vista Hospital, the city's crown jewel and one of its largest employers, mark the main commercial district along Lake Mead Boulevard.

Except for the 200-bed hospital, which has expanded and made improvements in recent years after the city talked its owners out of moving the facility elsewhere, downtown North Las Vegas lacks distinguishing commercial establishments. No highly regarded ethnic restaurants attract the valley's culturati. No bookstores, music stores, antique shops or movie theaters draw anyone from outside the immediate vicinity. The only relief from the urban hodgepodge is along Civic Center Boulevard, where City Hall and the city library serve as an oasis of visual serenity amid the clutter. A newcomer to Las Vegas who settles elsewhere in the valley would have few reasons to venture into this distinctly working-class area. Two large hotel-casinos, the Texas Station and Fiesta, sit on the city's western edge, miles from the urban core. Another hotel-casino, the Cannery, is several miles north at Craig and Losee.

The older residential neighborhoods range from zoning nightmares to pleasant lower-middle-class enclaves. The zoning frights, in an area called Arrowhead Estates, north of Lake Mead Boulevard, are a result of undisciplined city planning in the '60s and '70s. Seeking to grow any way it could, the city had an anything-goes approach that resulted in single-family houses, duplexes, fourplexes and small apartment buildings built cheek-by-jowl. What's more, Dyal noted, the city did not require those who built the multifamily residences to have enough parking spaces to accommodate residents or to dedicate inconspicuous locations for garbage dumpsters. The result: unattractive neighborhoods that attract low-income residents and absentee landlords. "People started selling their homes or using them as rentals," Dyal said. "The character of those blocks changed."

The neighborhoods south of Lake Mead were another story. College Park, built by Pardee in the early '50s, and other neighborhoods benefit from sound zoning. The homes were mostly small and mostly single story, and many of them did not have garages. They were the valley's starter homes of the '50s and '60s, perfectly nice places to live at the time. Today, many of the houses north of Rancho High School remain attractive and well-maintained, but most of them have bars on the windows, a telltale sign of persistent crime problems.

West on Carey Avenue, outside the downtown commercial corridor, the city takes on another role: host to the unsightly yet vital realities of urban living such as salvage yards, towing impound lots and other semi-heavy industries that aren't much concerned about their grimy appearance. Somehow, a modest residential neighborhood was built right next to this industrial wasteland, many of the houses directly across the street from the wrecking yards now abandoned.

Except for a couple of new fast food restaurants and North Vista Hospital, there's not much evidence in old North Las Vegas of recent progress. It's a certainty that things in general have improved since the '80s—Lake Mead Boulevard is a bustling commercial district—but the degree of improvement is relatively meager. Driving through the area today is very much like traveling back in time. It has a distinctively 1970s feel to it, which may be charming in its way but generally leaves one feeling it's been left behind in the valley's growth boom.

Jacque Risner, North Las Vegas community development director, acknowledged the city's efforts in older areas have focused on small revitalization projects rather than wholesale redevelopment. The city has allocated funds for new gasoline stations, fast food restaurants and senior housing projects, and invested tax dollars in building new homes. But unlike Las Vegas, where downtown redevelopment is associated with large, high-profile projects, downtown North Las Vegas hasn't attracted a similar level of private sector investment. "We have to do our steppingstones before we are going to attract a big developer down here," Risner said. "It's more about one brick at a time."

But former city manager Dyal said the older neighborhoods need to be reinvented. "I came to the unhappy conclusion that somewhere someday we'd wake up with a pot of gold and buy up entire blocks to turn that thing around," he said. "North Las Vegas needs a sense of place built where you now have rundown old rentals. You have to raze that stuff and build something that's so compelling that people want to go there and buy there."

## Origins

And yet, North Las Vegas, old and new, has come a long way from its origins. In 1917, a Utah rancher named Thomas L. Williams bought 140 acres north of Las Vegas for $8 per acre. He subdivided 100 of those acres into seventy-nine lots. He attracted residents who liked the absence of taxes, building restrictions and license requirements. Williams envisioned a community founded on libertarian principles of rugged individualism and freedom from government interference. The only rule: no blacks.

While Williams's segregated subdivision, roughly where Jerry's Nugget stands today, grew slowly during the 1920s, it prospered during Prohibition, when it became the center of bootlegging in the valley. In fact, bootleggers bought thirty-one of Williams's seventy-nine lots and built their homes over basements where they kept their stills. Allegedly, a maze of tunnels was dug connecting speakeasies in the city. Law enforcement of Prohibition in neighboring Las Vegas did not extend into rough-and-tumble "North Town."

About the same time, the construction of Hoover Dam, during the darkest hours of the Depression, drew thousands of the nation's unemployed to Southern Nevada. Those who did not secure jobs at the dam squatted in makeshift camps, one of the largest of which was in North Las Vegas. Living in shacks made from mud, cardboard and beer bottles, the residents of "Hoover City" effectively doubled the population of North Las Vegas.

The small community, first officially called Vegas Verde but later renamed North Las Vegas, got its first post office in 1932. During the Depression, it attracted low-cost housing, a trademark of the city to this day. But even with its slow development into a distinct entity, North Las Vegas had a population of 2,000 by the start of World War II. The war stimulated growth in the city, as the nearby gunnery range (now Nellis Air Force Base) prompted the construction of off-base housing and commercial services for military families. The city incorporated in 1946 with an official population of 2,875.

From the beginning, North Las Vegas was behind the curve. Its first mayor, Horace Tucker, was a businessman with a severe drinking problem and a propensity to wave guns around. Tucker's reputation as a "mean drunk"—one acquaintance said he was known to "drink seven quarts of liquor in one day"— kept him in office only a few months before he was replaced. In later years, Tucker was implicated in two separate murders at his home. Tucker's antics seemed to set the tone for North Las Vegas politics. In the early '50s, Mayor

Earl Webb and three members of the City Council were indicted for accepting kickbacks.

Through this period, the city did not have political leaders who sought to take advantage of the dramatic changes happening in Las Vegas. The city's streets were dismal, its public services meager, and not much was being done about it. That changed in 1960 when Clay Lynch was hired as city manager. Under Lynch's progressive direction, North Las Vegas became the fastest-growing community in Nevada. The city issued an $8.6 million bond issue for water and sewer facilities in 1963. A year later the city issued a $1.6 million bond to improve more than twenty miles of streets. In 1965, the city obtained federal funds to build its $1.8 million city hall and library complex on Civic Center Drive. During this period, the city also spent millions on "slum clearance," bulldozing much of the decrepit refuse of its free-for-all origins. In the early '70s, Lynch pulled off a major coup, with the aid of Assemblymen Paul May and Dave Branch, convincing the state to build Clark County Community College (now College of Southern Nevada) on eighty acres of city land along East Cheyenne Avenue.

While Lynch was adept at obtaining federal funds for local projects, he also was a visionary in terms of city expansion. In 1962, he spearheaded the city's annexation of twelve square miles of largely undeveloped land north and west of the urban center. This move sparked a heated war with Las Vegas and Clark County, which also wanted the land and went to court to get it. North Las Vegas ended up with most of it, creating the region north of Cheyenne Avenue that has been its primary growth area since 1990.

Lynch had even grander visions, moving in 1969 to annex another thirteen square miles in the northeast valley—the Sunrise Manor area that includes Nellis Air Force Base. The proposal met stiff opposition from county commissioners, who sued and eventually won back the land in a ruling by the Nevada Supreme Court.

Sadly, Lynch's impressive career ended in scandal. He had always been a controversial figure, sidestepping bribery charges in 1967. But in 1975 he resigned under pressure. Critics accused him of misusing city property and attempting to write off personal bills to the city. But those specific complaints were simply a side effect of what those close to Lynch called a "personality change" fueled by alcohol and valium. He got divorced shortly after his resignation and took up with an exotic dancer twenty-three years his junior. On May 3, 1977, Lynch shot himself in the forehead with a .22 revolver.

After Lynch's resignation, the city continued to be a focus of controversy. The first successful recall election in state history removed Mayor C.R. "Bud" Cleland and two council members from office in 1976. The police union spearheaded the recall after controversies over the lack of a pay raise and the firing of dozens of police officers and firefighters, ostensibly because they were no longer needed after the failure to annex the Sunrise Manor area.

In the late '70s and early '80s, the city focused intently on industrial development, succeeding in turning Losee Road between Cheyenne and Craig into a vibrant industrial hub. The city also tried schemes to improve its image. In 1978, City Councilwoman Cynthia Baumann promoted a plan to change the city's name to "Industrial City" or "Nellis." Advocates said "North Las Vegas" did not distinguish the city from its larger next-door neighbor. The issue made it onto the election ballot in 1981, with voters being given the option of either "Vegas Verde" or "North Las Vegas." The latter name prevailed.

The city's philosophy in the late '70s and early '80s was to attract industry and let residential development naturally follow. But it didn't work out that way, and by the late '80s the city had what could only be called a housing shortage. Middle-class folks who worked in North Las Vegas did not live there. Even many city government employees lived elsewhere. The lack of new residential development resulted in part from the city's poor reputation with home builders. For one thing, it insisted on ranch estates zoning—half-acre lots rather than the smaller urban lots that builders could get in neighboring jurisdictions. (The smaller the lot, the higher the profit.) Horse-owning homeowners in the city's northwest area built a vocal coalition against the denser zoning that builders wanted in the late '80s, but the City Council eventually bucked the rural group and started approving the kinds of subdivisions that were commonplace in Las Vegas, Henderson and North Las Vegas's new centerpiece, Eldorado.

## Closing the gap

Today, and perhaps forever more, North Las Vegas is a city divided between old and new. Much like Henderson and Las Vegas, North Las Vegas is two distinct places that have little in common. People who live in the newer areas do not shop downtown. Unless they have specific business at City Hall or the Justice Court, they rarely if ever venture into the southern portion of the city. Until North Las Vegas opened a satellite library branch in a West Craig Road storefront in 2001, most residents opted to use the Rainbow Library in Las Vegas.

The makeup of the City Council, too, reflects this shift of perspective. Not so long ago, all the council members lived in the older part of town. In more recent times, only one of them resided in the downtown area. That's not to say older areas are being neglected as a result, but human nature suggests elected officials will be most interested in the well-being of their own neighborhoods.

Of course, newcomers to the valley often are unaware of political boundaries. As a result, some of those who move to Eldorado and Aliante do not immediately realize they live in a separate city from world-famous Las Vegas. At one time, when North Las Vegas offered little in the way of civic pride, that knowledge may have mattered. But to the city's credit, the distinction doesn't mean as much anymore.

That fact was hammered home in January 2004 when the city held its eighth annual State of the City luncheon at the Texas Station hotel-casino. A full house of business executives, public officials and citizens turned out for the event, which included high-tech video productions shown on three screens and a speech from Mayor Michael Montandon, who rather effortlessly extolled the city's current virtues and future prospects. Montandon discussed projects that his predecessors in the mayor's job could only dream about. For example, he mentioned the city's $29.5 million Justice Facility—the largest public works project in city history—slated to open in 2005. Montandon emphasized that this facility was being built in the downtown area. He mentioned a planned recreation complex in a flood detention basin that would include a lighted baseball field, soccer field, basketball courts and the city's first skateboard facility. He mentioned that the city was getting two new fire stations—one opened in late 2003 and another broke ground that year—after not seeing a new one for ten years. And he noted that the city was home to several major restaurant chains, meaning residents no longer had to leave the city for a bite to eat. Montandon's only regret was that the city still did not have a new car dealership.

But while Montandon's litany of government and commercial projects played a big part in his presentation, they seemed almost mundane compared with what the city's future seemd to hold. Montandon pointed out that while North Las Vegas was the nation's second-fastest-growing city, with a population rapidly approaching 150,000, its eighty square miles were only thirty percent built out. By 2020, he said, the city expected its population to exceed 500,000. Montandon mentioned two major projects on the horizon. First, there was the plan to transform the venerable Craig Ranch Golf Course into a 150-acre regional park. The federal Bureau of Land Management had allocated $38 million to purchase the golf course and give it to the city. The course, with hundreds of mature trees, is an idyllic place not only for family picnics and long walks, but for public events attracting thousands of people. Once completed, it will be the northern valley's answer to Sunset Park, the large county park in the southern valley. Second, Montandon mentioned that another large piece of federal land, 2,600 acres just east of Aliante, would be put up for auction in 2005, with plans for another large master-planned community.

But perhaps the biggest news about North Las Vegas on that January day was not mentioned in Montandon's speech. Newspaper reports revealed that the University of Nevada, Las Vegas, landlocked at its 337-acre Maryland Parkway campus, was talking about building a second campus in the northeast part of the city. The city and university planned to ask the BLM for 640 acres, which, under federal law, could be obtained for educational purposes for just $10 per acre. All involved agreed the second UNLV campus was a long-range project but they hoped construction of some facilities could start in three to five years.

Alas, North Las Vegas's ambitious outlook in 2004 was derailed just a few years later by the real estate collapse and national recession. Home foreclosures spread across the valley, but the newer subdivisions of North Las Vegas were particularly hard hit. Construction of residential neighborhoods screeched to a halt. High unemployment throughout the valley was even higher in North Las Vegas. City government suffered deep layoffs and $60 million in budget cuts. The city was unable to balance its budget in 2010, prompting discussion of the state having to take over the municipality's financial affairs. The city still was struggling to balance its budget in 2012. The opening of Craig Ranch Regional Park was delayed until 2013, and an entry fee was being considered to help pay for operations and maintenance. Olympia Group purchased the BLM parcel next to Aliante in 2005, but its $1 billion Park Highlands master-planned community soon was put on long-term hold. Needless to say, talk of the university campus and half-million population faded.

Still, North Las Vegas persevered, buoyed by the knowledge that its counterparts in Las Vegas, Henderson and Clark County were dealing with some of the same challenges. The city was no longer the valley's outcast.

In 2011, North Las Vegas reached a long-sought threshold: With an official population of 223,873, it inched past Reno to become Nevada's third-largest city. When state demographer Jeff Hardcastle released the population figures, showing North Las Vegas trailing only Las Vegas and Henderson, City Manager Tim Hacker took the opportunity to boast to the *Las Vegas Review-Journal*: "We believe it reinforces what we've been saying: North Las Vegas has come of age."

While North Las Vegas will struggle alongside the valley's other cities to emerge from the recession, its best days still could be ahead of it. Unlike Las Vegas, which has a limited potential to grow, many square miles of North Las Vegas have yet to be developed. In addition, North Las Vegas has been the valley's most successful jurisdiction in terms of building a diverse economic base. It is becoming a hub for technology and green businesses. Industry, rather than tourist entertainment, is likely to be the city's hallmark in coming decades.

A major coup for North Las Vegas was its selection to host Southern Nevada's new Veterans Administration hospital, the first to be built in the United States since the early '90s. Years in the works, the $600 million hospital stood seven stories high and covered 1.3 million square feet. Opened in

August 2012, it had 210 beds for a range of medical uses, as well as the most advanced technology to treat the community's more than 200,000 veterans. The hospital would employ more than 1,800 people, but North Las Vegas officials saw that as just the beginning. They believed its opening would spur additional medical facilities to locate nearby.

# CHAPTER 8

# The Federal Role: Balancing Act

You can't discuss Las Vegas history without mentioning the federal government and its various roles in the valley's development. Faceless though they sometimes are, the feds show up in just about every chapter of this book, nudging Las Vegas forward. Often, Las Vegans credited with making things happen have merely followed a course set by politicians and bureaucrats thousands of miles away.

It's unlikely, in fact, that Las Vegas ever would have blossomed into a modern metropolis without federal help. Start with Hoover Dam. The Great Depression might have sunk the town for good if not for the infusion of millions of dollars and thousands of jobs to build the dam from 1930-35. When the dam was completed, the town faced another crossroads, but along came World War II, and the federal government plopped two major defense projects in the valley: the Las Vegas Air Gunnery School (now Nellis Air Force Base) and the Basic Magnesium plant. After the war, the community faced the prospect of losing thousands of workers as both federal projects shut down, but both ended up being saved. The Korean War created a newfound need for pilot training, and Nellis Air Force Base was born. Initially, the government wanted to dismantle the Basic Magnesium plant in Henderson, but local leaders convinced federal officials that it would be better to convert the facility for peacetime uses. And as the Cold War with the Soviet Union heated up, the government located its nuclear bomb testing program sixty miles outside Las Vegas, creating yet another federal lift for the lucky city.

225

"Federal spending, and lots of it, triggered the rise of modern Las Vegas," historian Eugene Moehring wrote in *Resort City in the Sunbelt*. "Like towns across the Sunbelt and West, Las Vegas benefited from a sudden outpouring of federal reclamation, relief, and, after 1939, defense programs. More importantly, the dam builders, soldiers, and defense workers brought to town by Uncle Sam patronized the city's fledgling casinos, laying the foundation for Las Vegas's resort industry."

As Moehring noted, Las Vegas was not unique among Western towns in enjoying the benefits of government largesse. But one difference between Las Vegas and everywhere else is important. The biggest thing the feds did to boost Las Vegas was not writing a check or building a large structure or road. It was an act of doing nothing. At a time when gambling was looked upon as sinful, when police were cracking down on illegal gambling dens in cities across the country, Nevada legalized gambling—and, for the most part, the feds looked the other way. In the decades since the legalization of gambling in 1931, members of Congress, U.S. attorneys general and other federal authorities have taken an interest in Nevada's primary industry, probing here and there for reasons to shut it down. But for more than eighty years, Nevada has been a state where people can place bets without worrying about officers busting in the door. That, more than anything, is why Las Vegas has become a major city.

The federal government has been involved in Las Vegas's development in other ways as well. It was the feds who established the law that divvied up Colorado River water, ensuring a share for Nevada that allowed it to support a population far beyond what local groundwater could supply. It was the feds who made a land trade with Howard Hughes, giving him the vast acreage that eventually became Las Vegas's premier master-planned community, Summerlin. And it was the feds who turned over tens of thousands of acres to the young city of Henderson in the '50s and '60s to help it grow and prosper.

Land management, in fact, has been the federal government's second most important role in Las Vegas (besides leaving the gamblers alone). It's a well-worn fact that the feds control more than eighty-five percent of Nevada. This fact boils the blood of the state's libertarian types who think all that public land should be in private hands. But the truth is that the government has been fairly accommodating with its Nevada holdings. Mining and grazing occur on public lands across the state, and federal land in more urban areas is frequently sold or traded to allow for private use.

But to its credit, the federal government has kept the bulldozers off certain areas with significant ecological and recreational value. It's likely that if these areas were not under Washington's control, if they were left to the designs of local entrepreneurs, they would not have been preserved. So, in a sense, one of the government's roles has been to protect us from ourselves. As a result, an array of beautiful places around Las Vegas, including Red Rock Canyon, Mount Charleston, Lake Mead and the Desert National Wildlife Range, are available for everyone to enjoy.

## Red Rock Canyon

Growth and development decide most matters in the Las Vegas Valley, but environmental preservation also has been a priority in recent years. Considering the pressure to free up public lands around the city for development, federal officials have been surprisingly successful in protecting large swaths of environmentally and aesthetically important terrain.

This is quite an achievement when you consider the public's initial response to the Mojave Desert. Just like the frontiersmen who first ventured into Nevada, they see desolation. They may be impressed by the towering mountain ranges, but they are turned off by the absence of leafy trees, grassy meadows, lakes and streams—the essential elements of "back home." Even some locals still find it difficult to appreciate what the desert has to offer.

Others, however, have come to love the hidden and not-so-hidden attributes of the Mojave, and they have found abundant examples around Las Vegas. Red Rock Canyon, fifteen miles west of Las Vegas on the east side of the Spring Mountains, is the premier example. Red Rock is perhaps the most striking feature of the Mojave, its brilliant red, orange and yellow layers of sandstone and limestone setting it apart from the otherwise monotonous landscape. Red Rock also is home to dozens of springs, which attract an array of wildlife, including mountain lions, foxes and desert bighorn sheep. Hundreds of years before white men set foot in the valley, Native Americans occupied Red Rock's shady alcoves, leaving evidence of their presence in the form of extensive petroglyphs and pictographs.

Red Rock's environmental riches probably were of little concern to federal land managers at mid-century when billionaire Howard Hughes moved to acquire thousands of acres along the western edge of the Las Vegas Valley. Hughes traded a patchwork of railroad properties in Northern Nevada for what was then remote acreage west of Las Vegas. Hughes envisioned his 25,000 acres of new holdings as the site of an airport or aircraft research center, but he never acted on this impulse. As Hughes's extensive business operations were sold or revamped after his death in 1976, company executives decided to develop the land west of Las Vegas into a master-planned community. Local environmental groups raised concerns that the acreage spread well within Red Rock Canyon—in fact, the western edge of Hughes's parcel was just 200 feet from the visitor center. Rather than arrogantly forge ahead, Hughes executives agreed to a land swap in 1988 that protected the property within Red Rock Canyon from development while giving the company desirable property closer to Las Vegas. Hughes executives were not entirely selfless in their motivation, since they knew they would benefit from marketing their new community as being at the doorstep of Southern Nevada's most striking natural area.

Two years later, Red Rock Canyon received further protection with its designation, in a bill signed by President George H.W. Bush, as an 83,100-acre national conservation area. While this designation expanded Red Rock and helped to ensure development would never compromise it, it also tripled federal funding for facilities and trails and to enforce regulations.

Efforts to protect Red Rock date at least to the early '60s, when a state parks commission asked the Bureau of Land Management to protect key features of the canyon. In 1964, President Lyndon Johnson allocated $72,000 to build camping and picnic sites within Red Rock. And in 1967 almost 62,000 acres were designated as the Red Rock Canyon Recreation Lands, the first site in the nation where the BLM became involved in the management of a recreation area. The BLM's oversight of the canyon got off to a rocky start, though, as the agency lacked funds to adequately police the area, where vandalism was rampant. In the early '70s, state parks officials proposed that the state assume control of Red Rock Canyon. The state had recently purchased a historic 530-acre ranch within Red Rock—also once owned by Howard Hughes—that became Spring Mountain Ranch State Park, and officials saw acquiring all of the canyon lands as a logical extension of that effort. Congress, however, never approved legislation to transfer the land.

The conservation area's boundaries more than doubled in size in legislation approved in 1994, and more acreage was added in 1998. Red Rock's boundaries widened once more in 2002, when Howard Hughes Corporation agreed to another land exchange. It traded 1,082 acres in the Red Rock foothills for 998 acres of flatter terrain within the valley. Following that exchange, the Red Rock Canyon National Conservation Area totaled 197,000 acres.

The value of protecting Red Rock Canyon cannot be overestimated. It's what business folks like to call a win-win situation. This environmental jewel is protected, but it also serves as a tourist attraction. Red Rock draws more than one million visitors annually, including hikers, bicyclists and rock climbers from all over the world, as well as a steady stream of sightseers motoring along the thirteen-mile Red Rock loop road.

One possible encroachment into Red Rock Canyon—home builder Jim Rhodes's proposed 2,000-acre hilltop development on an old gypsum mine property—faced vocal and sustained opposition from environmentalists throughout the first decade of the new century.

Another key area receiving federal protection in the '90s was the Spring Mountains, home to 11,916-foot Mount Charleston. The mountain range west of Las Vegas had been a summer retreat for Native Americans for hundreds of years, and it was a popular recreation spot for Las Vegans dating to the late nineteenth century. J.T. McWilliams, who built the original Las Vegas townsite in 1904, was an early property owner within the range and built some of the first recreational and camping facilities in Lee Canyon. As part of the Toiyabe National Forest, the Spring Mountains long enjoyed U.S. Forest Service oversight, but President Clinton signed a bill in 1993 creating the 316,000-acre Spring Mountains National Recreation Area.

## Public land disposal

In recent years, the feds have taken an even greater role in determining Las Vegas's future by basically deciding where development will occur next. In the '90s, the sprawl finally approached the edges of private land holdings in the valley. Developers worried that if federal lands were not made available for private use, Las Vegas growth could stop.

The Bureau of Land Management owned tens of thousands of acres scattered across the Las Vegas area. Rather than trying to manage the hodgepodge of large and small parcels, most of them surrounded by development, the BLM marked them for "disposal." In the past, the BLM engineered massive, complicated land swaps in which a developer seeking a prime federal tract would buy up environmentally sensitive properties elsewhere and exchange them for the developable land. Across the country, the BLM executed more than 1,200 exchanges between 1988 and 1999. But the land exchanges came under heavy fire in the mid-'90s when an investigation showed taxpayers were losing millions of dollars in lopsided swaps. The general sentiment was that influential developers were taking advantage of BLM officials. A U.S. General Accounting Office report cited a damning example: In one exchange in Nevada, a private party acquired seventy acres of federal land valued at $763,000 and sold the parcel the same day for $4.6 million.

One of the most controversial land swaps involved Del Webb Corporation's efforts to obtain 4,700 acres of public land where the Anthem master-planned community stands today. The exchange came under fire from government watchdog agencies, which said Del Webb's early appraisals undervalued the public land by as much as $9.1 million. The agencies also criticized Del Webb's heavy-handed lobbying tactics. A second appraisal increased the value from $43 million to $52.1 million. Even at that higher figure, however, many observers felt Del Webb was getting a great deal, paying half as much per acre ($12,210) as other developers were paying for nearby land on the open market. Del Webb, meanwhile, argued that it was a fair price considering it was investing $250 million in infrastructure to prepare the acreage for development.

Nevada's congressional delegation, led by Senator Richard Bryan and Representative John Ensign, came up with a solution to the land exchange controversy: Taking a cue from the original auction that created Las Vegas, they proposed to sell the BLM's 27,000 disposable acres in the valley to the highest bidders and use the proceeds to buy valuable habitat and riparian areas in private hands. Under the Southern Nevada Public Lands Management Act, signed by President Bill Clinton in 1998, the auction proceeds stay in Nevada rather than being deposited in the federal treasury. Eighty-five percent of the auction revenues are used to buy environmentally sensitive lands and fund improvements on public lands, while ten percent goes to the Southern Nevada Water Authority and five percent to a state education fund.

Environmentalists complained that the Southern Nevada Public Lands Management Act would contribute to urban sprawl in Las Vegas. But long-time activist Jeff van Ee pointed out that the auctioned lands would have been disposed of anyway. "The pressure has always been there to sell these lands, and in the past the proceeds would disappear into the federal treasury," he said. "And once they disappeared, it was difficult to get federal money to buy environmentally sensitive lands in Nevada. Now the money stays within Nevada."

Starting in 1999, the BLM auctions, held twice per year, quickly became public spectacles, with hundreds of people—bidders and curiosity-seekers alike—crowding into meeting rooms to witness tens of millions of dollars being spent in a heartbeat. And the theory that auctions would bring the government more money than land swaps proved true, as the bidding process often significantly increased the final sale price for a piece of public land. Critics soon noted that the auctions were creating artificially high land values in Las Vegas, thereby making homes more expensive.

The first auction, in November 1999, reflected the competitive atmosphere that would come to characterize the auctions. The BLM sold twenty parcels totaling 105 acres for a combined $9.4 million. The average price per acre was $90,000. This auction soon would prove to be small potatoes as the BLM began to put larger tracts up for bid. At the next auction in June 2000, the BLM netted $16 million for a total of 120 acres—or $133,000 per acre. Still, this total was dwarfed by the auction in May 2001, at which the BLM put up a choice 1,905-acre parcel in North Las Vegas. A bidding war ensued, and the winner was a partnership between American Nevada Corporation (developer of Green Valley) and Del Webb Corporation (developer of the Sun City retirement communities) that paid $47.2 million for the land, or about $25,000 per acre. The partners did not waste any time in starting construction of the Aliante master-planned community.

The escalation wasn't over yet. The North Las Vegas auction looked like child's play after the November 2002 auction, during which Focus Property Group won a bidding war for a 992.5-acre parcel in the southwest valley. Focus, headed by John Ritter, agreed to pay $159 million for the land, or a whopping $160,000 per acre. Why did he have to pay so much? "The real estate market has changed," losing bidder Guy Inzalaco told the *Las Vegas Review-Journal*. "The cost of land in this valley since the North Las Vegas sale has just taken off." In 2004, Ritter started building the Mountain's Edge master-planned community on the BLM land, plus other contiguous land the company already owned. Despite its huge expenditure in 2002, Focus Property Group wasn't done. The next year it was the winning bidder for 485 acres in the northwest valley with a price tag of $113.5 million. Focus added this property to its other holdings and developed it as the Providence master-planned community.

The BLM's hitting streak with the auction process hit a snag in the fall of 2003 when a 1,940-acre parcel on the western edge of Henderson did not sell. Potential bidders knew the price tag would be high, but they were more concerned with the requirements the city of Henderson had placed on development of the land. To develop the land as Henderson wanted, with parks, fire stations and affordable housing, they said it would be impossible to turn a profit. As a result, no one bid on the property, which had been appraised at $250 million—more than five times what American Nevada/Del Webb had paid just two years earlier for the similarly sized North Las Vegas acreage. For their part, Henderson officials said the problem wasn't the infrastructure demands but the BLM's appraisal. Still, the Henderson City Council later voted to remove the affordable housing requirement from the BLM parcel in hopes of attracting bidders the next time it came up for auction. Sure enough, when the same property returned to the auction block in June 2004, it attracted considerable interest, and bidding skyrocketed well beyond the appraised figure. When the dust settled, Focus had purchased the 1,940 acres for an incredible $557 million, or $287,113 per acre.

Over its first nine auctions (plus seven online-only auctions), the BLM sold 5,656 acres for $700.5 million—a huge chunk of money, most of it dedicated to preservation and recreation endeavors within Nevada. By law, percentages of the proceeds also went to education and to the Southern Nevada Water Authority. After the June 2004 auction, which brought in $707 million altogether, the BLM had obliterated the $1 billion sales mark, which was its original goal for selling *all* of the 27,000 acres designated for disposal.

Through January 2012, the public land auctions had generated an incredible $2.79 billion. Add in nonauctioned land disposals and interest earned on revenues, and the act had generated $3.34 billion. Almost all of the proceeds were distributed to protect habitat, create parks and trails, and help fund Lake Mead restoration. A state education fund had received $152 million.

The BLM established committees to take suggestions for environmentally sensitive lands to acquire and projects to fund. The BLM purchased an array of parcels across the state, many of them privately held properties surrounded by national parks, forests and other public recreation areas. Some critics have argued that too many of the acquisitions have been in Northern Nevada. Ashley Hall, a former Las Vegas city manager, penned an op-ed piece for the *Review-Journal* in 2003 in which he argued that proceeds from selling land in the Las Vegas area should be spent not to preserve distant Lake Tahoe, but to "secure additional expansion of Red Rock Canyon National Conservation Area, the Valley of Fire [State Park], the Mount Charleston recreation lands and severely needed facilities on the usable beaches around Lake Mead and Lake Mohave, where few presently exist."

Federal decision-makers cited three reasons that millions in land acquisition funds have found their way north: 1) the northern part of the state includes many ecological treasures worth preserving, including Lake Tahoe; 2) Northern Nevada property owners tended to be more willing to sell and 3) Northern Nevada parcels were considerably cheaper than those in the southern part of the state. Long lists of Southern Nevada "inholdings" have been identified for acquisition, but many of them either were not on the market or the owner was asking an outrageous price. Also, BLM officials noted that tens of millions had been allocated for improvements at Lake Mead, Red Rock Canyon, Mount Charleston, the Clark County Wetlands Park, regional parks and trails and other public recreation areas.

The national recession and real estate meltdown that stopped Las Vegas growth essentially put public land disposal on hold. Demand disappeared. The BLM sold a grand total of twenty-six acres of public land in 2009. After a decade of headline-grabbing auctions and big-dollar improvement projects, the party was over. But it was fun while it lasted.

### Wilderness protection

Another key piece of federal legislation, the Clark County Conservation of Public Lands and Natural Resources Act, was signed by President George W. Bush in November 2002. It furthered the goal of making sense of Southern Nevada's land jigsaw puzzle. Senator Harry Reid was credited with ushering the multifaceted bill through the Senate, while Congressman Jim Gibbons pushed it through the House. On the environmental side, the law added 440,000 acres in Clark County to the national wilderness system, including parts of Mount Charleston west of Las Vegas, the McCullough Mountains south of Henderson and the Muddy Mountains northeast of Las Vegas. Although environmentalists had sought wilderness protection for more than two million acres in Clark County, the final bill was considered a major achievement, locally and nationally, because it represented one of the few expansions of wilderness in the United States in recent years. Wilderness designation is anathema to many conservative politicians because heavy recreational uses, such as off-road vehicles, are banned within these areas. The success of the Nevada wilderness expansion can be attributed largely to Reid attaching it to a larger bill containing goodies for a variety of constituencies. The law also created the Sloan Canyon National Conservation Area south of Henderson. This 48,400-acre region encompasses the northern part of the McCullough Mountains and helps to protect hundreds of fine examples of Native American rock art. In early 2004, scientists completed a survey of Sloan Canyon and found at least eighty prehistoric sites, some linked to the fabled Anasazi civilization that populated the Southwest more than 1,000 years ago.

But protecting the environment was only part of the 2002 law. It also satisfied the growth lobby by opening tens of thousands of acres of public land for future disposal in the Las Vegas Valley and beyond. For example, the law identified about 500 acres near the Anthem master-planned community to be sold at auction, with the proceeds dedicated to funding the Sloan Canyon conservation area. It also dedicated 14,000 acres of public land in the Ivanpah Valley south of Las Vegas for a cargo airport. Clark County aviation officials envisioned the need to relieve the pressure on McCarran Airport. They see the Ivanpah airport taking over cargo transportation duties, while McCarran continues to serve travelers. The Ivanpah plan also calls for development to progress south along Interstate 15. The project had been gaining steam until the recession resulted in declining passenger traffic at McCarran. Original plans to open the Ivanpah airport by 2017 were pushed back to at least 2025.

The large-scale disposal of public lands around Las Vegas had critics. The sales were unheard of in other parts of the country, according to Janine Blaeloch, director of the Western Land Exchange Project, a watchdog group. Blaeloch said she could understand the BLM disposing of small parcels within the Las Vegas urban area. "It doesn't make sense to keep the tiny fragments of land that they have," she said. "Those small fragments are not providing any habitat value." But Blaeloch said the disposal of large blocks of land on the Las Vegas periphery was another matter. "I think there needs to be more consideration of what the environmental consequences are going to be," she said.

Blaeloch, whose group was a major critic of public land exchanges, supported the auction process. "It's been a solution in terms of taxpayer losses suffered under the land exchange program," she said. But Blaeloch worried that Southern Nevada was too eager to hand out public lands to developers, noting that the usual process of conducting environmental assessments of prospective disposal lands was not being followed. "We're talking about the wholesale disposal of habitat," she said.

The dilemma had many characteristics. First of all, the BLM was in an odd position in Southern Nevada. For all intents and purposes, a federal agency that historically had focused on rural ranching and mining issues was functioning as the largest real estate agent in the state. This was a whole new world for BLM bureaucrats, and they were bound to make mistakes. On a related note, it was particularly irritating to environmentalists that the BLM, of all federal agencies, was taking on this role. Historically, the BLM has been the least environmentally sensitive federal agency, tending to side with conservative ranching and mining constituencies over idealistic environmentalists. If, for example, the U.S. Fish & Wildlife Service was handling public land disposal in Southern Nevada, one presumes that habitat preservation would be given greater attention.

Still, all this land changing hands in Southern Nevada created a geography that made a little more sense than it had a decade earlier. The areas most logical for development—primarily within the urban area—are slated for development, while many of the areas most appropriate for preservation have been protected. Considering the pro-development mindset in Southern Nevada, it's amazing to realize the metropolitan area is surrounded by federally protected recreation, conservation and wilderness areas: Lake Mead National Recreation Area to the east, Desert National Wildlife Refuge and Nellis Range to the north, Red Rock Canyon National Conservation Area and Spring Mountains National Recreation Area to the west and Sloan Canyon National Conservation Area to the south. Hardcore developers may grumble, but the protection and availability of these regions for public enjoyment enhances the quality of life in Southern Nevada for current and future generations. There always will be a need for more adjustments in the public vs. private land puzzle, especially as the Las Vegas Valley fills in and developers begin prospecting in adjacent valleys for good land to build on. As long as federal decision-makers continue to demand a proper balance between development and preservation, Southern Nevada will grow in a reasonable manner.

### Yucca Mountain

Over the past eighty years, the federal government has boosted Las Vegas's economy in a variety of ways. But one of the government's "investments" in Southern Nevada—the proposed Yucca Mountain high-level nuclear waste repository—could have a detrimental effect on the community. Local officials worry that the operation of a radioactive waste dump just ninety miles away could dissuade tourists from visiting Las Vegas and people and businesses from moving to Southern Nevada.

After World War II, at the dawn of the Atomic Age, government scientists went to work figuring out how to use nuclear fission for civilian purposes. The 1954 Atomic Energy Act made it a national goal to encourage the widespread use of atomic energy, and the first nuclear power plants came on line in the late '50s. Soon, there were dozens of them all over the United States.

From the beginning of commercial nuclear power, scientists believed deep underground salt beds were the best places to store highly radioactive waste. The National Academy of Sciences recommended underground storage as early as 1957. But nothing was done to address the issue. In 1970, in response to increasing concerns about the lack of a policy for waste disposal, the Atomic Energy Commission said it would develop a permanent repository in an abandoned salt mine near Lyons, Kansas, northwest of Wichita.

"It aired its plans without conducting thorough geologic and hydrologic investigations, and the suitability of the site was soon challenged by the state geologist of Kansas and other scientists," according to the Nuclear Regulatory Commission's website. "The uncertainties about the site generated a bitter dispute between the AEC on the one side and members of Congress and state officials from Kansas on the other. It ended in 1972 in great embarrassment for the AEC when the reservations of those who opposed the Lyons location proved to be well-founded."

Needless to say, history has repeated itself with the Atomic Energy Commission's successor, the Department of Energy, and its efforts to put nuclear waste in Nevada. The Nuclear Waste Policy Act, signed into law by President Ronald Reagan in 1983, called for a nationwide search for geologic formations capable of containing high-level nuclear waste for 10,000 years. The law said three sites would be considered in separate geographic regions— the Northeast, Southeast and West—and they would be studied and presented to the president, who would choose the best location. But after influential Northeastern lawmakers objected to the prospect of building a nuclear waste dump in their area, the DOE unilaterally took the Northeast out of consideration. And when President Reagan thought he might need Southern votes in his 1984 re-election bid, the Southeast was withdrawn, leaving only the strongly pro-Reagan West in the running. In 1987, Congress modified the Nuclear Waste Policy Act, making Yucca Mountain, ninety miles north-west of Las Vegas, the sole site to be studied. This legislation became known locally as the "Screw Nevada bill."

Since then, the DOE has been studying the site, digging tunnels and conducting experiments, while state-funded scientists have tracked evidence showing Yucca Mountain to be a questionable location for a nuclear waste dump storing 77,000 tons of spent fuel pellets. Frustrated by slow progress on Yucca Mountain, the nuclear power industry and its congressional allies tried during the '90s to designate the Nevada Test Site, adjacent to Yucca Mountain, as a "temporary" or "interim" waste storage site—a maneuver aimed at sidestepping the research into whether Yucca was a safe option. But Nevada officials were able to block Congress from moving forward with the scheme, largely because of President Bill Clinton's ties to state leaders.

### Sound science?

The DOE was studying Yucca Mountain on the premise that it's a good place to store high-level nuclear waste for 10,000 years—one estimate of the amount of time it takes for the waste's deadly radioactivity to dissipate to a non-deadly state. The hard volcanic nature of the mountain and its dry, remote location, the thinking goes, reduce the likelihood that the waste would be exposed to the environment.

But research shows that Yucca Mountain is not as solid and stable—or as dry—as previously thought. It is in an active earthquake zone, for one thing. Nevada ranks third in seismic activity behind California and Alaska, and several faults run through or near Yucca Mountain. The mountain's volcanic origins suggest that over a period as long as 10,000 years, it could erupt again. Studies also show that a leak of nuclear waste stored in Yucca Mountain—per-haps caused by an earthquake—could infiltrate nearby groundwater supplies, eventually exposing thousands of people to radioactivity.

State scientists argue that in the past thermal water has risen within the mountain and could do so again. The concern is that a future upwelling of water, triggered by an earthquake or volcanic eruption, could flood the repository and corrode the metal waste canisters, allowing deadly radioactivity to be carried off into the groundwater used in nearby communities such as the Amargosa Valley.

Meanwhile, there's the cask issue. The waste would be transported to Yucca Mountain in steel casks and stored there. The DOE touts its cask models as very strong and unlikely to leak or corrode. But state scientists say their studies show the casks could indeed corrode and leak in a matter of hundreds of years.

The DOE scientists have an attitude that they can make Yucca Mountain work. They have been presented with a challenge and intend to solve it. Originally, Yucca Mountain was preferred because it would provide geologic barriers—the dry, hard volcanic rock—to keep radioactivity out of the environment. But today, in light of many studies showing Yucca Mountain's natural shortcomings, the DOE's efforts are focused on creating engineered barriers to prevent leakage.

Environmentalists and Nevada officials are coming from the perspective that there's no way to adequately solve the nuclear waste problem with current technology. In addition, environmentalists and Nevada officials do not have great confidence in the DOE's abilities to do the job right.

## Transportation dangers

The safety of transporting the high-level nuclear waste to Yucca Mountain is an issue that Nevada has tried to exploit to its advantage. The DOE contends it can transport the waste to Nevada with minimal risk of accident and almost no chance of the waste canisters cracking open and contaminating communities in, say, Ohio or Nebraska. The DOE does have a good transportation safety record for the low- and mid-level radioactive waste that it has been carting around the continent in recent decades. But state officials say the high-level waste, to be transported by truck and train, would travel through parts of forty-three states to get to Yucca Mountain, and common sense and statistical probability tell you there will be accidents—especially when human fallibility is involved. Nevada scientists say the possibility of an accident in which nuclear waste canisters are breached should be a wake-up call for citizens and their congressional representatives across the country who are otherwise uninterested in the repository issue. The Nevada Legislature and Clark County Commission spent millions on a national advertising campaign highlighting the dangers of nuclear waste transportation.

Bob Loux, director of the Nevada Agency for Nuclear Projects from 1985-2008, called transportation the project's "Achilles' heel." A handful of high-profile accidents involving trains and trucks carrying hazardous cargo gave fresh ammunition to nuclear waste opponents. The accident that received the most attention from anti-nuclear forces was a derailment of a freight train in 2001 in a tunnel beneath Baltimore, Maryland. The train carrying hazardous chemicals burned for several days at temperatures of up to 1,500 degrees. If the train had been carrying nuclear waste, opponents suggested, the steel casks designed to protect radioactive waste could have been breached. "I hope everyone recognizes the tremendous tragedy that was just barely averted in Baltimore," Nevada Senator Harry Reid told reporters after the derailment. "Hydrochloric acid is bad, but not as bad as nuclear waste. A speck the size of a pinpoint would kill a person."

The September 11, 2001, terrorist attacks in New York City and Washington, D.C., combined with fears of more terrorist attacks, reinforced concerns about the risks of nuclear waste transportation. Yucca Mountain critics maintain it is safer to simply keep the waste where it is—in security-guarded concrete vaults at the nation's 103 reactor sites.

### Yucca politics in Nevada

Polls consistently have shown that a large majority of Nevadans oppose the federal government's plan to dump nuclear waste in Nevada. The majority view is that Nevada should fight to the very end, never give up the battle. This position holds that a nuclear waste dump would be disastrous for Nevada. It would be an environmental abomination, putting Nevadans at risk, and have a devastating effect on Las Vegas tourism. Many tourists surely would be frightened away by the thought of a deadly radioactive waste dump just ninety miles from the Strip. This view also is founded on the belief that Nevada can win its war against the pro-nuclear forces with strong scientific arguments and political and legal clout.

But some in Nevada were ready to make a deal. Led by the likes of former Governor Bob List, as well as county commissioners in Lincoln and Nye counties, this group believed the state could not win the fight. Yucca Mountain was the only site being studied, they've noted, and the waste would come eventually. Knowing that, this group believed Nevada should try to get something for its agreement to accept the waste. Pro-Yucca forces suggested Nevada could receive hundreds of millions of dollars for highways, schools and other public services in exchange for accepting the dump—a windfall for a cash-strapped state. Labor officials touted the high-paying jobs that would come with the construction of a nuclear waste dump.

The fight-to-the-end types responded that if Nevada showed any willingness to compromise on the dump, or even considered taking any blood money, the fight would be lost for sure.

## Yucca politics in Washington

In the nation's capital, the long-running Yucca Mountain battle must seem bizarre to some observers. It's a case of one of the most powerful lobbies in Congress—the nuclear utilities—being beaten back time and again by environmental groups and little ol' Nevada. This doesn't happen very often. Nevada could have lost big time in the '90s when there was a push in Congress to store nuclear waste "temporarily" at the Nevada Test Site. Pro-nuclear members of Congress, pressured by nuclear utilities in their home states, introduced a bill to store the waste in Nevada right away and then shift it to Yucca Mountain once the larger issues were settled. President Clinton put that idea on ice. How strongly Clinton felt on the nuclear waste issue never was clear. Probably not very. But he had some good friends in Nevada who lobbied him hard, and it worked. Clinton went to law school with *Las Vegas Sun* Editor and land developer Brian Greenspun and stayed at Greenspun's Henderson house a few times during his years in office. Greenspun contributed heavily to Clinton's campaigns and once stayed in the White House's Lincoln Bedroom. Clinton also was close to former Nevada Governor Bob Miller and casino mogul Steve Wynn.

Nevadans supporting Vice President Al Gore for president in 2000 expected him to continue Clinton's policy of skepticism about Yucca Mountain, if not downright opposition to the project. But when George W. Bush took office, the anti-nuclear forces feared the worst. They were right to be concerned, because, despite Bush's vow during the campaign to base decisions about Yucca Mountain on "sound science," he quickly went to work to get the repository approved and opened.

First, Bush called for fast-tracking new nuclear power plants as part of his plan to solve what he called an energy crisis rivaling the shortages of the 1970s. A bevy of new plants would increase the pressure to build a dump at Yucca Mountain. Then Bush's DOE, under Secretary Spencer Abraham, accelerated studies of Yucca Mountain's suitability.

An unlikely turn of events initially thwarted Bush. A Republican member of the narrowly divided Senate, Vermont's James Jeffords, changed his party affiliation, in part at Reid's urging, and the Democrats took control of the upper chamber. That made Reid the majority whip—the second most powerful person in the Senate. Reid confidently announced that any talk of a nuclear waste dump was dead for that year.

But the tide turned against Nevada soon after that. In February 2002, President Bush formally recommended Yucca Mountain as the site for the nuclear waste dump. In April, Nevada Governor Kenny Guinn vetoed the recommendation, a procedure provided for in the original repository legislation. But a month later the House of Representatives voted 306-117 to override Guinn's veto, approving the Yucca Mountain project. Two months after that, the U.S. Senate concurred by a 60-39 vote.

That was a dark period for Yucca Mountain opponents, but it did not mark the end of the fight. In 2003 the state of Nevada filed half a dozen federal lawsuits challenging Yucca Mountain on environmental and constitutional grounds The state's lawyers felt they had strong legal arguments, especially the point that forty-nine states had placed an undue burden on one state against its will, a violation of the Tenth Amendment.

But when the U.S. Court of Appeals for the District of Columbia heard Nevada's case in January 2004, the reception was decidedly cool. The appeals court judges appeared to have all but ruled out Nevada's constitutional challenges, which, if successful, could have been a knockout blow to the repository.

However, the judges seemed receptive to the state's complaints about how the Environmental Protection Agency had relaxed health and safety standards for Yucca Mountain.

In July 2004, the Court of Appeals confirmed that perception, dealing the DOE another serious setback by siding with Nevada on the EPA standards issue. Although the court ruled against the state on several constitutional arguments, it said the EPA's 10,000-year standard for protecting the public from radiation leaks was arbitrary and too short, perhaps by hundreds of thousands of years. Nevada political leaders declared victory, suggesting the decision may be enough to kill the Yucca Mountain project. However, that assessment seemed premature, as nuclear lobbyists started plotting their next plan of attack, possibly through legal appeals or by seeking relief from Congress. More than $12 billion, much of it derived from fees paid by nuclear utilities, had been spent on the Yucca Mountain project. It was unlikely that such a substantial investment simply would be written off because of an appeals court vote.

There's no question, however, that the court decision resulted in another delay for the project. The lengthy process of licensing Yucca Mountain was expected to get started in late 2004 when the Department of Energy was to submit its application to the Nuclear Regulatory Commission. The court ruling postponed that application indefinitely until the EPA standards were resolved. The DOE's oft-stated goal of opening Yucca Mountain by 2010 had already seemed unrealistic, but the court ruling all but assured a later opening date.

Paul Craig, a physicist and engineering professor at the University of California, Davis, resigned from his seat on the federal government's Nuclear Waste Technical Review Board in early 2004, citing a desire to speak more freely about dangers posed by the DOE's plans for Yucca Mountain. Craig contended that the repository is poorly designed and could leak waste into the environment. He focused his criticism on the DOE's plan to store the waste in a high grade of stainless steel canisters. "The science is very clear," Craig told reporters. "If we get high-temperature liquids, the metal would corrode and that would eventually lead to leakage of nuclear waste. Therefore, it is a bad design. And that is very, very bad news for the Department of Energy, because they are committed to that design." Craig said if the DOE had to adopt a different design for storage at the dump, as he believed it would, the project would be delayed for years.

Nevada leaders welcomed that scenario. They believe every delay in the Yucca Mountain project increases the odds in favor of an alternative to underground storage. Scientific advances suggest that in the future the waste could be transformed or reprocessed through chemical processes into a less-deadly substance.

Transmutation is the new alchemy in science circles, and federal and state officials are taking a keen interest. Transmutation reduces the volume and toxicity of nuclear waste by bombarding it with neutrons. As a result, the storage time would be reduced from 10,000 years to about 300 years. Congress has been increasing funding for transmutation research, from $5 million in 1999 to $34 million in 2002. University of Nevada, Las Vegas scientists were involved in transmutation research.

But transmutation is no panacea. First of all, the waste still would have to be stored safely for hundreds of years, although maybe not in a central repository such as Yucca Mountain, but at a series of regional sites that might not have to meet the same safety standards. Second, transmutation would be billions of dollars more expensive—far more costly than simply sliding metal canisters into underground tunnels in the desert. But transmutation could offset some or all of the costs by producing energy in the process. The strongest critics are environmentalists who say transmutation would be used as an argument for building more nuclear power plants. Unlike Nevada political leaders, many environmentalists not only oppose nuclear waste disposal, they oppose nuclear power generally.

### The never-ending story

Despite Bush's support, Yucca Mountain was dealt another heavy blow when Harry Reid became majority leader of the U.S. Senate in 2007. Nevada's senior senator vowed to starve the dump project financially, and he did so over the next few years. Yucca's demise seemed even more certain when Barack Obama was elected president in 2008. A year later, Obama's

Energy secretary, Steven Chu, announced, "Yucca Mountain as a repository is off the table." In 2011, the project shut down entirely.

The odds of nuclear waste ever being stored within Yucca Mountain seemed extremely long. In 2012, the Blue Ribbon Commission on America's Nuclear Future, co-chaired by former Indiana Rep. Lee Hamilton, called on Congress to take a new approach to solving the nuclear waste problem. "We can continue along to fight the same battles we have fought for decades with no conclusion, or we can step back and try to chart a new course," Hamilton told a congressional subcommittee.

The commission recommended a "consent-based" strategy to find a state willing to accept the waste. Congressional Republicans responded by insisting it's too early to give up on Yucca Mountain, but Hamilton, who served in Congress for thirty-four years, offered a historical perspective:

"Our view is we've had thirty to forty years' experience, and as a country we have not been able to reach a solution. You can blame whoever you want. I suspect there is blame to go around. The fact is, the process we have been following has not worked for whatever reason, and it continues to roll up huge costs to the American taxpayer. If you stand around and insist on Yucca, Yucca, Yucca, which people have been insisting on for a long, long time but have not been able to pull it off, we think the result of that is an impasse."

Reid took the opportunity to administer Yucca Mountain's last rites. "The Yucca project is dead, and the sooner all Republicans realize this, the sooner we can finally develop a nuclear waste policy that protects all Nevadans and Americans," he said.

And yet, Yucca Mountain still had a feint pulse. Steve Sebelius, political columnist for the *Las Vegas Review-Journal*, assessed its status. "It's defunded, dormant and on life support, but it's not defunct," he wrote. "That's because Reid and Obama can no more speak for Congress than the Nye County Commission can speak for the state of Nevada. And the last time anybody checked, the Nuclear Waste Policy Act of 1982 is still the law of the land."

What to do with the nation's high-level nuclear waste had been debated and studied for fifty years, but a solution remained elusive. Somehow, some way, the small state of Nevada had managed to fend off nuclear waste for twenty-five years, and during that time had pulled off a neat trick: The project the state had so vociferously opposed had employed thousands of Nevadans and infused millions of dollars into the state.

By 2012 it appeared the state's leaders could legitimately declare victory. Yet many Nevadans remained wary of doing so, knowing the ever-shifting political winds still could turn against them.

# CHAPTER 9

# Lap of Luxury: Las Vegas Goes Upscale

When Las Vegas was founded as a railroad town in 1905, businesses operated out of canvas tents. Luxury lodgings consisted of a tent in which hanging pieces of cloth separated the beds. With no air conditioning, a constant dust haze, pungent horse manure odors, pesky flies and rough characters walking the streets, Las Vegas was not a place that lent itself to ostentation. Indeed, Fremont Street wasn't paved until 1925. It was the twentieth century, yet the early residents of the new town lived a decidedly nineteenth century lifestyle. Many early investors in Las Vegas, such as William Andrews Clark, the mining mogul who built the railroad and developed the townsite, did not actually live there.

By contrast, at that time in American history, being rich meant extravagant East Coast estates, elegant parties for hundreds where the finest of everything was served, and "the pomp and circumstance of society," as Frederick Lewis Allen observed in *The Big Change*. "These people had more money than they knew what to do with, and they were engaged in a competition to see who could toss it about most superbly," Allen wrote in his history of the years 1900-1950.

Clark, for whom Clark County is named, lived in Montana until 1907, when he built a mansion on Fifth Avenue in New York City with more than 100 rooms, plus servant quarters. In *The First 100*, A.D. Hopkins described the Clark abode: "The main banquet room had a marble fireplace fifteen feet across and was roofed with wood from Sherwood Forest; a breakfast room had 200 carved panels, none of the same design. Clark filled his mansion with original Gothic tapestries and paintings gathered in Europe."

This, to be sure, was a far cry from the modest lodgings in Las Vegas. The first "elite" residential area was on Fremont Street between Fourth and Fifth streets, where the railroad's local boss, Walter Bracken, built an attractive gray stone house. This remained the city's high-end district until at least 1930, when many nice homes were built in the old Las Vegas High School and John S. Park neighborhoods, though they would barely qualify as middle class by modern standards. In those days, living in Las Vegas was a hardscrabble existence—even for those with money. When Nevada leaders sought to attract wealthy new residents by promoting the state's friendly tax structure, Reno and Lake Tahoe were the primary beneficiaries.

Susan Berman, in her memoir *Lady Las Vegas*, recalled her family's move to the tiny desert town from the Midwest in the mid-'40s: "There was no opulent Spanish Trail area like today where Vegas millionaires live. … There were no luxurious gated golf course developments. There weren't even any two-story houses that represented the Midwest stability my mother craved." Berman, whose father, Davie, was a mob-connected casino operator alongside Bugsy Siegel, moved to what was then the best neighborhood in town—South Sixth Street. "My mother called the realtor—there was only one in town—and found the only Tudor-style house: small, brown and white, with two bedrooms and two baths, which my father paid $7,000 cash for in 1945. It had a fireplace in the living room, maybe the only available fireplace at that time."

During the city's gambling boom in the '50s, as the city's prosperity created more wealthy people and attracted others to the desert, houses started getting bigger and more elegant. But the city still boasted nothing that rivaled the mansions found in more established areas of the country. And those with the means to build them here didn't bother. Howard Hughes, one of the world's richest men, owned a small, nondescript house a few blocks off the Strip in the early '50s. (Of course, impressive houses were never a priority for Hughes, whose second Las Vegas residency, in the late '60s, occurred in a window-blackened room at the Desert Inn Hotel.) Downtown casino owner Benny Binion's ranch house on Bonanza Road, long vacated but still standing, echoed the rustic flavor of the TV show *Bonanza*. Binion, a Texan, was more at home on a horse than a throne. Many of the city's elite were not particularly interested in showing off their wealth, some in the interest of keeping a low profile. If Las Vegans enjoyed a white-collar income at that time, they retained a blue-collar mentality.

Nevertheless, a few enclaves for the wealthy developed in the '50s and '60s. Five specific areas became synonymous with the good life: Rancho Circle, on Rancho Drive near Alta Drive; Desert Inn Estates, east of the Desert Inn Hotel (now Wynn Las Vegas); the Scotch 80s, off Rancho Drive south of Charleston Boulevard; the Las Vegas Country Club, near Maryland Parkway and Vegas Valley Drive; and Sierra Vista Ranchos, near Sunset Park.

Rancho Circle was the first neighborhood to cater to Las Vegas's elite. In the '40s local pioneers Bob Griffith and Bob Kaltenborn paid the Union Pacific Railroad $10,000 for eighty acres, and showplace residences on one-acre lots (sold for $1,500 each) started rising on what was then the city's western edge. The early residents included many casino owners and executives, as well as movers and shakers from other industries. Perhaps the most famous Rancho Circle resident was Phyllis McGuire, lead singer of the McGuire Sisters. McGuire often called her neighborhood "Las Vegas's little Beverly Hills."

Joy Bell, a well-known interior designer and native Las Vegan, remembered trick-or-treating in Rancho Circle in the '50s (two decades before guard gates were installed). One house she always hit twice was that of legendary socialite Mitzi Hughes. "This was my dream home," Bell recalled. "We always came to her house twice because she gave the best stuff." In 2001, Bell fulfilled a lifelong desire and bought Hughes's house, which is reminiscent of luxury housing in Palm Beach, Florida.

While many Rancho Circle homes remain impressive, it's the lush landscaping that catches visitors' attention first. "We have trees that are just huge," Bell said. And over the decades, Rancho Circle maintained its prestige, with an average home value of well over $1 million. A new generation of owners, many of them doctors who want to live close to centrally located hospitals, refurbished the homes or tore them down and built newer, larger ones. "There's been a resurgence," Bell said. Richie Clyne, president of the Rancho

Circle homeowners association, described the neighborhood as "like living in Central Park in New York City." "It's a park-like setting," he said. "The tree-lined streets, the whole nine yards."

The Desert Inn Estates and Las Vegas Country Club, which got started in the early '50s and '60s respectively, were the first areas to offer a lifestyle revolving around a golf course. Both benefited from their proximity to the emerging Strip, as they were home to well-known resort bosses and show-room entertainers. Bob Maheu, Howard Hughes's right-hand man during the reclusive billionaire's eccentric tenure in Las Vegas, lived in an ostentatious mansion in Desert Inn Estates. The Las Vegas Country Club, built by casino operator Moe Dalitz and others, featured Regency Towers, the city's first high-rise condominiums. While the Desert Inn Estates homes disappeared after they were bought up and torn down by casino developer Steve Wynn, the Las Vegas Country Club persevered. It is still home to some of the most well-known individuals in local business and entertainment.

## Las Vegas Country Club

The mastermind of the Las Vegas Country Club was a New York entrepreneur named Marvin Kratter, who once owned the Boston Celtics. In 1965, Kratter bought 480 acres from Joe W. Brown for $11 million. The land, east of the Strip, was home to a money-losing horse-racing track. Kratter envisioned building the city's first opulent country club there. He helped fund the construction by selling sixty acres of the property to Kirk Kerkorian, who later built the International Hotel (later Las Vegas Hilton) there.

Kratter's vision became reality on October 20, 1967, when the 7,125-yard golf course opened for play. A few months later, the country club opened, quickly becoming a second home for Las Vegas's top dogs as well as visiting celebrities. A regular presence on the course in those days was singer Dean Martin.

Although the country club had made a splash, it was not profitable, and Kratter's free-spending ways got him into financial trouble. In 1970, he sold the property to the Paradise Development Company, a local partnership of Moe Dalitz, Irwin Molasky, Merv Adelson and Allard Roen. The new owners brought a more professional and attentive approach to managing the property.

"We took it over and brought better business practices to it," said Molasky, in an interview for *The Las Vegas Country Club: Chronicle of an Icon*, by Brian Hurlburt. "We stopped all the free stuff."

Although Dalitz was deeply connected to organized crime during his lifetime, many remember his association with the country club fondly. He was a constant presence at the club in his later years. Hurlburt wrote: "At the club he was Moe, the grandfatherly figure who would spend his own money on upgrades—including the indoor tennis center—and do anything to make the place more enjoyable for the members."

Under new management, the Las Vegas Country Club flourished, and it soon became a place to live as well as to play. The Regency Towers, the city's first residential high-rise, was home to some of the city's most prominent citizens. Closer to the ground, the club hosted an array of houses and condo complexes. One prominent homeowner was Frank "Lefty" Rosenthal, the notorious casino operator who was the subject of the Martin Scorsese movie *Casino*.

The Scotch 80s developed in the '50s on eighty acres originally owned by the city's first mayor, Peter Buol. The acreage could have been developed much earlier, as Buol obtained the land in 1913 and planned to build residential lots in partnership with Scottish investors—thus the name. But the project fell through a year later when Buol's Scottish partner died and then World War I precluded the transfer of funds from British banks, according to *Water: A History of Las Vegas*.

Like Rancho Circle, the Scotch 80s' most prominent feature is dense foliage—especially mesquite and cottonwood trees. The neighborhood's rustic feel reflects its early years, when many residents had horses. Famous residents included car dealer Fletcher Jones Sr. and casino mogul Steve Wynn, who resided in the neighborhood until the early '90s, when he built a mansion at his exclusive Shadow Creek golf course in North Las Vegas. While doctors flock to Rancho Circle, the Scotch 80s seems to be more appealing to lawyers, such as the neighborhood's most famous resident, Las Vegas Mayor Oscar

Goodman, who has lived there since 1976. In the '90s, Scotch 80s successfully appealed to the city to close off the streets to public access to prevent shortcut-seeking motorists from disrupting the neighborhood's tranquility.

Sierra Vista Ranchos, the most remote of the early upscale neighborhoods, developed in the mid-'60s, catering to the "horsey set," as *Las Vegas Review-Journal* society columnist Dorothy Huffey described it. The large estates are adjacent to what once was the valley's premier farm, owned by Asian-American pioneer Yonema "Bill" Tomiyasu. Moving to Las Vegas in 1916, Tomiyasu grew a variety of fruit and vegetables on his spread. In addition to serving local restaurants, Tomiyasu provided food for Hoover Dam workers in the '30s and the Army Air Gunnery School during World War II. Later, he and his son, Nanyu, or "Tomi," adapted to changing times by operating a nursery business, selling trees, shrubs and their expertise to local landscapers. A legal battle over an unpaid loan cost Tomiyasu the 100-acre farm in the mid-'60s. It soon was subdivided, and large ranch-style homes cover much of the property. Next door is the guard-gated Sierra Vista Ranchos, whose famous residents have included singer Robert Goulet, actress Totie Fields and comedian Pat Cooper, as well as notorious rap music producer Marion "Suge" Knight. A well-known neighboring property is Casa de Shenandoah, the ranch owned by singer Wayne Newton.

### Spanish Trail

The first development that changed the nature of how the wealthy could live in Las Vegas was Spanish Trail. The guard-gated golf course community at Tropicana Avenue and Rainbow Boulevard was for years the premier address in Las Vegas, and remains among the valley's most fashionable neighborhoods.

Interestingly, while Spanish Trail introduced a whole new chapter to Las Vegas development history, it was not the product of some newcomer bringing fresh thinking to town. It was the brainchild of an old-time Las Vegan, Joe Blasco, who made his money in gravel pits and mobile home parks long before venturing into the luxury housing business. Blasco emigrated to the United States from Spain when he was five years old. He grew up in the East, but eventually found his way to Southern California, where he became an engineering contractor. In 1952, Blasco secured subcontracting work on an ammunition storage project at the former marine base at Lake Mead, launching a five-decade career in Southern Nevada.

Blasco obtained the 640 acres that became Spanish Trail from the same place where developers of other Las Vegas planned communities got theirs: the federal government. Blasco got the land in 1953, not longer after Howard Hughes secured the property that would become Summerlin and William Peccole acquired the land for Peccole Ranch. He ran a gravel operation there.

When the gravel business became too competitive, Blasco and his sons decided to build homes on the land. Development started in 1983, after the Blascos commissioned a market study that indicated strong demand for an upscale golf course community. An initial investment of $10 million went into building the golf course, which features rolling terrain, 1,500 mature trees and six lakes. "We went for mature landscaping because we didn't want to say this will be a great golf course in a few years," Jose Blasco, Joe's son, told the *Las Vegas Review-Journal* in 1984. "We wanted to say this is a great golf course right now."

Spanish Trail represented Las Vegas's first attempt to replicate what appealed to the wealthy about places like Palm Springs, California, and Scottsdale, Arizona. In a 1985 interview, Jose Blasco acknowledged that was their intention: "We went through Palm Springs," he told the *Review-Journal*. "We were there for five days watching everything and picking out the high points and bad points. We took all the things we liked and put them into this." One early Spanish Trail marketing slogan was, "Move Over, Palm Springs."

The project was immediately popular, satisfying pent-up demand from local doctors, lawyers and business owners seeking security and a country club lifestyle. One early selling point was that Spanish Trail featured the first new golf course built in Las Vegas in fifteen years. In a 1986 *Review-Journal* interview, local developer Ernie Becker Jr. said he and his wife, Kathy, were moving to Spanish Trail because they liked the fact that it is a "self-contained" community. "There's no place in town that has the atmosphere which is available at Spanish Trail," Becker said. Security also was a big draw. Tom Harmon of Desert Construction said, "What's so nice is you can walk to the clubhouse for dinner or lunch. Then I can go for a walk around the golf course any time

I want and not worry about being mugged." Las Vegas socialites flocked to Spanish Trail, friends following friends to the development. Tito Tiberti, a longtime local contractor, explained why he built a large home there: "We wanted an area we felt would have protection, and the town has been very short on that type of development. Also, it has the clubhouse, and my family thought it would enjoy being a part of the club. Thirdly, we have a lot of friends out there and we feel very comfortable." While Spanish Trail attracted many locals, it also drew home buyers from New York and California.

Spanish Trail is wrapped around a twenty-seven-hole golf course designed by legendary golf course architect Robert Trent Jones Jr. The property is surrounded by eight miles of wall, with just two guard-gated entrances. The housing ranges from townhouses and relatively modest tract homes to the largest estates in the valley. Those who got in on the ground floor of Spanish Trail were extraordinarily smart—or lucky. Townhomes in the earliest phases were priced as low as $120,000, and patio homes could be purchased for $155,000. These were fairly steep prices for Las Vegas in the early '80s, but, until the real estate bust, the smallest suburban tract home in the valley cost tens of thousands more.

Today, Spanish Trail remains one of the elite addresses in Southern Nevada, even if trendy new enclaves now overshadow it. Its most famous property owners were Prince Jefri of Brunei, whose sixteen-acre compound cost $60 million, and major league pitcher Greg Maddux, a local boy whose precision hurling made him a lock for the Baseball Hall of Fame. The community also is home to many old-time Las Vegas movers and shakers, as well as newcomers who are expanding and renovating their homes to make them even bigger and more luxurious. A good example is the home of retired Los Angeles judge Harry Peetris and his wife, Mary. In 2002, the Peetrises spent $650,000 to expand their home by 2,400 square feet to enclose their pool. Looming twenty feet above the water is an eighty-four-inch television screen on which a top-of-the-line projector displays crystal-clear images.

Spanish Trail set in motion a profound movement in Las Vegas toward a more modern, sophisticated lifestyle. The community showed wealthy Las Vegans they didn't have to leave town for luxury, and it showed out-of-towners that Las Vegas could offer a place to live that met their high standards. "It opened up a lot of people's eyes," said Steve Bottfeld, president of Marketing Solutions, which performs consumer and economic research in Las Vegas.

It wasn't long after Spanish Trail started that Steve Wynn conceived the Mirage Hotel, which sparked the upscale trend on the Strip. At the same time, Transcontinential Properties started finding traction in building the long-planned Lake Las Vegas in Henderson. These projects signaled a new era in Las Vegas. It was no longer a dusty railroad stop or a mob money machine. It was a place to enjoy the suburban good life.

Spanish Trail got the ball rolling, but the luxury residential market really took off in the early '90s, when the city experienced a building boom of unprecedented dimensions. With the whole world watching, Las Vegas transformed itself from quaint neon oasis to major resort destination—and population center. Companies with no ties to the casino industry had ignored Las Vegas, but now they were taking notice of the city's untapped economic opportunities. A revved-up national economy fueled by the dotcom boom didn't hurt. "As we approached the million [population] mark, the national chain retailers began seeing what was happening," Bottfeld said. "That's when we saw the rapid growth here of Walmart, Home Depot, Lowe's, RC Willey, Kohl's. Those are national stores that we really didn't have a lot of until the late '90s. Walgreen's put up twenty-seven stores here in a period of five years. Suddenly, because of the population mass, we began to be seen differently." (By 2012, Walgreens had more than fifty stores in the Las Vegas area.)

At the same time, the community started attracting national home builders such as KB Home and Richmond American, which increased the quality of residential architecture and offered an array of attractive new options for home buyers. Those companies also were able to market their products to an audience beyond the Las Vegas Valley. The development of the Green Valley and Summerlin master-planned communities raised the bar for suburban living, and each offered upscale neighborhoods rivaling the luxury of Spanish Trail. The valley's explosive growth, the casino industry's shift to a more sophisticated tourist market and a booming national economy combined to make Las Vegas an attractive place to build a dream home. It didn't hurt that

Nevada has no state income tax and that building in Las Vegas could be done for half the cost of doing so in California.

During the boom period, probably the best-known luxury home builder in Las Vegas was Christopher Homes, which was responsible for many of the leading golf course neighborhoods in master-planned communities such as Summerlin, Green Valley and Southern Highlands. Chris Stuhmer got his start in the early '80s building individual custom homes. Spurred on by the success of Spanish Trail, he incorporated Christopher Homes in 1987 to fill a void in the construction of luxury production home neighborhoods. These are upscale neighborhoods for wealthy people who want to avoid the hassles of building a custom home. Stuhmer's first project was Palm Canyon in the Painted Desert planned community at U.S. 95 and Ann Road. His next was Palm Valley in Green Valley. The first of his many Summerlin neighborhoods was Hillpointe in 1991. But Christopher Homes was just getting warmed up for the projects that would really put the company on the map, starting with Country Club Hills, on the TPC golf course in Summerlin, in '92, and Country Rose Estates, also in Summerlin, in '95. The crowning achievement was Palisades, on Summerlin's Canyons TPC golf course, which opened in '98. The company won local, regional and national awards for the designs of its Palisades models.

Christopher's reputation was based on combining excellent architecture and interior design with strict attention to detail. "The attention to interior design was something that no one really ever saw in Las Vegas," said Erika Geiser, longtime vice president of marketing for Christopher Homes. "We bring the architects and designers together in the design phase to make the home work right." Another key element of Christopher's success was that it gave its buyers a wide range of options. The phrase "production home" suggests a regimented process of building rows of homes exactly alike. But Christopher was among the first builders in town to essentially offer semi-custom production homes. "We came up with thirty different floor plan varieties for each house plan," Geiser said. "It is a difficult thing to manage as a builder. There are issues with permits and inspectors. Coming from a custom background, catering to the client gave us a competitive advantage."

When Christopher Homes started in the late '80s, its luxury homes could be picked up for as little as $150,000. By the early 2000s, the low end in its neighborhoods was more than $400,000. The average price in its Christopher Collection neighborhood in Southern Highlands in 2002 was $950,000. The market was changing, however, and Christopher Homes changed along with it. The company returned to individual custom home building, in part because master-planned communities had, for a variety of reasons, stopped building neighborhoods around golf courses. It also began to build some smaller luxury homes for empty-nesters and single professionals who don't need 6,000 square feet. The prime example was The Villas in Southern Highlands. These smaller homes "offer all the architecture of a larger home for buyers who don't need a larger home," Geiser said. "In the past, if you wanted a really nice home, you had to get a large one."

Geiser said Christopher Homes's customer base remained fairly constant throughout the company's existence: fifty percent local, twenty-five percent from California and twenty-five percent from other parts of the country. Real estate broker Ken Lowman, who came to Las Vegas in 1995, said the market for homes above $1 million was thirty to thirty-five percent Californians. But he was seeing more and more people from other parts of the country as well. "People come out here to visit Las Vegas and they look into the idea of having a home here," he said. "They see everything that's going on here and it reassures them about what they should do."

The neighborhoods sporting the largest, fanciest houses tend to be scattered along the valley's southern and western edges. The Macdonald Highlands master-planned community in Henderson is in the foothills of the McCullough Mountains, with lots offering some of the most incredible views in the valley. Green Valley has The Fountains, Legacy and Quail Ridge. Anthem has its country club, and Seven Hills has The Estates. Southern Highlands, at the far south end of the valley west of Interstate 15, features a majestic golf club neighborhood. In the southwest valley is Rhodes Ranch. Just west of Spanish Trail is Spanish Hills Estates, with an array of mansions, including one once owned by tennis star Andre Agassi, sitting amid a hilly landscape. The Red Rock Country Club, Tournament Hills and The Ridges are among the elite addresses in Summerlin, while Canyon Gate Country Club and Queensridge are the high-end neighborhoods in Peccole Ranch. The northwest valley has Painted Desert and a few smaller luxury enclaves, but it is better known for individual ranch estates. The first true luxury homes in North Las Vegas were built in the Aliante master-planned community. Far removed from the urban bustle, in the far southeast part of the valley, is Lake Las Vegas, an exclusive planned community surrounding a 320-acre man-made lake and several golf courses.

## High-rise condos

The upscaling of Las Vegas housing echoed the upscaling of Strip resorts in the '90s. "With hotels like the Mirage, Bellagio, Venetian and Mandalay Bay, it began to increase the awareness of Las Vegas in the minds of higher-end people," said John Riordan, vice president of sales for the Turnberry Place high-rise condominiums on Paradise Road. Instead of having a second home in Palm Springs or Scottsdale, California's wealthy started choosing Las Vegas, with the absence of a state income tax serving as a strong incentive.

The first businessman to take advantage of these factors was Irwin Molasky, a longtime Las Vegas builder responsible in part for major landmarks such as Sunrise Hospital, the Boulevard Mall and the Las Vegas Country Club. Molasky said he first pursued the idea of building a high-rise condominium in Las Vegas years earlier, but "we didn't have the market for it here." He didn't forget about the idea, however, and when he came across a great piece of property in the Hughes Center at Paradise and Flamingo roads in the mid-'90s, he decided the timing was right.

The result: Park Towers, one of the nation's most luxurious high-rise condos. Molasky, along with a well-heeled partner, casino developer Steve Wynn, hired top-notch architects and interior designers and used the finest materials for the two twenty-story towers. He bought antiques from France and Italy. On-site services were a key attraction of Park Towers, with concierge desk, spa, fitness center, theater, library, business center and beauty salon. Molasky charged $700,000 and up for the units, but they sold quickly. "I think we succeeded beyond our wildest dreams," Molasky said of the eighty-four-unit high-rise.

*Sun, Sin & Suburbia: The History of Modern Las Vegas*

Why did Park Towers work in 1998 when it couldn't two decades earlier? "There wasn't a population base of people who could afford those units," he said of the earlier period. In the late '90s, he said, "the economy was better, and people didn't want to drive all the way to Green Valley or Summerlin."

Turnberry Place came along on Molasky's heels. The developers, the Florida-based father-son team of Don and Jeffrey Soffer, identified Las Vegas as having many of the same characteristics as 1970s Miami, where the company built many high-rise projects. "The amenity in Florida is the ocean," Riordan said. "Here it's the concentrated couple miles of the Strip." Miami became a second home for New Yorkers. Las Vegas has become a second home for Californians.

Most of Turnberry's buyers were millionaires from Los Angeles or the Bay Area who most likely owned their own businesses. "They have a certain amount of freedom of travel," Riordan explained. "They can pretty much do whatever they want to do from a financial point of view." They also relish what Las Vegas offers. "They love the shopping, the great restaurants, and the gaming is always part of it," he said.

Turnberry residents are different from those who build or buy in the suburbs. "They aren't interested in golf course communities in Summerlin or Green Valley," Riordan said. "They want a more urban environment. They don't want the aggravation of having people take care of their homes and their pools. They just want to come and go, shut the door and not worry about it."

The average Turnberry condo owner spends ten to twelve weeks a year in Las Vegas. But Riordan said many of them intend to retire to their second home in the future. In the meantime, while they may not qualify as full-fledged residents, they are making a significant contribution. "They are paying property taxes whether they are here full or part time," Riordan noted. "And when they are here, they aren't cooking too many meals at home. They're out on the town. They probably are making a greater impact in twelve weeks economically than most people who live here year-round."

What's more, Riordan said, Turnberry's part-time residents haven't contributed to the urban sprawl that afflicts Las Vegas in the form of traffic congestion, air pollution and crowded schools. By building up rather than out, and in a highly urbanized area, local governments didn't have to spend money building streets, utilities or schools. "The infrastructure was all here to begin with," he said.

With 800 units spread across four towers, Turnberry was one of the largest high-rise condo developments in the western United States. Its success spawned numerous other high-rise condo projects, all within view of the Strip.

In the early 2000s, before the real estate bust and national recession, Riordan was bullish on the "Manhattan-ization" of Las Vegas. "There's a lot of growth potential in the high-rise market," he said. "We'll see great leaps over the next five to ten years." Riordan believed Las Vegas could support 800-1,000 high-rise units per year. "California is such an enormous state with great wealth," he said. "And Las Vegas is still a very affordable place to live relative to California."

Alas, while Turnberry and a few others succeeded, the "Manhattan-ization" of Las Vegas never materialized. Although the collapse of the real estate market was a big factor, it wasn't the only one. For all the optimistic talk of a major shift to urban living, most Las Vegans still preferred a more traditional suburban lifestyle, luxury or otherwise.

### The creative element

Las Vegas enjoyed a strong luxury housing market for several years, but one frequently heard critique was that many of the high-end houses failed to inspire from an architectural standpoint. Rather than hiring respected architects to design unique homes, the valley's big spenders often settled for cookie-cutter designs—the same white stucco walls and red tile roofs that you'd find in any Las Vegas subdivision. "A lot of the large-scale custom homes are just tract homes on steroids," architect Bing Hu said. "There's nothing special about them; they're just big. I hate to see people spend $3 million and not pay attention to the architecture."

Street of Dreams Incorporated went a long way toward changing that mindset in Las Vegas. The company, based in Woodinville, Washington, put together luxury home tours. An upscale neighborhood was selected, and top architects and interior designers collaborated to create a street of unique homes, completely furnished. Once the homes were completed, visitors lined

*Sun, Sin & Suburbia: The History of Modern Las Vegas*

up to check out the bold designs and latest trends. The homes were then put on the market and could be moved into after the tours were over. Street of Dreams's first four home tours in the Las Vegas Valley occurred between 1998 and 2004. The first two, in 1998 and 2000, were located in the Seven Hills community in Henderson. The third and fourth, in 2002 and 2004, were in Macdonald Highlands, also in Henderson.

The 2002 Street of Dreams featured four houses in the foothills of the McCullough Mountains. All four emphasized contemporary architectural trends, consciously departing from the Mediterranean and Old World Tuscany styles so prevalent in Las Vegas. They also took full advantage of the panoramic views available from their locations 1,000 feet above the valley floor. The houses shared other themes: elaborate water features such as fountains and waterfalls; huge north-facing windows, some reaching from floor to ceiling; organic materials such as slate, ledgestone and limestone, reflecting—and attempting to blend with—the desert setting; and indoor/outdoor living features, designed to make outdoor spaces as comfortable and appealing as indoor spaces. The largest home at 8,250 square feet, "Dragon's Oasis," worked hard to integrate itself into the natural environment. Built by California custom home builder Greg Gevorkian, the house was wedged into the rocky hillside. The front of the three-story house reflected this location, with boulders, native plants and a river striving to emulate the environment. "We wanted to make the home belong to that hill," Gevorkian said. "We want it to look like the house is coming out from inside the mountain."

With Macdonald Highlands, Rich Macdonald, a veteran local developer, was spearheading one of the last low-density planned communities to be built in the Las Vegas Valley. When Macdonald Highlands was completed, there were fewer than 1,000 housing units within its 1,200 acres. Land became too expensive and scarce to allow for such expansive golf course neighborhoods in the future.

When he started the development, Macdonald figured his customers would be mostly Californians, but it didn't work out that way. "I've seen as much interest in the local market as outside," he said. "There's a pent-up demand among locals for something like this." He echoed Spanish Trail's founders when he said high-end home buyers were now choosing Las Vegas over traditional good life enclaves such as Palm Springs.

Despite the success of Macdonald Highlands, Macdonald agreed in 2003 that the next big thing in Las Vegas would be high-rise living, and he wanted to get into that business in the future. "Instead of going out and buying thousands of acres of land, our focus is more on good locations of property that's close in," he said. By "close in," Macdonald meant near the Strip—or, as he quipped, "close to the steel mill." And Macdonald saw the high-rise future in more affordable units than had been built so far. Where Park Towers and Turnberry Place condos were all more than half a million dollars and many of them exceeded $1 million, Macdonald predicted high-rise units in the $200,000-$300,000 range would be the next frontier. This proved true, especially after property values plummeted in 2007.

In the headier days before the crash, most planned high-rise projects had not focused on that more mainstream market. For example, Turnberry Place had partnered with the MGM Grand hotel-casino on a large high-rise on the site of the long-closed Grand Adventures theme park. Units at The Residences at MGM Grand ranged from $350,000 to $1.5 million. The Metropolis high-rise, which was being developed by Houston-based Randall Davis, had units ranging from $400,000 to $1.7 million. Del American Incorporated of Orlando, Florida, was attempting to bridge the gap with its mid-rise project, Vegas Grand, where units started at $200,000.

This more affordable price range also was the rule for planned high-rise condo towers in downtown Las Vegas. One key to former Mayor Oscar Goodman's downtown redevelopment plan was high-rise housing. The market, however, was not high-rollers seeking second homes in the gambling capital. It was the lawyers, casino middle managers and government employees who worked downtown and were tired of the long commutes to Summerlin, Green Valley and other distant suburbs.

High-rise living is not for everyone, but substantial growth in this type of housing could have a positive impact on the community as a whole, Turnberry's Riordan argued: "I think most city planners throughout the western United States will tell you they would like to encourage more high-rise development in the urban parts of their cities. The biggest problems Western cities face are pollution and congestion. They're all in the same boat. There has been enormous growth over the past fifteen years, and almost all of it has been single-family homes. The costs have been enormous. Now we're seeing high-rise development throughout the West, in Denver, Seattle and other cities. People don't want to be thirty miles out in the suburbs. They want to be near the cultural centers. City planners are pleased with us being here."

Clearly, Las Vegas is no longer the frontier. Urban amenities are plentiful, from dependable electricity and a steady stream of clean water coming out of the faucet to some of the world's finest entertainment and dining options. Housing in the valley is as attractive and diverse as anywhere in the American West. A young couple can find an affordable starter home in any corner of the valley, eventually move up to a nicer neighborhood to raise the kids and then, if prosperity permits, buy or build the home of their dreams. Or, if they no longer want the hassle and cost of maintaining an estate, they can move into a luxury condo overlooking the Strip, coming and going as they please throughout the year. At each stage, the options are numerous. New or used. Urban or suburban. Tract house or custom. Rambling ranch house on big lot or two-story on small lot. Master-planned community, stand-alone subdivision or uncharted acreage on the valley's edge. Perhaps the only living option not available in the valley is a farm, though a couple of them were still struggling to hang on in the northwest valley.

The valley's affordability allows working-class families and retirees to buy comfortable homes and millionaires to own bigger, fancier palaces than they could afford in other cities. And while the '90s are recognized as the valley's super-boom period, housing construction and sales actually increased in the new century. Where the '90s boom was tied directly to megaresort construction, this was not the case in 2003. Las Vegas growth was taking on a life of its own, increasingly independent of the Strip.

Low mortgage interest rates offset a recessionary national economy as 2003 set records for home sales locally. A total of 25,230 new home sales were recorded in 2003, far exceeding the previous record of 22,940 in 2001. Resales totaled 49,792 in 2003, trouncing the previous high mark by thirty percent.

This frantic demand for houses meant at least two things. One, people putting their homes up for sale often had several bids on it that same day—at or perhaps in excess of the asking price. And, two, home prices rose quickly. With little or no standing inventory of homes for sale, prices rose as demand dictated. The median price of a new home jumped twelve percent in 2003 to $209,611, while resales increased 14.6 percent to $180,000. The 2003 numbers also confirmed that Las Vegas was rising rapidly on the list of preferred retirement locales, as the top-selling neighborhoods were Sun City Anthem, Siena and Sun City Aliante—all age-restricted communities.

Regardless of income level, real estate was a hot topic in Las Vegas. Residents here, unlike their more settled counterparts in, say, the Midwest, were a restless and ambitious bunch. It was common for a couple to buy a home and then sell it in just a year or two, moving up to a larger one a few miles away. It was a case of keeping up with the Joneses gone overboard. Residents could be completely happy with their new home, yet unable to suppress the urge to check out the model homes in the new subdivision nearby. Or, if the couple was satisfied with their current address, they sought to improve what they had, putting in backyard pools, new flooring and other home improvements that enhanced their quality of life but—often more important to them—increased their resale value.

It wasn't always this way. In the city's pioneer days, simply having a roof over your head was an achievement. The first actual subdivisions in Las Vegas consisted of small, plain houses close to the city center that served a practical purpose—protecting people from the elements. Times change. A house in Las Vegas became an economic and/or aesthetic statement, a reflection of your personal tastes and a measure of your standing in the world. And there were no limits to the size of that statement, as the growing number of mansions in the valley illustrated.

The feverish enthusiasm for real estate crumbled in 2007 when the market bubble burst and home values plummeted. Rather than seeking the next level of luxury, many Las Vegans, even the most well heeled, struggled just to hold on to what they had.

# Chapter 10

## Transportation: Better Late than Never

In the nineteenth and early twentieth centuries, Las Vegas was an important pit stop on the way to other places. In the latter half of the twentieth century, Las Vegas became one of the world's most popular destinations. In both periods, transportation was a huge issue for Las Vegas.

Las Vegas first attracted non-native people as an unlikely oasis amid a harsh desert that vexed Western pioneers seeking the lush promises of California. Though not the first non-native to see the Las Vegas Valley, John C. Fremont is credited with putting it on the map. In 1844 Fremont led an expedition that traveled through Las Vegas. The group camped where two large springs gushed from the ground and fed deep, clear streams—near present-day U.S. 95 and Valley View Boulevard. In his report on the trip, published in 1845, Fremont described Las Vegas, including a now-famous comment about the spring water: "The taste of the water is good, but rather too warm to be agreeable; the temperature being 71 in the one and 73 in the other. They, however, afford a delightful bathing place."

Fremont's report, printed by Congress, was a best seller in its day, a must-read for anyone migrating to the West, and soon Las Vegas became a popular camping spot on what was known as the northern arm of the Old Spanish Trail. Las Vegas's plentiful water came as a great relief to many who suffered mightily trudging through the desert. Visiting Las Vegas in 1849, Mormon pioneer Addison Pratt wrote in his diary: "Oh! such water. It comes just at the termination of a fifty-mile stretch without a drop of water or a spear of grass."

265

When the United States acquired the territory that encompassed Las Vegas in 1848, the Old Spanish Trail ceased to be a New Mexican trade route. But it continued to be used by Mormons traveling from Salt Lake City to Southern California and became known as the Mormon Trail. In 1852, mail from Salt Lake City to Southern California started traveling through Las Vegas. In 1855, Mormon leader Brigham Young dispatched a group of church members to Las Vegas to build a settlement, in part to protect immigrants and mail carriers from hostile Indians and rustlers.

Las Vegas continued to be a popular stopping point for travelers through the rest of the nineteenth century, but with the turn of the century it entered a new phase of its existence, this one also linked directly to transportation. With mining activity heating up all over southern and central Nevada, railroads were needed to haul freight from the mining camps to cities. (Another reason was to get in on the Los Angeles market—which also is tied in to transportation.) In 1905, Montana mining mogul William Andrews Clark built a railroad from Salt Lake City to Southern California—running through Las Vegas. What's more, Clark selected Las Vegas as a division point on the rail line, which meant it would have shop facilities, a roundhouse and other amenities. Soon after trains started using the railroad, a town developed around the new division point. Stanley Paher, in his book *Las Vegas: As It Began—As It Grew*, describes the hustle and bustle of this burgeoning transportation hub:

"The fantastic amount of freight and stage traffic which churned the thoroughfares of both Las Vegas townsites would stagger the modern mind. Especially around sunrise, but continuing throughout the day and night, a steady procession of eight- to twenty-animal teams, drawing high-wheeled freight wagons each loaded with immense quantities of supplies and equipment, whiskey, animal feed, machinery, and more whiskey, struck out for Bullfrog and adjacent camps, or returned with empty wagons and one or two trailers for another cargo."

Las Vegas was strictly a railroad town until the early '20s, when a bitter strike resulted in the railroad company cutting back its facilities in the still-small community. Looking for ways to keep the town from drying up and blowing away, city fathers turned to tourism. This prospect was viable only

266          *Sun, Sin & Suburbia: The History of Modern Las Vegas*

if visitors could get to Las Vegas. To that end, air service between Salt Lake City and Los Angeles started making regular stops in Las Vegas in 1926. The first landing strip was Rockwell Field, near present-day Las Vegas Boulevard and Sahara Avenue. Air travel to Las Vegas improved significantly in the '40s when the valley hosted an Army Air Corps base that trained pilots for action in World War II. Also in the '20s, as car travel increased dramatically nationwide, the federal government built a highway, U.S. 91, between Salt Lake City and Los Angeles—taking a route through Las Vegas rather than a competing option that would have coursed through Searchlight.

Ever since those early days when the first planes touched down in the valley and the first cars arrived on a paved highway, the city has worked tirelessly to improve its transportation facilities to entice and satisfy visitors. McCarran Field, which opened in 1948, has expanded a dozen times since then and become an international airport. A new $2.4 billion international terminal opened in 2012. To this day, local tourism officials agonize that the highway linking Las Vegas to Los Angeles—now known as Interstate 15—is not wide enough to accommodate the large numbers of cars coming and going between the two metropolises.

But while easing the transportation crunch for visitors has been a top priority for at least seventy-five years, officials have given a lot more attention over the past two decades to improving transportation options for the valley's skyrocketing population. Traffic congestion suddenly became an issue in Las Vegas in the '80s, as the population began to overwhelm the skeletal network of streets and highways. But it wasn't until the '90s that community leaders embarked on three major transportation projects designed to be long-term answers to the burgeoning crisis of getting from one place to another in Las Vegas.

## Citizens Area Transit

The first city bus system in Las Vegas started its engines on August 20, 1942. Vegas Transit Company had three routes: one running along Fremont and Main, one venturing to the Westside and one cruising west on Charleston to the county hospital. A year later, Vegas Transit had six buses on the road. The Tanner family of Los Angeles, which also ran the local cab company and the Avis rent-a-car franchise, later operated the bus system. In 1965, the Tanners sold out to Henry Burroughs, and the city renewed Las Vegas Transit System's exclusive twenty-five-year franchise to furnish the community with public transportation.

Over the years, Las Vegas Transit was often described as "better than nothing," which surely was true. But "better than nothing" left many neighborhoods in the valley unserved. In 1974, the system operated twenty-one buses on twelve routes that traversed the city's major streets, such as Sahara Avenue, Charleston Boulevard, Rancho Drive and Boulder Highway. People living between those thoroughfares, however, were forced to walk a mile or more to catch a bus. And if bus service was needed after ten p.m., forget it. The private company, which needed to make a profit to stay in business, simply could not provide the level of transit service available in other cities. Lack of funding led to an aging bus fleet with inadequate air conditioning and radio communications. The system's bread and butter was its highly profitable route along the Strip, but the company lost money on routes extending into residential areas.

Residents of West Las Vegas, the predominantly black neighborhood west of Interstate 15 and north of Bonanza Road, were particularly vocal in their criticism, especially after Las Vegas Transit suspended service to the area in 1969 after a period of racial violence. In 1974, the NAACP filed a lawsuit, contending that where the company made bus service available in the valley constituted discrimination against blacks. A few years later, the transit system was sued on grounds that it provided inadequate service for the elderly and disabled.

By the time a consulting firm examined the Las Vegas Transit System in 1979, the company's fleet had dropped to sixteen buses, and the study concluded that Las Vegas had one of the worst mass transit systems in the country—and one of the most expensive to ride at seventy-five cents. The consultant estimated that at least 110 buses would be needed to provide adequate mass transit in the valley. A year later, the Junior League of Las Vegas released a report that painted a scathing portrait of the transit operation and blasted the city for not acting to make it better.

City and county officials were pondering creation of a public transit system as early as 1974, arguing that the community was losing out on a fortune in federal funding by relying on a private service. Numerous studies recommended improvements. Las Vegas City Commissioner Ron Lurie was a persistent advocate of a public transit system, but tight-fisted state and local lawmakers repeatedly rejected proposals to dedicate tax dollars to expand the system.

In 1981, the state's so-called Futures Commission said the key issue facing Clark County was mass transit. "There is an urgent need for the expansion of mass transit in Las Vegas," commission Chairman Morton Galane said at the time. "I think we're facing a crisis situation here." The state Legislature that year approved placing a question on the 1983 election ballot asking voters to approve a quarter-cent sales tax increase to finance a bus system expansion. Voters, coping with a national recession and embracing President Ronald Reagan's tax-cutting rhetoric, responded with a resounding no. Although the question might have lost anyway, it didn't help that it had to compete on the ballot with a bond issue to pay for the Metro Police Department's computerized communications system. In a 1984 article in *The Nevadan*, the *Las Vegas Review-Journal*'s Sunday magazine, A.D. Hopkins summarized the dilemma: "Las Vegas Transit is simultaneously a symbol of Las Vegas's urban future and of its voters' small-town thinking. It is widely maligned for inadequate routes, yet citizens have overwhelmingly voted against a tax increase which would make better service possible."

Las Vegas continued to suffer with its privately run bus system into the late '80s, despite accelerating growth that made Las Vegas Transit's attempts to serve the valley look even more ridiculous. Trolleys began operating within the downtown area in a modest attempt to address the problem, while local officials considered proposals to establish a system of mini-buses serving residential areas. The latter idea generated little enthusiasm, however.

In 1990, the Las Vegas City Council, frustrated by its inability to exert any control over the private bus company, rescinded its franchise agreement with Las Vegas Transit System and vowed to work with the Clark County Regional Transportation Commission on a new mass transit system.

The community's embarrassing record on mass transit in the '70s and '80s reflected a huge leadership vacuum during that period. City officials constantly agonized over the system's inadequacy, yet they chronically passed the buck and offered excuses for why it was the best that could be done. At the same time, county commissioners and state lawmakers kept their distance from mass transit, letting the city take the heat. All the while, the city's poor, disabled and elderly suffered with the nation's least adequate bus system, one that devoted most of its resources to the Strip, serving tourists traveling from one resort to another.

Barry Perea, who ran Las Vegas Transit in the '70s and '80s, said local politicians would tell him, "We don't want the transit system, it's a money loser." When Councilman Lurie, a rare individual who did want the city to take over mass transit, pushed a tax increase to support the move on the 1983 ballot, another faction was heard from. "The business community didn't really want it done," Perea recalled. "They actually mounted a campaign against it. They didn't want government stepping into private business at that point. These business guys knew that once the government got involved, taxes would go up and the subsidy would be unending."

The leadership vacuum was filled in 1990 by County Commissioner Bruce Woodbury, a lawyer from Boulder City. Woodbury saw that with the opening of the Mirage and Excalibur resorts, and more on the horizon, the valley's growth was accelerating at a pace not seen in decades. He saw that Las Vegas was on the verge of becoming a genuine metropolitan area that needed to shed its small-town thinking and prepare for the future. Woodbury spearheaded an ambitious proposal to raise money for all of the valley's transportation needs.

Later that year, county voters passed Question 10, a $100 million-per-year package of tax hikes designed to ease mounting traffic congestion in the valley. Unlike the 1983 ballot question, which focused solely on mass transit, the 1990 measure provided funding for an array of transportation projects, including street and highway improvements, airport facilities and a comprehensive mass transit system. Because it called for modest tax increases in a variety of areas—tourists and developers would pay as well as residents—combined with the promise of wide-ranging traffic improvements, Question 10 was palatable

*Sun, Sin & Suburbia: The History of Modern Las Vegas*

for voters, sixty-four percent of whom endorsed it. Question 10 actually was an advisory measure, so the tax package still required approval of the state Legislature in 1991. The strong support for the question, however, made that largely a formality.

Citizens Area Transit was born. After Question 10's passage and legislative approval, the Regional Transportation Commission set out to buy new buses and create a route system. It hired ATC/Vancom, an Illinois-based company that operated transit systems in other cities, including Phoenix, to run the day-to-day operation. CAT launched in December 1992 with 128 buses on twenty-one routes that stretched to all corners of the valley, while maintaining a strong presence on the busy Strip. Glitches were common in the new system's initial months. CAT had to adjust schedules and routes to better reflect the reality of how long it took to get from one stop to another and serve larger numbers of riders. In its second year, CAT expanded its routes to twenty-nine, covering more areas of the valley. High demand on the Strip routes led to overcrowding, a problem that was addressed by the purchase of larger buses. Total ridership in 1993 was 14.9 million, a huge leap from the Las Vegas Transit System era. Soon, CAT was gaining accolades for its cost-effectiveness. In its first full year of operation, 1993, CAT ranked eighth nationally for cost-effectiveness in a study by the University of North Carolina-Charlotte's Center for Interdisciplinary Transportation Studies.

In 2012, CAT, now called RTC Transit, had 379 vehicles running on thirty-six routes. With more than 54.9 million riders per year, it was the nation's eighteenth largest bus system. It also had a separate paratransit system providing door-to-door service for disabled riders. In 2004 it launched its MAX rapid transit system on Las Vegas Boulevard North. MAX provided rail-like service in a dedicated bus lane. RTC Transit later opened a handful of park-and-ride facilities and set up express bus routes to assist commuters. An organization called Walk Score put together a formula that ranked Las Vegas twenty-third in the country for best public transit. The community had come a long way in a relatively short period to earn that ranking.

Despite all the expansions and refinements, the system was not perfect. There were good drivers and those who could use an attitude adjustment in dealing with customers. There were late buses. There were still areas of the valley without sufficient service. But no one who remembered the meager Las Vegas Transit System would have suggested a return to the old days. Perea described Woodbury as a "real visionary" who did a "great service to the whole community." Although the formation of CAT doomed Las Vegas Transit, Perea was glad it happened. "It had to be done, no doubt about it," he said. "I'd hate to think where the city would be today without CAT."

## The beltway

Dennis Cederburg, deputy director of the Clark County Public Works Department, kept an old map in his office. He came across it some years ago while looking for something else in the Public Works offices. It wasn't dated, but he believed it was drawn in the early '60s. The map shows the main streets and highways in the Las Vegas Valley at the time with an addition: a dotted line tracing a proposed route for a "belt road" encircling the city.

The map is a fascinating trip into Las Vegas's not-so-distant past. Flamingo Road does not venture west of Interstate 15. Rancho Drive is called Tonopah Highway. North Las Vegas Airport is called Thunderbird Field. U.S. 95 does not exist, though the mapmaker has drawn in a possible route that would follow Boulder Highway in the southeast valley.

The "belt road" route is equally intriguing. In some places, it closely follows what eventually was built in the '90s, but in other places it is quite different. For example, the '60s-era southern stretch would have been farther south than the current route, hooking into Blue Diamond Road for part of its route. The northern stretch, meanwhile, would have been closer in, roughly following where Ann Road is today. The western leg appears to be about right, though the map is not specific enough to show any roads west of Rainbow Boulevard The eastern leg appears to follow the path of modern-day Hollywood Boulevard. All in all, the old map makes more of a square shape, while the current route is more oval.

The map reveals that local transportation planners were thinking about a beltway decades before it became a reality. It suggests, furthermore, that at least some officials had an inkling more than forty years ago that Las Vegas eventually would grow into the metropolis it is today. But Cederburg's old

*Sun, Sin & Suburbia: The History of Modern Las Vegas*

map obviously did not lead to concrete action. Beltway-style roadways also were considered in the '70s, primarily as routes to haul hazardous and nuclear wastes around the city. But it was not until the '80s that the idea really took hold. Marty Manning, Clark County public works director from 1986-2005, said a beltway was being discussed when he came to town in '86. "It was more of an idea than anything else," he recalled. "It was not part of any transportation plan." That would change quickly when beltway discussions began in earnest in 1988-89.

Funding remained an issue, however. The federal government was a likely prospect, but local planners knew the bureaucracy and uncertainty of obtaining federal funds could prevent the project from getting done in a timely manner. Las Vegas was growing by leaps and bounds, and it would need a beltway as soon as possible. The solution was Question 10, the same funding mechanism that fueled the bus system and a variety of street and highway projects in the valley. Question 10 allowed the Public Works Department to sidestep the federal government and proceed more quickly with the project. Planners estimated that building the beltway using federal funds would delay its completion until 2025. Using strictly local money, they figured the project could be completed by 2012.

A fifty-one-mile beltway route was roughed out in a C shape around the valley (the plan did not include an eastern leg because more than 1,100 homes would have to be demolished to create it), and the county began buying land to establish a right of way. This process started early for two reasons: to avoid the prospect of subdivisions and businesses being built on land slated for the beltway and to buy the properties before prices skyrocketed. At the same time, the county held numerous public meetings to receive input on beltway route alternatives.

The county focused first on the southern part of the beltway. Green Valley was exploding in the early '90s, and the upscale master-planned community's one drawback was poor freeway access. Green Valley residents had a long drive along surface streets to get to either Interstate 15 to the west or U.S. 95 to the east. The thinking then was that the western and northern beltway legs could wait as long as a decade for the growth to create a need for them.

Work started with the airport connector. McCarran officials had identified a pressing need to provide a second access point for the increasingly busy airport besides Tropicana Avenue. The answer was to build a highway from Interstate 15 running east along the southern edge of the airport. The highway then turned north, and a tunnel was dug beneath the runways to get to the main terminal.

Next on the agenda was a segment of the southern beltway from Warm Springs to Windmill Lane. Then the county marched southeast through Henderson, eventually hooking up with U.S. 95.

The game plan in the early years of construction was to build the beltway one segment at a time. This is how the entire southern segment was constructed. But while this made sense from the standpoint of doing the job right the first time and providing maximum traffic capacity, it meant the western and northern segments would not be usable for many years. This was a problem both politically and practically. Politically, representatives of the city of Las Vegas were perturbed that their constituents were paying for the beltway but getting nothing for their money. Practically, western and northern growth—primarily in the Summerlin master-planned community—was accelerating at a comparable pace to Green Valley's.

At the urging of Las Vegas Councilman Matthew Callister and County Commissioner Paul Christensen, whose districts encompassed the northwest valley, a compromise was devised in 1996. Rather than build the full beltway one segment at a time, a partial beltway would be constructed on a faster timeline. Basically, frontage roads would be built first on the western and northern segments, giving those areas a beltway ten years ahead of the old schedule. The partial beltway segments would have traffic signals at some intersections and forty-five mph speed limits, but at least they would provide an outlet for frustrated motorists.

Piece by piece, year by year, the beltway started to fill out. But with each completed segment, traffic volume grew to the point that rush-hour congestion started to become an issue. Another troubling problem was that drivers were regularly exceeding the forty-five mph speed limits and causing accidents, treating the beltway like a highway instead of the regular thoroughfare that

*Sun, Sin & Suburbia: The History of Modern Las Vegas*

it truly was. As a result, they were not ready for traffic signals that would not typically exist on a highway. Between March 1999 and April 2002, there were 340 accidents on the beltway, 115 of them causing injury and seven ending in deaths. The most high-profile accident ended in the death of longtime *Las Vegas Sun* newspaper executive Sandy Thompson, who was killed in August 2002 when an SUV driver ran into the back of her car while she was stopped at a red light at the beltway's intersection with Far Hills Avenue. The county responded to the spate of fatalities by improving signage along the beltway to give motorists better notice of upcoming intersections.

The accelerated beltway, now known as Interstate 215, was completed in December 2003 with the opening of the final 4.5-mile segment from Lone Mountain Road to El Capitan Way in the northwest valley. Under the accelerated plan, more than fifty miles of road—some full beltway, some half beltway, some frontage road—took about ten years to finish at a cost of $875 million. The county spent a little more than a fourth of that money, $256.5 million, to buy 600 parcels of private property (in the end, only eighty-seven houses were demolished). The county also obtained about 2,500 acres of public land from the Bureau of Land Management for the project.

But the beltway, while drivable from end to end, was far from finished. The county worked next on building out all segments, adding lanes and eliminating traffic signals. It concentrated first on one of the partial beltway's busiest segments, from I-15 west to Buffalo Drive, to relieve bottlenecks.

By 2012, a few sections of the beltway, especially in the northern valley, were still under construction, and other improvements were envisioned, such as a new, improved interchange with U.S. 95 in the Centennial Hills area. It seemed likely the beltway could not be called "finished" until at least 2015.

At completion, the beltway's price tag would exceed $2 billion.

In scope and in cost, the beltway is the single largest public works project in Nevada history. More importantly, it is one of only a few examples of local officials showing planning foresight. At least as early as 1988, they saw that Las Vegas was on the verge of explosive growth and would need a major new highway to accommodate the hundreds of thousands of new suburban residents. Parts of the beltway simply kept pace with growth. Other segments actually were ahead of the growth curve—a rare occurrence in Las Vegas.

In the end, the same thing can be said about the beltway that Barry Perea said about Citizens Area Transit: One would hate to see what the valley would be like today without it.

## Las Vegas Monorail

The monorail that debuted on the Strip in July 2004 had its roots in the late '60s, when the county and city first considered building a monorail linking the airport, Strip and downtown. In 1971, the county signed a contract with a consortium led by Oklahoma investor A.J. Kavanaugh to pursue the idea, but the process bogged down in controversy. A local taxicab company, fearing the impact on its bottom line, questioned the financing plan for the monorail, while environmental groups questioned its value in battling air pollution. In 1973, 1,000 people jammed the Las Vegas Convention Center's East Hall for an all-day town hall meeting on the pros and cons of the monorail plan. Soon after, the *New York Times* dispatched a reporter to check out the controversy. After outlining the opposing viewpoints, the reporter provided succinct insight into why the monorail plan had generated so much attention:

"Everybody here seems to agree that Las Vegas, the nation's fastest-growing metropolitan area during the 1960s, and still growing, should do something to decongest its roads. Even though it has six lanes, the Strip roadway becomes stubbornly congealed with automobiles during many of the twenty-four hours the casinos remain open. Much of the time, Las Vegas suffers from inversion conditions that clamp sort of an atmospheric lid on the Strip, preventing auto emissions from rising into the sky. At these times, the desert air becomes so fouled that tourists strolling from one air-conditioned casino to another can taste the pollution."

Despite these troubling conditions, county and city officials voted in 1974 to scrap the monorail project, saying it lacked public support and they were not convinced it was economically feasible. But the city of Las Vegas picked up the ball in 1977, proposing a "people mover" linking the three tourist areas. The city's plan differed in that it would have used seventy-foot-long wheeled vehicles traversing city streets. Traffic signals would be controlled to allow the people mover smooth travel. It also would have been much cheaper than the county project at an estimated $10 million. City Public Works Director Larry Hampton, who conceived the "Silver Express" system, said the vehicles would be "plush, comfortable [and] well air-conditioned ... so that even a person attired in formal dress will feel that the express is a socially acceptable mode of transportation."

Hampton's plan went nowhere. In 1984, however, the city renewed its interest in mass transit technology, advertising in the *Wall Street Journal* for companies interested in developing an automated people mover linking Cashman Field and downtown. The theory at City Hall was that companies would leap at the chance to showcase new transportation technology in Las Vegas—at no cost to city taxpayers. And the city was right: Sixty-seven national and international firms expressed initial interest in the project, including General Electric, Westinghouse and (remember these names) Bombardier Inc., the Canadian company that had built the Disneyland monorail, and HSST Corporation, a Japanese firm.

The city elected in 1985 to contract with Las Vegas People Mover Associates, a consortium headed by Magnetic Transit of America, a German company developing a magnetic levitation train system. In addition to running the monorail between downtown and Cashman Field, plans developed in 1986 to integrate a station into a planned library and children's museum complex to be built next to the transit line on Las Vegas Boulevard North. The company also expressed interest in eventually expanding its system to the Strip and McCarran Airport.

In 1987, HSST, which had dropped out of the city bidding, announced plans for a magnetic levitation train linking Caesars Palace on the Strip with the Union Plaza downtown, using the Union Pacific Railroad right of way. HSST wanted to exhibit its new technology in Las Vegas. That proposal met with immediate opposition from Las Vegas People Mover officials, who said the Japanese project would violate their contract with the city. HSST also had an ulterior motive: The company planned to build the Las Vegas train to get its foot in the door for a proposed high-speed train linking Las Vegas and Southern California.

Both projects intended to use magnetic levitation techology. The vehicles would hover half an inch above their guideways. They would not have wheels; electromagnets would propel them silently forward. Different versions of the technology were tested successfully in Germany and Japan but Las Vegas would be the first American city with a mag-lev system, and the first place in the world to operate one commercially.

A groundbreaking ceremony for the $60 million People Mover was held in January 1988, with Lieutenant Governor Bob Miller proclaiming, "Walt Disney would have loved the Las Vegas People Mover. Today we are breaking ground on Tomorrowland right here in Las Vegas." But construction did not actually begin until the following year, when eighty-foot steel girders were placed along the rail line.

Meanwhile, HSST changed its plans, focusing on the Strip corridor. It abandoned the railroad right of way and decided against extending to downtown. By doing that, it would not violate the city's contract with the People Mover. The new route would start at the Tropicana Hotel and run north along Industrial Road to Circus Circus. But then HSST ran into opposition from Strip resort executives who were not convinced the train would improve traffic congestion. By 1990, Mirage Hotel owner Steve Wynn was arguing that a Strip train was a "crackpot scheme" and a "stupid idea."

Fighting between the two companies became fierce, with each trying to politically derail the other's project. In 1988, HSST officials called a press conference to hand out photographs and translated German news reports about a crash of a People Mover test train in Berlin. HSST spokesmen suggested the "unfortunate accident" might mean the company's Las Vegas train would be unsafe. People Mover officials responded by accusing HSST of "gutter tactics." It also announced that it wanted to extend its train system to the Strip and the airport, putting it in direct competition with HSST.

In the end, neither project got off the ground. People Mover construction stopped in 1990, citing an array of financial and political reasons for the project's demise. A dozen support columns erected during construction eventually were torn down, while a partially finished 5,500-square-foot station attached to the Las Vegas Library was converted into library administrative space.

HSST struggled along for a few more years, eventually convincing Wynn and other resort industry leaders to drop their opposition by shifting the route to Interstate 15 instead of directly behind the casinos. But in 1993, HSST withdrew its plan, citing an inability to obtain financing during an economic downturn in Japan.

But the seeds of an idea had been planted, and ever-worsening traffic congestion in Las Vegas, especially in the Strip corridor, kept alive the idea of a rail-based mass transit system. The first monorail on the Strip, connecting the MGM Grand and Bally's, was the brainchild of then-MGM Grand President Bob Maxey. As the story goes, Maxey was flying over the Strip corridor when he noticed a clear right of way along Audrie Lane between the MGM Grand and Bally's. Figuring a monorail could connect the Strip's two busiest corners and help both resorts bring in customers, he called Bally's Chairman Arthur Goldberg and sold him on a joint venture. Using refurbished Disney World cars, the $25 million, privately funded monorail opened in 1995, carting visitors eight-tenths of a mile along the east side of the Strip. The train soon was carrying 14,000 passengers per day.

But the MGM-Bally's monorail merely served as a harbinger of bigger things. Other casino companies built monorails between their Strip properties. The person who advanced the idea of a larger private monorail was Bob Broadbent. The former county commissioner actually had been a vocal critic of the early '70s monorail project, but after he retired as longtime director of McCarran Airport, the casinos tapped him to spearhead a plan to extend the MGM-Bally's monorail down the Strip.

About the same time, the Clark County Regional Transportation Commission was drafting plans to build a publicly owned monorail from McCarran to Cashman Field Center. For a time, whether the public or private monorail would win out was unclear, but funding issues clearly favored the private plan. The casino-backed project appealed to the state to issue $650 million in bonds to finance the project. Once the company agreed to take out private insurance to cover most of the costs if the monorail went belly up, the state agreed to issue the bonds. With the County Commission approving the private plan in 1998, the RTC assumed the role of making sure the private monorail's technology would mesh with future monorail plans in the valley.

The initial casino-backed plan would have extended the monorail north to the Las Vegas Hilton and Las Vegas Convention Center. But soon the project grew, reaching north to the Sahara Hotel, with seven stations along the four-mile route: MGM Grand, Bally's/Paris, Flamingo, Harrah's/Imperial Palace, Las Vegas Convention Center, Las Vegas Hilton and Sahara. Ground was broken in August 2001, with construction progress most evident along the monorail's northern section on Paradise Road, where pillars rose up in the middle of the street.

The monorail started carrying passengers along the Strip in July 2004. In its first full year of operation, 2005, it was projected to provide 19.5 million rides, or 53,000 per day, taking a substantial number of cars off the roads—and pollution out of the air—within the resort corridor. While most of the riders were expected to be tourists, officials expected some resort workers, especially those who used the bus to get to work, to use the monorail.

The monorail was a rare public-private achievement—becoming a reality when so many previous proposals had died on the drawing boards. The key, it seems, was that the project was locally conceived and executed; no out-of-town hucksters were involved. The monorail required highly competitive casino companies to work together—not a simple matter, especially consider-ing past squabbles over the HSST project. But the companies came to see that all would benefit from the monorail. It also required the county's Regional Transportation Commission to put a major piece of its regional master plan in the hands of a public-private entity, the nonprofit board that oversees the monorail. Taking a cue from their funding strategy for the beltway, local officials realized the privately funded plan could be done more quickly and without burdening taxpayers. County officials gained confidence from a pub-lic-private partnership working well in the CAT system. And in the end, they felt confident that Broadbent, who oversaw major expansions at McCarran Airport, was capable of doing the project right.

As ambitious as the monorail was, it was envisoned as just the first piece of a larger plan aimed at improving traffic congestion in Las Vegas. Extending

*Sun, Sin & Suburbia: The History of Modern Las Vegas*

the monorail 2.3 miles to downtown was next on the agenda. This $454 million downtown extension aimed to use a combination of federal and private funds. Local officials hoped that besides providing additional commuting options, this second leg, slated for completion by 2007, would funnel more tourists to Fremont Street. Phase three would connect the Strip monorail to the airport, possibly by 2012. This would provide visitors with seamless transit from airport to hotel. Although this leg seemed like a natural to build right away, it came with a major complication: It would have a detrimental effect on taxicab, limousine and rental car businesses. Despite strong opposition from those industries, a monorail extension to the airport seemed likely. There also was the possibility of a monorail leg running along the west side of the Strip. The west side was where HSST officials met stiff opposition, but circumstances had changed. In the mid-2000s, the resorts on the east side of the Strip owned the casinos on the west side. The first evidence of a west side monorail would be a spur to the Stardust, after which a west-side line could run down Frank Sinatra Drive.

The RTC's monorail ambitions didn't end with serving the tourist centers. The agency envisioned the monorail system hooking into a light rail line extending into the northwest valley along either Rancho Drive or the U.S. 95 corridor. This would serve workers commuting to jobs in the downtown area and on the Strip. The agency also had plans for a commuter rail to Henderson, using an old Union Pacific Railroad spur. These were long-range visions, but they stood a better chance of becoming reality than the pie-in-the-sky proposals of the '70s and '80s.

But it didn't take long for lofty visions of a vast monorail network to fall to earth.

Enthusiasm for the monorail took a hit just weeks after it opened thanks to a pair of mechanical mishaps that prompted temporary shutdowns of the system. First, a sixty-pound wheel assembly fell off a moving train and plummeted to the street, forcing a six-day shutdown (and $500,000 in lost revenue). Then, a day after resuming service, a small piece of a drive shaft came loose and fell to the ground, triggering another prolonged shutdown and extensive evaluation of the system. The problems were blamed on Bombardier Corporation, the Montreal firm that built and operated the monorail. Public confidence in the system was shaken to the extent that the Regional Transportation Commission announced that plans for the downtown extension were put on hold until the monorail was running safely and smoothly. Despite the setbacks, County Commissioner Bruce Woodbury remained optimistic about the monorail's long-term prospects, telling the *Las Vegas Sun*, "I think we'll not only have a second phase, but a third phase and fourth phase as well."

Although he had been dead-on with other transportation projects, Woodbury misjudged the monorail. He was hardly alone. The monorail's ultimate misfortune didn't end up being mechanical problems, however, but the fact that not enough people wanted to ride it. Simply put, it didn't go where people wanted to go.

From the start, ridership fell short of projections, and before long the system encountered financial difficulties. In 2009, with the recession adding to the misery, monorail officials tried to boast of having carried more than thirty-seven million riders since opening. But based on initial projections, that figure should have been exceeded in the first two full years of operation, not the first five.

Unable to make a bond payment, the monorail started seeking taxpayer aid to help keep the train rolling. Critics came out swinging.

"The well-connected, amply paid honchos who rammed this through the public process lied to us from Day One," wrote George Knapp, television journalist and columnist for *Las Vegas CityLife*. "They exaggerated ridership and revenue figures from the get-go, but used those bogus numbers to con investors into buying the bonds and weaseled the state into backing them. A train that travels only to a couple of casinos, a train that does not reach to the airport or downtown or anywhere else, is never going to compete with bus lines and limos and taxicabs and good old-fashioned family cars. Financial failure was always in the cards."

In January 2010, the monorail filed for Chapter 11 bankruptcy protection, hoping to restructure its bond debt. Almost two years later, after the monorail had secured support from its creditors, a bankruptcy judge nonetheless rejected the monorail's reorganization plan, saying it left the company $40 million short in its ability to survive.

"The monorail essentially asks the court to allow it to float along until it sinks, suggesting that when it ultimately sinks, the court need not concern itself with how creditors will make it onto the life raft—or even whether there will be a life raft available," Judge Bruce Markell wrote.

In 2012, the monorail planned to return to court with a revamped bankruptcy reorganization plan. But regardless of whether the monorail emerged from bankruptcy, it was a project with a dim future. Considering the monorail's tortured history, the odds of securing funds to extend the line to McCarran Airport were somewhere between long and impossible. The monorail's future ruined the otherwise sensible notion of providing a mass transit line in the Strip corridor.

The Strip needs mass transit, but it has to start over. The monorail was a faux pas, a bad first draft, a mistake. The problems with the monorail are plain to see in hindsight. It's too far away from the Strip. It only runs on the east side of the resort corridor. It doesn't go to the airport. It doesn't go downtown. It's too expensive to ride.

If the monorail had run down the middle of Las Vegas Boulevard—as early supporters of a Strip people mover envisioned—it undoubtedly would have had a lot more customers. Not only would it have served a larger customer base, but it would have been a bigger tourist attraction. What would you rather look at while riding the monorail, the ugly backsides of the Strip resorts or the shiny front facades, flashing signs and gawking tourists? No contest.

The business management books all agree on this point: By all means, try new things, but if something isn't working, cut your losses and try something else. You see this philosophy in action in Las Vegas all the time, from the MGM Grand completely replacing its lion façade to Treasure Island revamping its pirate show. Reinvention is the city's mantra.

The monorail didn't work, but that doesn't mean something better is doomed to the same fate.

## Fast train to California

Talk about your big ideas. How about a train between Las Vegas and Southern California, one that could whisk gamblers to the casinos in about two hours?

It's not a new idea. Talk of a high-speed train linking the two places had been discussed for three decades. But the idea didn't gain traction until 2009, when the DesertXpress, brainchild of local public relations guru and political operative Sig Rogich, came to life.

With Rogich taking the lead and garnering the support of U.S. Senate Majority Leader Harry Reid, the DesertXpress project overshadowed a long-sought magnetic levitation train. Reid had long supported the maglev project but switched his allegiance. He said he did so because the maglev project had languished for thirty years with no chance of getting built, while the DesertXpress had a legitimate chance of happening. Critics said Reid's support for the DesertXpress was politically motivated, a move to gain influential support for his 2010 re-election campaign.

Politics aside, both projects faced high hurdles.

The maglev train would terminate in Anaheim, while the DesertXpress would stop in Victorville. The maglev train would go 300 mph, while the DesertXpress would employ conventional motorized technology and top out at 150 mph. The DesertXpress would cost $6.5 billion while the maglev would cost $12 billion.

Originally, backers insisted the DesertXpress would be privately funded—requiring no taxpayer support. But when the recession closed off lending options, the DesertXpress changed course and sought a $4.9 billion loan from the federal government to help build the train. Transportation Secretary Ray LaHood endorsed the project, touting the jobs it would create, while Victorville officials envisioned an elaborate train station surrounded by hotels and restaurants.

But skeptics were plentiful. A fundamental question had yet to be sufficiently answered: How many Southern Californians really want to ride a train from Victorville to Las Vegas? If relatively few want to take the train to Las Vegas, a lot of money could be wasted.

"It's insanity," Thomas Finkbiner of the Intermodal Transportation Institute at the University of Denver told *USA Today*. "People won't drive to a train to go someplace. If you are going to drive, why not drive all the way and leave when you want?"

A few other points:

• Most residents of the American Southwest own cars. They drive almost everywhere, and they aren't accustomed to relying on other forms of transportation. The mass transit culture of New York City, say, just hasn't gained traction yet in this part of the country.

• For many Southern Californians, driving to Las Vegas is a time-honored pastime, memorialized in Hunter Thompson's book *Fear and Loathing in Las Vegas* and the hit movie *The Hangover*. We know there's something about driving across the Mojave Desert that appeals to Southern Californians cooped up too long in the smog-draped hives of humanity hugging the Pacific. It takes them four to six hours to make the journey, just enough time to shake off their daily anxieties and gear up for a rip-roaring weekend in the gambling capital. And when they get there, they don't have to pay for or hassle with taxis or rental cars.

• The highways linking Southern California with Las Vegas have some issues but for the most part motorists move along at a steady clip. It's not like the highways are so rough or narrow or congested that they represent a deterrent to making the drive.

• Flying between Southern California and Las Vegas is cheap and easy. The flights are short, and the airlines offer affordable rates. There are several different airports in Southern California to choose from, giving most everybody a convenient option.

• Starting or ending your train trip in Victorville, eighty miles from downtown L.A., doesn't make a lot of sense. There are practical reasons why the train would stop short of the big city, among them the thicket of physical obstacles to going farther. Still, nothing against Victorville, but it isn't many people's idea of a vacation destination. If you live in Las Vegas and want to visit Southern California, you don't think of stopping in Victorville unless you have family there. No wonder critics dubbed the DesertXpress the Train to Nowhere.

Considering these questions, is it possible there's no pressing need or demand for a high-speed train?

Maglev train advocates said their project would carry an initial passenger load of forty-three million per year. DesertXpress supporters believed their train would carry ten million. DesertXpress later slashed its first-year projection to three million riders. But what if the estimates are overly optimistic? Consider the Las Vegas Monorail, which sold itself based on ridership estimates that, even in the best of economic times, it never came close to achieving. And consider Amtrak, which ceased service to Las Vegas in 1997 primarily because of low ridership.

Despite the skepticism, the prospect of high-speed train travel between Las Vegas and Southern California had appeal on several fronts. If millions of people rode a maglev train between Las Vegas and Southern California instead of driving or flying, it would be good for the environment. Even the motorized train would be a net gain.

Additionally, advocates envisioned the DesertXpress eventually hooking into a proposed bullet train network connecting Los Angeles and San Francisco. But the vast scope of that California project—at least $68 billion, with forty-eight miles of tunnels through mountains—spurred even more criticism than the Las Vegas project.

In the end, observers said the train would have to be an incredible bargain to attract a fair share of the Southern Californians now driving or flying to Las Vegas. Both projects said they would be "competitive" with other modes of transportation, perhaps $100 for a roundtrip ticket. But "competitive" was a vague promise. Southern Californians noted a common practice of saving money by filling a vehicle with four, five or more people to make the trek to Las Vegas. If they took the train instead, each would have to buy a ticket.

## Interstate 11

Digital prophets love to talk about people all over the world being connected to one another without leaving the comfort of their recliners, iPads perched on their laps. This vision of virtual connectedness suggests that the

286                     *Sun, Sin & Suburbia: The History of Modern Las Vegas*

need to physically move from one place to another to accomplish various tasks is a thing of the analog past.

Of course, this is fantasy on most levels of human existence. Consider online shopping. While it's true that a Las Vegan is able to shop for shoes while seated in front of her home computer, that's far from the end of the story. Once the credit card information is entered and the purchase button is clicked, the next phase of the process begins, and it doesn't involve magically squeezing the shoes through a fiber optic line. The shoes must be shipped to Las Vegas from wherever they're being stored. They likely start their journey on a truck, transfer to an airplane, then return to a truck to be carried to somebody's front door.

This transportation goes on endlessly. Shoes are flying all over the country as customers seek just the right pair for their feet. And it's not just shoes, of course. It's the large majority of products we buy and sell.

Transportation of goods, services and people is a huge piece of the world marketplace, and it's not going away no matter how many promises the digital gurus make. Quick and efficient transportation is an essential element of a vibrant economy.

Over the years, Las Vegas has invested heavily in and benefited greatly from improvements in air travel. But it has lagged in the development of highways linking to the region's other population centers. The most egregious example is the hodgepodge surface route between Las Vegas and Phoenix.

Historically, Las Vegans' orientation has been to the west. Los Angeles, Anaheim, San Diego—these are the regional centers that come to mind. Phoenix rarely makes the list, and the highways available to get there reflect this neglect. It's a meandering 300-mile trip, and it takes longer than it should.

You'd think Las Vegas and Phoenix would be natural bosom buddies, joined at the hip economically and culturally. You'd think Las Vegans would be big fans of the Cardinals, Suns and Diamondbacks. But mostly they aren't. The absence of an efficient north-south transportation route is a primary reason.

In 2008, a movement emerged to build "Interstate 11" as the last major piece of the interstate highway system. Las Vegas and Phoenix are the last large, neighboring cities in America not connected by an interstate. The idea gained momentum in Arizona and Nevada. The first step in the process debuted in 2010: the $114 million Hoover Dam bypass bridge spanning the Colorado River. The Mike O'Callaghan-Pat Tillman Memorial Bridge saved truckers from having to endure long detours to avoid the dam. Commuters and tourists saved time as well, avoiding the Homeland Security checkpoint and the winding, narrow highway crossing the dam.

The bridge represented a big improvement to the Las Vegas-Phoenix corridor, but it was only one piece of the puzzle. Several stretches of roadway still needed to be expanded to four-lane divided highway, and a $500 million highway bypassing Boulder City was needed not only to eliminate another traffic slowdown but to preserve the tranquility of that small community.

The full plan for Interstate 11 was even more ambitious. "The vision for this highway is to ultimately connect Phoenix to Seattle through Las Vegas," Las Vegas transportation consultant Tom Skancke wrote in 2010. "Looking at where Las Vegas sits on the transportation grid, our city is strategically positioned to become a U.S. port of entry, thus becoming a global partner with China, India, the United Kingdom and other nations."

Naturally, finding money to build Interstate 11 was the primary impediment. But unlike the high-speed train, few questioned the underlying value or viability of the highway. Federal and state governments started work on establishing the regulatory framework for Interstate 11. In 2012, Congress officially designated Interstate 11 between Phoenix and Las Vegas in a transportation reauthorization bill.

Las Vegas stood to benefit dramatically if Interstate 11 came to pass. It could boost tourism as well as connect the city in new ways to national and international commerce. Brookings Mountain West, a think tank, pointed out that creating the segment of Interstate 11 between Las Vegas and Phoenix wasn't as ominous an undertaking as it might have seemed:

"Most of the route of the would-be I-11 currently consists of near-interstate-grade highway. A few critical improvements, such as a bypass around Boulder City and a full interstate-gauge interchange at I-40 in Kingman, would complete the link. The all-important bridge over the Colorado River just south of

*Sun, Sin & Suburbia: The History of Modern Las Vegas*

Hoover Dam was completed in 2010, so the most costly and difficult section of what will become Interstate 11 has already been built."

While Brookings minimized the scope of the project, post-recession political realities suggested that actually getting it done—and done right—would require a considerable degree of leadership and cooperation.

## The net effect

While the bus system and beltway were the boldest transportation projects of the modern era, they were not the only productive endeavors to address Las Vegas traffic. Other major projects included the Desert Inn Super Arterial, providing a nonstop east-west thoroughfare crossing Interstate 15 and the Strip; the expansion and reconfiguration of the Spaghetti Bowl, improving traffic movement through the I-15/U.S. 95 interchange; the widening of U.S. 95 through the northwest valley and the construction of numerous interchanges and overpasses to accommodate growing traffic volume; the Summerlin Parkway, which provided a link from the giant planned community to U.S. 95 and the beltway; endless improvements to I-15; pedestrian bridges on the Strip, clearing tourists off several busy intersections; the extension and widening of countless major streets in the valley; and the computerized coordination of traffic signals to improve traffic flow.

And yet, traffic congestion remained a chronic issue in the Las Vegas Valley, even after growth slowed to a trickle. Traffic planners said that without all the improvements, gridlock would be far worse, diminishing the quality of life for residents and impeding the conduct of business. No doubt that was true. But it's also fair to say Las Vegas has always been playing catch-up when it comes to transportation.

This, however, is nothing unusual for a metropolis of two million people. Where Las Vegas really fell down was in creating a safe environment for bicycle riders and pedestrians. The city's sprawling nature was the primary deterrent, as distances between destinations made walking or cycling realistic for only the most hardy or desperate souls. The summer heat makes either alternative even less inviting. Bicycles are seen on Las Vegas streets, but their numbers are small compared with many other cities. The biggest problem is the hostility that bicyclists encounter on Las Vegas roadways. Bicycle lanes are sparse, and drivers tend to see bicycles as an impediment to their forward progress. Reckless and arrogant motorists have turned the metropolitan area into one of the nation's most dangerous for pedestrians, who literally put their lives on the line when they venture across major thoroughfares. In 2011, an organization called Transportation for America ranked Las Vegas the sixth most dangerous city for walking.

Traffic planners can do only so much about human behavior, but they could do more to enhance the environment for cyclists and pedestrians. Not everybody can afford to drive everywhere they go, and, more importantly, not everybody wants to. Whether it's to reduce auto emissions or improve personal health—or both—the choice to pedal or walk should be a more attractive one in Las Vegas.

# CHAPTER 11

# The Reckoning: Riches to Rags

Almost nobody saw it coming. It was as if a tornado had somehow eluded meteorological detection and swept into town without notice. In that sense, it was more like an earthquake, striking without any warning. Las Vegas was completely caught off guard by the real estate bust and the national economic meltdown that followed. This could be said of the whole country, of course, but Las Vegas was hit harder than most other places, fell farther and was among the least prepared to deal with the effects.

Las Vegas was booming like never before, which is saying something for a community that had enjoyed long periods of growth and prosperity throughout its history. The future looked as bright as the past. "We went on as though this boom would continue forever," said Michael Green, a history professor at the College of Southern Nevada. "Alan Greenspan used the term 'irrational exuberance,' and in some ways that describes the situation in Las Vegas. This community had suffered through downturns before, but not in the lifetimes or careers of many of those making government or economic policy in the early and mid-2000s. So there seemed to be no little voice in their heads warning them."

With no little voices rising above the din, casino companies, developers and civic leaders forged ahead with ambitious plans to transform Las Vegas into a world-class city. Las Vegas entrepreneurs have always been willing to take risks, but the amounts of money they were leveraging on the future were beyond the scale of anything that had been imagined before. The best

291

example was MGM's CityCenter—an $8.5 billion colossus that promised to take Las Vegas to the next level as an international resort destination.

Full of confidence and ignoring historical perspective, Las Vegas neglected one of the most enduring truths of human existence: What goes up must come down. This lesson of Physics 101 also applies to economics, and Las Vegas learned it the hard way in the first decade of the twenty-first century.

In hindsight, it all looks so obvious. Certainly we should have seen that the real estate bubble would eventually burst. We should have recognized that Wall Street was playing with fire, and putting everything at risk. Yet, before the fall, the finest minds in Las Vegas didn't recognize the city's precarious position. Or, if some did see it, they didn't heed it or do anything to cushion for the impact.

Part of this blindness surely was a case of intoxication. Not actual drunkenness, although, this being Las Vegas, there probably was some of that. Rather, Las Vegans were intoxicated by the energy, activity and money flowing like a raging river through the valley. For more than two decades, Las Vegas was the fastest-growing metropolitan area in the country, a beneficiary of international economic prosperity, as well as cultural and demographic shifts. Ambitious business and political leaders gulped from this overflowing stream of good fortune to build their empires. Grappling with the present demanded their full attention, leaving little time to ponder the bigger picture. This inebriated view was reflected in the tone of the first edition of this book, published in 2004—at the peak of the city's economic vitality.

Some of this blindness was forgivable, the result of a laser focus on competing in the here and now. After all, at its peak Las Vegas was building one new house per hour, one new school per month, so just meeting demand understandably took precedence over more rarified concerns. But many of those pocketing profits in Las Vegas simply did not care about the city's long-term prospects. Like the miners of yesteryear drawn to Nevada's rich veins of gold and silver, the plan was to extract the resources as quickly as possible and pick up stakes as soon as they ran dry. This rape-and-scrape mentality did not cause Las Vegas's economic collapse, but it accelerated and deepened the fall.

Finally, Las Vegas possessed a special form of hubris, a belief, largely without basis, that it was immune from the inevitable ups and downs of the U.S. economy. The popular phrase was "recession-proof," a myth derived from the notion that the innate human desire to gamble would always supersede the effects of economic downturns. The grain of truth in this myth—that gambling is, indeed, a time-honored human impulse—hardly justified a belief that the Las Vegas train would continue chugging along regardless of what happened to the economy nationally or internationally.

But Las Vegas suffered from a severe lack of historical perspective. The general opinion was that Las Vegas would continue to grow at a rapid rate, that property values would continue to rise, that the demand for more—and more opulent—gambling resorts was limitless. And even if economic growth slowed a little bit, the thinking went, it surely would never again stagnate or shift into reverse. Las Vegas believed it had figured out how to outwit history. Rather than respecting the laws of gravity, Las Vegas embraced something closer to the fanciful belief in perpetual motion.

In reality, Las Vegas was highly susceptible to outside influences. The hotel-casino building spree in the '50s eventually outpaced demand. A few casinos closed, and others barely survived. The national recessions of the late '60s and early '80s flattened Las Vegas's growth curve. The September 11, 2001, terrorist attacks gave the city a vivid glimpse of what could happen. The Strip all but shut down for several weeks after 9/11, as air travel tightened and pensive Americans adopted a wait-and-see attitude toward extravagances such as gambling and vacations. The resulting casino layoffs were quick and widespread. But the city bounced back fairly quickly, reinforcing an undeserved confidence that Las Vegas could shrug off economic hits.

But Las Vegas discovered just a few years later that it was far from recession-proof, that it was, in fact, among the most vulnerable places in the country to economic fluctuations. The city's economic reliance on tourism and construction meant it depended almost entirely on outside forces to keep the money flowing. The economic dramas that unfolded on the national stage between 2007 and 2011 could not have been worse for Las Vegas.

One Las Vegas business leader who readily admitted he failed to see the economic rapids looming ahead was John Restrepo, a consultant and chairman of the Nevada Economic Forum, which is charged with gauging future tax revenues for the state Legislature. Restrepo filed for personal bankruptcy in November 2010. "It happened so fast," Restrepo told the *Las Vegas Review-Journal.* "My personal situation was just like the national situation. Nobody saw this coming. Wall Street didn't see it, the Fed didn't see it. Do you really think the MGM would have built CityCenter if their top financial guys saw this?"

Declaring bankruptcy was hardly an unusual step in Las Vegas after the financial crisis, as Nevada led the nation in bankruptcy filings. Restrepo, who owns a consulting company, said he tried hard to avoid it by cutting his expenditures, but he ended up tapping his savings to pay off his debts.

It was a common story, in Las Vegas and beyond, and Restrepo doesn't believe any one thing should be blamed. "This recession has behaved like no other in history," he said, "and it continues to do things that are unexpected."

The national media, always intrigued by what's new in Las Vegas, jumped on the city's economic troubles. In January 2011, *The Economist* magazine printed an article titled, "Party Over." Citing the city's nation-leading unemployment and home foreclosure rates, the magazine cleverly summarized the situation: "This desert valley, which once represented the most extreme pleasures in American consumerism, now has the most severe hangover."

*The Economist* pondered whether Las Vegas would ever recover: "The question is whether there will ever be a complete recovery, or whether something more fundamental has changed, threatening the existence of places that rely directly or indirectly on gambling."

While *The Economist* concluded its assessment on a more upbeat note, the same couldn't be said for a gloomy front-page article by Adam Nagourney in the *New York Times* printed just a few months earlier, in October 2010. This article, too, pursued the hypothesis that Las Vegas may never fully recover. "Although gaming dropped with the economy, don't automatically assume that when the economy comes back people will start gaming at the same level," Keith Foley, a senior vice president at Moody's Investor Services, told the *Times*. "This is a highly discretionary form of spending. People lost their savings."

The *Times* also quoted Billy Vassiliadis, the longtime Las Vegas advertising and political guru, who argued that there was more to the equation than simply leading gamblers back to the tables. "There was a time twenty-five years ago that if tourism rebounded, the state rebounded," Vassiliadis said. "That isn't the case anymore. The other side of the economy here is going to be harder. There needs to be some real, thoughtful, deliberate effort to rebuild an economy here. It isn't going to happen by itself."

The *Times* story hit a nerve in Las Vegas, where Nagourney was accused of purposely ignoring signs of economic recovery. His chief critic was Doug Elfman, nightlife columnist for the *Las Vegas Review-Journal*. Elfman, who spent many hours every week getting an upfront view of how the economy was affecting the Strip, suggested Nagourney should have taken a closer look before filing his tale of doom and gloom. By 2010, restaurants, nightclubs and showrooms were filling up on a nightly basis again, Elfman reported.

"Those of us who grace the Strip regularly know that, in the past year, everything from car traffic to foot traffic has gone from dismal to jamming," Elfman wrote. "Any decent journalist could have discovered all this if she came to Vegas for a week to report a front-page story for the *New York Times*." Elfman responded to the *Times* article in part because he wanted to put up an impassioned defense of the many people on the Strip working hard to fend off the economic crisis. "Just like people in the rest of America, many people here have been working sixty hours a week, six days a week, on skeleton crews, to get the job done," he wrote.

About a year earlier, in August 2009, *Time* magazine weighed in with a cover story on the woes of Las Vegas. The article presented a fascinating contrast with a *Time* report from 1994.

On January 10, 1994, *Time* published a cover story titled "Las Vegas, U.S.A." The piece, written by Kurt Andersen, was prompted by the Strip megaresort boom and reflected the anything-goes optimism of that era. Andersen came to Las Vegas during "its biggest boom since the Frank-and-Dino Rat Pack days" and marveled at the "crazily go-go" fact that three huge resorts (Luxor,

Treasure Island and MGM Grand) had just opened within three months of each other.

Andersen wasn't blinded by the neon. He noted the city's high cancer and suicide rates, its lack of "civic engagement" and reluctance to fund social programs, its "water gluttony." However, Andersen, who would go on to become a best-selling novelist and host a popular public radio show, had a deeper point to make: The "hypereclectic, twenty-four-hour-a-day fantasy-themed party machine" that is Las Vegas, he submitted, "no longer seems so very exotic or extreme." Las Vegas was mainstream. "Las Vegas has become more Americanized," he wrote, "and even more, America has become Las Vegasized."

Back in those early days of the "Information Superhighway," a *Time* cover story was still a big deal. Andersen's story was discussed and dissected, praised and derided. But what it did locally was to give Las Vegans a sense that what was happening in their town was important. Las Vegas was on the cutting edge of the future—America was following the city's lead. And it was true to a large extent. Starting in late 1989, when Steve Wynn opened The Mirage, Las Vegas had become a national frontrunner in the race for fortune and glory.

Fast forward to 2009—roughly fifteen years after Andersen's cover story. *Time* put Las Vegas on the cover again, but the headline carried a different tone: "Less Vegas." This time, Joel Stein was called on to assess the state of Las Vegas. His article documented how the global recession had put the city in a tough spot. Growth was flat, home foreclosure and unemployment rates were high, and conventions had been canceled. "Just as Las Vegas was the epicenter of the extravagant consumption of the past twenty years, now it's the deepest crater of the recession over the last year," Stein wrote. "Las Vegas is on sale," he quipped, noting that hotel room rates had nosedived and restaurants were selling cheaper wines. The Las Vegas painted by Stein bore little resemblance to the economic virility Andersen described in 1994. Touring foreclosed homes trashed by their former owners, Stein concluded: "This is what an empire looks like when it falls."

Yet amid the gloom, Stein detected the distinctive Las Vegas persistence to look on the bright side. Hope, perhaps even confidence that Las Vegas would rise again, permeated the population. The ever-quotable casino kingpin

Sheldon Adelson told him, "If you believe what you read in the newspaper about us, we have one foot in the pail of bankruptcy and the other foot on a banana peel, and there's a high wind. It's all wrong."

Stein heard the city's optimism but he wasn't quite convinced. "It sounds a little hollow," he wrote, calling Las Vegas "the world's greatest ghost town in waiting." But he was wise enough to conclude that "a lot of people have gone broke betting against the people who run Las Vegas."

While Andersen sought to break new ground with his incisive look at Las Vegas in 1994, Stein merely did a workmanlike job of reflecting the obvious. He might have pursued a different path. He could have explored the line of thinking, shared by a fair number of smart people, that Las Vegas would come back strong. Las Vegas remained the best place in North America to address the human animal's insatiable desire for risk and release. Adelson pegged it: "There's no way this world will change. There's no way people are going to stop doing things they want to do."

But Las Vegas had fallen so far that its recovery would trail the nation's, perhaps by a year or two—or three. The real estate crash was too severe for that sizable aspect of the Las Vegas economy to pop back up off the mat, as it had done before. By late 2011, the resorts filled again with money-spending tourists but the casinos could not thrive until they shed their billion-dollar debts.

The second decade of the new century could end up looking something like the 1980s, a period of slow expansion on the Strip while the city continued to expand and mature around it. But consider what happened at the tail end of the '80s—Wynn built the game-changing Mirage. He was a believer in Las Vegas when others didn't see it. By 2019, and probably sooner, it's likely a new risk-taker will advance the city's economy in a profound way. At the very least, we can say with some confidence that Las Vegas will outlast *Time* magazine.

## Learning from Phoenix

In the spring of 2011, the *Las Vegas Sun*'s Michael Squires published a thought-provoking essay under the headline, "Is There a Reason for Las Vegas to Be Envious of Phoenix?" Squires, who had lived in both places, outlined contrasts and parallels between the desert Southwest's two largest cities, with the general assessment that Las Vegas had a long way to go to match the big-city achievements of its less-glamorous sister city.

Phoenix—twice as large as Las Vegas—has four major league sports franchises while Las Vegas has none. It has a light rail system, a world-class zoo and a revitalized downtown, while Las Vegas has no light rail, no zoo and a downtown redevelopment in its adolescence. Phoenix has embraced higher education, while Las Vegas is indifferent. In 2011, Phoenix enjoyed a major boost to its economy when Intel announced plans for a $5 billion manufacturing facility employing 10,000 people. Las Vegas is simply not in the game when it comes to manufacturing. "Like the orthodontist living next door, Phoenix seemed a tad boring, but was doing much better than we were," Squires wrote.

Las Vegas, of course, was no slouch in the postwar growth boom. After all, it grew quickly, from practically nothing to one of the world's top tourist destinations. The Strip is one of the world's visual marvels, and the various entertainments it offers manage to keep the interest of tens of millions of people every year. But while Las Vegas has been visionary when it comes to spectacles along Las Vegas Boulevard, it has lacked the vision thing beyond the resort corridor. "Las Vegas has been more driven by growth itself than vision," Squires wrote.

Las Vegas architect Eric Strain made the point that Phoenix has more residents who were born and raised there, and who therefore are more comfortable living in the hot, dry desert. "They've come to accept that when it's 110 degrees they can still live outside," he told Squires. "They have summer festivals and people swarm to them. We tend to want to leave when the summer arrives."

While Las Vegas was content to focus on one industry to fuel its economy, Phoenix did not have that luxury. As a result, it worked hard to build a diverse economic base built on a range of manufacturing. More recently, Phoenix jumped into the fields of technology, bioscience and renewable energy. Phoenix was able to attract these sophisticated industries because of its investments in Arizona State University, which advanced from its party school past to become a major research institution.

298     *Sun, Sin & Suburbia: The History of Modern Las Vegas*

Las Vegas, meanwhile, remained a one-trick pony. It does adult tourism better than anybody, but the very nature of this industry dissuades many other industries from taking the city seriously. "When you think about building an environment where you're trying to attract talented people, you can't be home to *The Hangover* and high-tech at the same time," Barry Broome, president of the Greater Phoenix Economic Council, told Squires.

In light of Phoenix's successes, it would be understandable for Las Vegans to feel glum about their city's prospects. Indeed, Las Vegas is likely to struggle for years to come with the fundamental challenge of transforming from a single-industry economy to something more diverse and stable. But on the bright side, Las Vegas is addressing some of its deficiencies in comparison with Phoenix. It finally has a large performing arts center. It is moving into the medical research field with the Cleveland Clinic Lou Ruvo Center for Brain Health. The relocation of Zappos.com to the old city hall is going to have a transformative effect on the downtown area. At least one of the several proposals to build a sports arena appears likely to actually happen.

Education is the one area where Las Vegas appears likely to continue lagging the competition. For reasons difficult to understand, Las Vegas has not recognized the link between a respected research-oriented university and economic development. It's a combination that Phoenix has identified and taken advantage of, but Las Vegas can't seem to make this vital connection. Las Vegas as a whole remains all but contemptuous of education, or at least of the idea of taxpayers properly funding it. Until Las Vegas is able to make this intellectual leap, it will remain in the economic and cultural shadow of its boring sister city to the south.

### The recession's epicenter

The news media's coverage of the economic downturn tended to focus on how it affected the big resorts and residential developers. Reporters seeking a fresher angle would have been wise to consult some experts in the street-level economy of Las Vegas, such as pawn shop owner Rick Harrison.

Harrison, of course, is not your average pawnbroker. He's the star of a reality television series, *Pawn Stars*, on the History Channel. But his family-owned

Gold & Silver Pawn on Las Vegas Boulevard near downtown stood on the front lines when the economy soured.

"This is the absolute epicenter of the Great Recession," Harrison wrote in his 2011 memoir, *License to Pawn*. "Unemployment went to almost fifteen percent, the construction industry came to a halt, and tourism took a nosedive. This leaves a lot of people in trouble."

Harrison told a story that vividly explained what happened when the bottom fell out of the construction business. "I stopped buying tools or taking them on pawn," he wrote. "We were filling up the back room with expensive power tools, and nobody was buying them. And when I say nobody, I mean *nobody*. It got to the point where I couldn't give away power tools."

As the once-mighty Las Vegas construction business disintegrated, workers who had long depended on their tools to make a living suddenly saw them as a commodity to sell to pay bills or feed the family. "When the economy took a dive, workers who had been laid off were coming into the shop by the dozen—they had nowhere else to go," Harrison wrote. "These guys might not have been real sharp at managing their money. They never thought it would run out, and God knows our schools don't do much when it comes to teaching financial responsibility. A lot of these guys were hoping to be able to get their tools back—the recovery was always just around the corner—but too often they never came back, and one day I looked around and we had about seventy-five saws in the back room. I would look at them and see more than lost tools; I would see broken dreams and a broken system."

In a good economy, Harrison said, about ninety percent of pawned items are recovered by their owners. But when the recession hit, that percentage dropped to eighty percent. It didn't drop more, Harrison said, because people in survival mode tend to find a way. "If there's one thing I've learned, it's that people will do what they have to do to make it work," he wrote. "It's amazing to me how resourceful people are when it comes to making a living and taking care of their families."

### Foreclosure capital

Although Las Vegas was not prepared to deal with the recession, it didn't cause the financial collapse. Las Vegas was as much a victim as a perpetrator.

*Sun, Sin & Suburbia: The History of Modern Las Vegas*

Forces beyond its control—and, frankly, with far greedier and more cynical intentions than the CEOs of Sin City—were responsible for the most severe economic downturn since the Great Depression. The geniuses of Wall Street—high-stakes gamblers of another stripe—were the perpetrators. And their weapon of mass destruction was the subprime mortgage.

As the journalist Michael Lewis explained in *The Big Short*, his narrative of the financial crisis, the creation of the mortgage bond market in the '80s "extended Wall Street into a place it had never before been: the debts of ordinary Americans." At first, this meant "the more solvent half of the American population." But in the early '90s, with the emergence of the "subprime" mortgage, the mortgage bond market expanded "into the affairs of less creditworthy Americans."

A subprime mortage is a home loan awarded to someone who, based on traditional requirements, would not qualify to receive one. Subprime mortgages offered the opportunity for lower-income families to realize the American dream of homeownership. Perhaps nowhere was the subprime mortgage more popular than in Las Vegas.

For decades, Las Vegas had a reputation for affordable housing. A key incentive to relocate to Las Vegas was the chance for a working-class family to purchase a nice house in a safe neighborhood. Las Vegas promoters regularly repeated the apocryphal story of the young couple working as hotel cook and maid being able to buy a comfortable place to raise their children. But in the early 2000s, Las Vegas home values increased dramatically, delighting existing homeowners but making it difficult for many working-class families to buy a home. Enter the subprime mortgage. With a modest income and poor credit rating, a couple could make a low down payment, or none at all, and move into a suburban house of recent vintage.

It was a recipe for massive foreclosure. When the real estate bubble burst, subprime mortgage holders found themselves in the toughest spot of all. They couldn't afford their houses in the first place, so when they lost their jobs, they walked away from their houses. Or, when their equity vanished, and with it the prospect of ever being able to sell their homes, they walked away. At the depths of the real estate bust, more than seventy percent of Las Vegas homes were "underwater," meaning the mortgage holder owed more than the property was worth.

A concrete example: The author of this book purchased a house in northwest Las Vegas in 2002 for $187,500. According to Zillow.com, the home's value in the summer of 2005 had reached $389,000. The owner was elated, of course. But that was the peak. The value started dropping—to $378,000 in 2006, $334,000 in 2007, $257,000 in 2008, $210,000 in 2009 and—oh boy—$155,000 in 2010. In the spring of 2012, the house's value had plummeted to $140,300—below what it sold for new in 1998, below what it was purchased for in 2002, and, most alarmingly, below what was owed on the mortgage.

Neighborhoods were pocked with empty houses. Yards went unmowed and weeds proliferated. Thieves stole appliances and copper wire. In some cases, squatters moved in, trashing the neglected properties. Construction halted right in the middle of development of some subdivisions and condominium complexes. It wasn't pretty. It was depressing and scary, especially for those who stuck it out in the worst-hit neighborhoods.

The hardest-hit neighborhoods were those on the valley's fringes—the new subdivisions that catered to first-time buyers and others drawn to the newness, security and presumed smart investment in a neighborhood far removed from the ills and aggravations of the urban core. Banks eagerly handed out mortgages to these folks, although many of them couldn't afford the terms. It turned out the neighborhoods on the fringes tended to attract the flightiest sort—untethered newcomers who had no qualms about abandoning ship when things got rough.

To be fair, some of them couldn't be saddled with all the blame for their predicament. In the overheated climate of the bubble, many home buyers were persuaded they could afford houses that were above their means. Often, the premise was that the home's value would rise quickly, building equity that could be converted into profit. The desire to enjoy the American Dream overwhelmed common sense.

The national real estate bubble started in 1997 and ended in 2006, according to Robert J. Shiller, a professor of economics and finance at Yale. "Home

*Sun, Sin & Suburbia: The History of Modern Las Vegas*

prices rose nearly ten percent a year on average in the United States from 1997 to 2006, long enough for many people to become accustomed to the pace and to view it as normal," Shiller wrote in the *New York Times*. "People who owned a home over that period had reason to feel pretty well off and proud of their investment acumen. That fed a contagion of optimism and helped to drive the speculative bubble, propelling the economy and the stock market in a feedback loop that repeated year after year."

Fast-growing home equity gave Americans confidence to spend and invest in other ways as well. Among other things, they obtained home equity lines of credit, and they loaded up their credit cards. "During the bubble, the sense of rising wealth and high expectations gave people a good reason to spend and a greater willingness to plunge into investment, too," Shiller wrote.

That optimism was crushed by the economic collapse. Americans, Shiller noted, were now reluctant to buy houses, even though prices and interest rates were low. This shortage of consumer confidence meant the economic recovery would be slow in coming.

Dennis Smith, owner of Home Builders Research in Las Vegas, had a front-row seat for the unfolding of disaster. Even before it happened, he didn't like what he was seeing. "It was too easy to get these houses," he said. "Everyone had this false sense of security. There were people talking about this. There was too much demand, and it's not going to be able to sustain itself. You could see it happening in California. Then it happened here, then it happened in Phoenix. Easy credit all of a sudden went to zero credit. Unfortunately it went further down than anybody projected. No one projected it."

According to Smith, the turning point for Las Vegas real estate was January 2006. "Sales demand was down, permits were down. We started to hear of cracks in the credit segment. There were rumors starting to fly that banks were starting to see late payments."

Who's to blame? Smith had a concise answer: "Everyone's to blame. There's one word: greed. ... A lot of these people thought they could refinance out of their situation because prices would continue to go up, right? But no. Nobody forced them to go in there and take that loan. You can't point a finger in one direction. It's the whole system, a perfect storm."

## A new normal

It's nearly impossible to pinpoint when the Las Vegas recovery began, but the all-important tourism and convention industries saw encouraging gains in the third quarter of 2011. The city welcomed more tourists and convention attendees, and visitors spent more money than they had during the recession's depths. Most important, the resorts were able to charge significantly higher room rates.

As early as September of that year, economists were sending positive messages. "We are turning a corner," said Perry Wong, chief economist for City National Bank. Wong warned, however, that the Las Vegas recovery would occur slowly.

"Uncertainty remains, but it appears the Southern Nevada economy has turned the corner," declared Bob Potts, assistant director of the UNLV Center for Business and Economic Research, in the final days of 2011.

Potts's proclamation was punctuated a few days later when more than 300,000 visitors—a record—rang in the new year in Las Vegas. The festivities resurrected the high-octane pre-recession energy on the Strip, with a massive fireworks show, iconic musicians performing in the showrooms and brand-name celebrities hosting parties in the nightclubs.

While gaming revived, the city's once-stratospheric construction industry continued to struggle, contributing to the high unemployment rate. Still, there was one sign of life: a dramatic increase in the buying of existing homes. This surge was a direct result of the bursting of the real estate bubble, which saw home values tumble to pre-2000 prices. Real estate affordability once again made Las Vegas an attractive place to relocate.

In August 2011, Trulia.com, a real estate listing service, ranked Las Vegas the best place in the country to buy a house instead of renting one. A few months later, Trulia.com's "Metro Movers Index," tracking where people are exhibiting interest in buying homes, showed Las Vegas registering twice as many inbound home searches from outsiders as outbound searches. "That's typical of cities that have seen huge price declines since the bubble burst and a high vacancy rate, so there are bargains," Jed Kolko, chief economist for Trulia.com, told the *Las Vegas Review-Journal*.

When the numbers for 2011 were tallied, it proved to be a banner year for Las Vegas home sales, with almost 49,000 existing houses and condominiums sold. About half the sales were cash-only transactions, reflecting the heavy involvement of deal-seeking investors. Also, about half the sales were homes purchased out of foreclosure.

Going into 2012, Las Vegas still had about 20,000 houses on the market, a significant decrease but still enough to prevent values from rising. "Even as sales return to life, there are so many homes on the market, or that could be put on the market, that sellers can't ask for much," Kolko said. As many as 100,000 houses still remained at risk of foreclosure in the next couple of years.

While Las Vegas homeowners who saw their values plunge might not agree, economists said the low prices would benefit Las Vegas in the long run. "Las Vegas is now a relative bargain," said Stephen Brown, director of UNLV's Center for Business and Economic Research. "This lower cost actually ... will help create future growth in Las Vegas."

The flurry of activity in the existing home market did not extend to new construction. In 2011, new home sales failed to reach 4,000. That was the lowest total ever recorded by Home Builders Research, which had started tracking new home sales twenty-three years before. It was a downright anemic tally compared with the nation-leading pace before the recession. In 2005, for example, Las Vegas saw 39,000 new home sales.

Experts were not optimistic that Las Vegas real estate would turn around anytime soon. Housing analyst Larry Murphy projected another 25,000 home foreclosures in 2012 and another ten percent drop in home values. The continuing drop in home values meant two-thirds of Las Vegas homeowners owed more than their homes were worth.

The state's soaring unemployment rate also appeared to be easing toward the end of 2011, with the rate falling from 13 percent in November to 12.6 percent in December and 12.3 percent in February 2012. But experts cautioned that unemployment percentages are often overly simplistic indicators of the actual jobs picture, as they don't take into account "discouraged" workers, those who are no longer seeking employment, or "underemployed" workers, those working part time who would like to work full time. Put all these categories together and one-quarter of Nevada's work force was unemployed or underemployed.

As a result of the persistent real estate crisis and few prospects for job growth outside of the tourism industry, optimism about a Las Vegas recovery was tepid at best. Nary a soul was willing to promise anything more than modest improvements in the Las Vegas economy in 2012 and 2013. The era of breakneck growth, of billion-dollar resort projects and sprawling master-planned communities, was over, replaced by a new normal for Las Vegas. The expansion of Las Vegas almost certainly would resume at some point, but perhaps never again at the frantic pace of 1990-2007.

The city's experts could not envision a scenario in which Las Vegas real estate returned to its euphoric bubble years. "Nobody sober would ever suggest we're going to get back to the peak," economic analyst Jeremy Aguero said in February 2012. According to Aguero, Las Vegas homeowners had lost an incredible $91 billion in equity since the market collapsed in 2006. "It's going to be decades or longer to recover the equity we lost," he said.

Las Vegas should have recognized that its growth could not be sustained, that circumstances of one kind or another would crash the party. But those who benefited from Las Vegas's economic vitality—the gamers, developers, contractors, politicians and media moguls—were so busy counting their money that they ignored the inevitabilities of history. They didn't save for a rainy day. They failed to prepare for the worst, and when the crisis came, they weren't ready. In short, they did pretty much the same thing as their counterparts on Wall Street and across the country. The difference was how far Las Vegas could fall.

### Signs of life

Still, by 2012 Las Vegas was feeling a little better about itself. Benefiting from modest improvements in the national economy, tourist traffic, gambling revenues and conventions were growing again. Nevada casinos collected more than $1 billion from gamblers in January 2012, a huge increase from the same month a year earlier. Taxable sales for February 2012 surged by 10.2 percent statewide, reflecting not only tourist activity but residents as well. "The mindset of consumers has moved beyond the recession," Brian Gordon of the

Applied Analysis research firm told the *Las Vegas Review-Journal*. "They're spending in spite of challenges that continue to loom."

One sign of Las Vegas's renewed confidence was its bristling response to ridicule. For decades, Las Vegas had endured the jokes of comedians and the slurs of critics. But during the heyday of the '90s and early '00s, Las Vegas had more admirers than belittlers. That changed when the recession struck, and Las Vegas was hardly in a position to defend itself from attacks, deserved or otherwise.

But in April 2012, the *Los Angeles Times* detected a renewed feistiness in Las Vegas. An article headlined "Town Pines for a Little Respect" documented a series of slights that had irked the city's defenders. "Commentators insist that America's once-swaggering devil-may-care mecca has rolled an ugly pair of snake eyes," reporter John Glionna wrote. The most vicious assault came from *Men's Health* magazine, which ranked Las Vegas the nation's worst city for men in financial distress.

"Have you heard about the new high-stakes game in Vegas?" the magazine asked. "It's a gamble called 'living there.' The economic downturn has been more like a flaming nose dive for the citizens of Sin City. Things are so bad, in fact, that we half expect to hear that Lady Luck has started turning tricks."

Not known for its vitriolic journalism, *Men's Health* must have thought itself terribly edgy to trash Las Vegas by employing gambling and prostitution metaphors. But for those enduring the economic downturn and working diligently to get the battered city back on its feet, this sort of snarky piling on seemed hackneyed and juvenile. It also echoed a century's worth of doubters, all of whom were proved wrong.

But would the doubters be proved wrong once more? Would Las Vegas find a way to end its worst streak of bad luck in the modern era? Or was the wild ride finally coming to an end?

# CHAPTER 12

# The Future: Hope Floats

*"Here's to Nevada, the 'Leave It' state. Ya got money you want to gamble?*

*Leave it here. A wife you want to get rid of? Get rid of her here. Extra atom*

*bomb you don't need? Blow it up here. Nobody's gonna mind in the slightest."*

—ISABELLE (THELMA RITTER),
*THE MISFITS, 1961*

O ne thing the economic challenges of 2007-2012 showed is that Las Vegas can take a punch. The city was pushed against the ropes and beaten bloody, but it didn't drop to the canvas. Unlike Nevada's nineteenth century mining camps that turned into ghost towns, Las Vegas proved it was here for the long haul.

But surviving and thriving were not synonymous.

Even as Las Vegas showed signs of recovery, it was equally clear it needed to do some things that for years it had refused to take seriously. With responsibility for two million people, it could no longer operate under the old terms, when Las Vegas enjoyed a unique position in the world economy. The dynamics had changed but Las Vegas had not adapted. In order to mature into a world-class city, it would have to take more cues from cities that had already reached that status. That meant focusing on education and economic diversification.

There was no doubt tourism would remain the city's primary industry for the foreseeable future. Las Vegas remained a masterful generator of spectacles

309

that drew people from all corners of the globe. It still could put on a hell of a party.

But tourism could no longer do it all, because Las Vegas was no longer unique. Gambling had spread across the country and around the globe. The domestic expansion took off in the '90s, and gambling exploded internationally in the '00s. The opening of casinos on Indian reservations and Midwest riverboats had not fazed Las Vegas, as some feared. In fact, they seemed to actually help by exposing more Americans to gambling and thereby making Las Vegas a desirable destination for more people.

The international growth of gambling, which took on proportions unheard of in the United States, was another matter.

## The waking giant

The man most closely associated with the rise of international gambling was Sheldon Adelson, owner of the Venetian and Palazzo resorts on the Strip. While Adelson was a big player in Las Vegas, he was a colossus in Asia.

Adelson's prominent role in expanding casino gambling in Macau and Singapore was well documented in Las Vegas, but the scope of what was happening half a world away often was difficult to grasp. The statistics boggled the mind.

The tiny city of Macau is the only territory of China where gambling is legal. The city enjoys this special privilege because it had been a Portuguese colony for centuries, and when the Chinese took over in 1999, they kept that aspect of its economy intact. Coupled with the dramatic rise of the Chinese economy, which allowed millions to shed the austerity of communism and pocket riches, Macau was poised for expansion.

What Macau lacked in size it made up for by serving the seemingly insatiable demands of high-rolling Asian gamblers. In a matter of just a few years, Macau's gambling revenues had surpassed those of the "gambling capital" of Las Vegas. By 2011 Macau's gambling wealth had left Las Vegas in a cloud of dust. In that year, Nevada's 334 casinos collected $10.7 billion in gaming revenues, while Macau's thirty-five casinos collected $33.5 billion.

Three Las Vegas casino concerns stood at the forefront of the Macau explosion: Adelson, Steve Wynn and MGM Resorts. But Adelson, one of

*Sun, Sin & Suburbia: The History of Modern Las Vegas*

the world's wealthiest individuals, was the most bullish of the trio, investing more than $8 billion in Macau, with plans to spend billions more. It was easy to justify: In 2011, Adelson's Macau properties generated $1.3 billion in earnings, while his Las Vegas resorts brought in $198 million.

Adelson also pioneered casino gambling in Singapore, where his resort generated a $1.2 billion profit in 2011. He also had plans to build a $35 billion resort complex in Spain, and he was pursuing deals to open casinos in Japan, Korea, Taiwan and Vietnam. Adelson had made his name in Las Vegas, but his financial interests had shifted to other corners of the globe.

Meanwhile, casino gambling in the United States was poised to expand dramatically in the new century. No longer were states tinkering with tin-shack Indian casinos or poker parlors. New resorts planned in prominent cities such as Miami, New York City and Toronto promised to rival the size and appeal of the top dogs on the Las Vegas Strip.

What did this mean for Las Vegas? Some naturally worried that the proliferation of beautiful casino resorts in every quadrant of the world would drain Las Vegas of its singular appeal. Others insisted the spread of gambling—even at the super-sized levels of the twenty-first century—was good for Las Vegas.

"New jurisdictions might have created marginal negative impact on Las Vegas at their outset during the heavy expansion period from the mid-1990s to the mid-2000s, but the Strip continues to thrive," Howard Stutz, gaming industry columnist for the *Las Vegas Review-Journal*, wrote in 2012.

What's more, Stutz said the fact that Las Vegas casinos companies were taking the lead in growing new markets would prove beneficial, as the profits would be sent home to the desert. Also, Las Vegas remained the source of industry knowledge, creating the city's greatest export. Stutz cited Bo Bernhard, executive director of the International Gaming Institute at UNLV, who asserted that Macau did not take jobs away from Las Vegas.

"Macau has actually created jobs in Las Vegas," Bernhard said. "Most of the major gaming corporations have Asian analysis departments. What this growth has done has made Las Vegas the corporate headquarters for the gaming industry."

While Bernhard identified a legitimate benefit of the global expansion, many Las Vegans could not help but wonder if their city had been tossed aside in favor of the industry's shiny new toys. While the Strip's Echelon Place and Fontainebleau resorts remained unfinished, and the Sahara sat shuttered, and the site of the imploded Frontier lay dormant, the casino giants invested billions elsewhere.

All the more reason for Las Vegas to supplement its casino-centric economy with a few new revenue streams.

## Online gambling

If the United States legalized online poker, which rose to the level of possibility in 2011, several major Las Vegas casino companies were gearing up to take advantage of it.

For years, people were able to gamble illegally on websites based in foreign countries. In 2006, for example, an estimated thirty thousand people in the United States were gambling online at any one time, spending as much as $4 billion per month. But in 2011 the Justice Department started cracking down on the illicit operations, resulting in a dramatic drop in U.S. online players. Poker is the most popular online game.

The crackdown deterred but could not dampen public demand, and the casino companies started angling to own the online gambling market if and when it was legalized. The first step was to establish regulations at the state level to allow Nevadans to gamble online. But of course that would be small money for companies accustomed to marketing to the world. And so MGM Resorts and Caesars Entertainment were among those lobbying Congress for a federal law to allow online poker nationwide. Nevada politicians supported the effort.

Gary Loveman, chairman of Caesars, was perhaps the biggest champion of the move, not surprising considering his company owns the annual World Series of Poker. He said online gaming has the potential to exceed estimates of a $5 billion market. "I consider $5 billion to be a conservative figure," he said.

Casino companies had identified a bigger trend—the rising popularity of video games—and were trying to figure out how to tap that audience. "Americans spend more money on video games, consoles and related equipment than on all casino gambling combined," the *Las Vegas Sun* reported. And that picture didn't include the profusion of smart phones and tablets—and the millions of apps used on them—that were drawing the attention of literally billions of people.

Still, not everyone in Nevada's gaming industry supported the push for online gambling. Adelson and Anthony Marnell III, president of the M Resort, spoke out publicly against it.

"I just can't see a scenario where you can truly secure that from young children," Marnell said. "Once it becomes legalized, it's taking it too far. I think you start to create addictive behaviors in the home that we can't see as operators. ... I know I'm not in the favor of the gaming industry perspective. I just think enough is enough. We don't need to push this farther into the home."

In addition to lending his name to the opposition, Adelson took his case to Washington, lobbying key Republican lawmakers in an effort to thwart legalization. Some hoping for quick legislative approval worried that Adelson's opposition would ruin their plans.

But David Schwartz, director of the Center for Gaming Research at UNLV, speculated that Adelson ultimately could not stand in the way of the public's demand to gamble online. He likened the situation to Prohibition, which was imposed through a political victory but eventually failed because of public sentiment.

"Outside of gambling, a great deal of our entertainment and commerce is moving online," Schwartz wrote in the *Las Vegas Business Press*. "Once buying music meant paying cash for a vinyl LP, taking it home and playing it on a home stereo system. Now, it's as simple as clicking a button in iTunes. We are shopping, banking and communicating with each other online. It seems nearly inevitable that those of who like gambling will, eventually, be doing that online, too."

While opinions differed, a more pragmatic position was voiced by Michael Gaughan, owner of the South Point hotel-casino south of the Strip. "I've always been somewhat against this but if it's going to come, I don't to be left at the station," he told the *Wall Street Journal*.

Efforts to legalize online poker failed in 2012, but advocates intended to keep applying pressure to get it done eventually.

## Diversify or else

The oft-cited reason for the recession's calamitous impact on Las Vegas was its lack of a diversified economy. The dependence on tourism and construction left the city vulnerable to economic earthquakes nationally and internationally. But Jeremy Aguero, principal of Applied Analysis, a local economic research firm, argued that Nevada had become more diversified in recent years than many believed. Citing examples such as Allegiant Airlines, Zappos.com and solar manufacturer Amonix, Aguero said Nevada led the nation in increased diversification between 2000 and 2010. However, Aguero acknowledged that Nevada remained the nation's third-least-diversified state behind Wyoming and Washington, D.C.

Aguero urged Nevada leaders to work harder to bring in more businesses in the areas of health care, information technology, logistics and aerospace. But he said it would be difficult to compete with other regions for these industries if the state does not build a better education system, which yields a more qual-ified work force. Emulating the successes of cities such as Seattle, Chicago, Denver and Dallas will require local investments that Las Vegas has given a low priority in the past. "They've invested more in their communities than we have, and they're reaping the benefits of that," he said.

Robert Lang, director of Brookings Mountain West, a UNLV-based off-shoot of the prominent Washington, D.C., think tank, said Las Vegas has a role to play in the technology arena. Las Vegas isn't likely to challenge Silicon Valley as an incubator of great innovations but it is ideal geographically to become a major location for digital data storage facilities. Why? Because it has fewer natural disaster risks than any other area on the continent, Lang said. It doesn't have tornadoes, hurricanes, floods or earthquakes that could jeopardize the vital data stored by governments and companies alike. Las Vegas officials could boast of one success story in this area already: a data center located near McCarran International Airport. *The Economist* magazine described the structure, which is the size of eleven football fields:

"Security guards dressed in ninja style, all in black and with tasers strapped to their thighs, confiscate the identity cards of visitors, then lead them through a series of gates into the so-called SWITCH SuperNap. Every part of the data center was custom-designed for optimal temperature control with blue vents for cool air, red ones for warm and everything looking futuristic. Computers, stacked neatly in cages, stretch out in long rows. They belong to the government, to eBay and Google, and to a growing number of other companies that could put their servers anywhere, but choose this spot in Nevada."

Lang suggested that lots of data could be stored very safely in Yucca Mountain, which has been all but abandoned as a nuclear waste storage site. And, he said, if Las Vegas were to become a major location for data storage, there are companies that would want to move there to be closer to their data.

Lang also said Las Vegas should do even more to attract trade shows to the city. He noted that ComicCon, which has grown into the entertainment industry's largest trade show, is running out of space in San Diego. Las Vegas is a logical place for it because of its ample floor space and long-standing linkage with Hollywood. But he suggested a bigger idea: permanent trade shows. Instead of putting up and taking down the big shows, why not keep them going year-round? This model was already happening at the furniture-focused World Market Center, he said, and would make sense for other industry events such as the Consumer Electronics Show.

Lang's underlying message echoed Aguero's: Nevada is grossly under-investing in higher education. Strong research universities are an economic generator on several levels, yet Nevada has been cutting rather than expanding. And this was happening while other Western states were improving the reach and prowess of their institutions. Educated people are more likely to be employed in the current economy, and they are more likely to be employable going forward.

### The next new thing

In a keynote address at the Nevada Press Association's annual convention in Winnemucca in 2009, now-retired state archivist Guy Rocha summed up the state's economic crisis with an ominous assertion: "We are searching for a future."

For decades, Nevada enjoyed being the only place where Americans could gamble without fear that federal agents were going to break down the door and arrest everybody. But with games of chance now legal in forty-eight states—and casino-style gambling prevalent across the continent—gamblers no longer had to journey to the desert for their fix. "We've gotta find a new horse to ride," Rocha said.

We've been here before, he noted, citing historical examples where the state economy slumped but a new industry was developed to fill the void. The Comstock mining boom put Nevada on the map in the nineteenth century, but when the mines played out, the state's population plummeted and its economy shriveled. With just 42,000 residents in 1900, Nevada parried with critics who suggested it should be stripped of its statehood.

A new mining boom in Tonopah, Goldfield and Ely revived the state soon after the century's turn, but Nevada dreamed up other revenue sources as well. Boxing, for example. Banned in other states, big-time fights brought thousands of people to Nevada. Between 1897 and 1910, Nevada was the nation's fight capital. But the boxing economy disappeared for decades after other states climbed back in the ring.

Relaxing the divorce laws was the next boon to Nevada's bottom line, but when other states eventually followed suit, Nevada lost its competitive advantage. No-sweat weddings drew eager couples to Las Vegas, but that industry eventually declined as other states caught on. Legal gambling turned out to be the state's cash cow for seventy-five years, but Rocha believed it was time to find our next new angle.

Rocha suggested that if Nevada had essentially the same mindset today as it did decades ago, it would legalize gay marriage and marijuana. Both would be economic boons to the state. But Rocha lamented that it's unlikely the state would take such steps today.

David Schwartz, director of UNLV's Center for Gaming Research, wasn't so pessimistic about the future of Nevada's casino industry, but he wasn't exactly bullish either. "People have been gambling for a really long time, and they will continue gambling," he said. "But there's a lot of competition that wasn't there before."

Still, finding something completely new to sustain Nevada economically wasn't what Schwartz had in mind. Rather, he saw potential in creating new experiences that tourists can't get anywhere else. He mentioned as an example "CSI: The Experience," an interactive attraction at the MGM Grand in which participants helped to solve a crime. On his blog, Schwartz put it this way: "Twenty years ago, having a big room full of slot machines with a coffee shop, buffet, steakhouse and lounge was relatively rare—there was a pretty big novelty factor in Las Vegas. Today, that's just not true."

While Schwartz saw Las Vegas exploiting cultural niches, economic analyst Jeremy Aguero suggested the city capitalize on its ability to host large events. "Southern Nevada has a competitive advantage whenever a group of people converge on a single location for a specific purpose for a limited period of time," Aguero said. "Think World Market Center for sports, medicine, entertainment, media, industry or government. [The future] is not going to be about more rooms, it is going to be about building more reasons to fill the rooms we have."

What the perspectives of Rocha, Schwartz and Aguero have in common is diversification—not necessarily of types of industry but of ways of thinking. Schwartz wants us to think small. Aguero wants us to think big. Rocha wants us to think new.

They're all right. Cleverness is a key to reviving Nevada's economy. Exploiting market niches requires a keen awareness of cultural trends and a willingness to take chances. Creating mega-events requires marketing savvy, proper facilities and community coordination. Building new industries requires political leadership.

The overarching message: Innovate or die.

"The enterprise that does not innovate inevitably ages and declines," the late theorist Peter Drucker said. "And in a period of rapid change such as the present ... the decline will be fast."

### Cracked crystal ball

Predicting the future—of Las Vegas or anything else—is a fool's errand. Consider the great wisdom of rockabilly singer Ronnie Hawkins. He once told a young singer from Memphis: "You've got to call yourself 'Rock' or 'Jack' or something. Anything as long as it's not 'Elvis Presley.'" Or how about Steve Ballmer, the Microsoft CEO, who in 2007 said, "There's no chance that the iPhone is going to get any significant market share. No chance."

The first edition of this book, released in 2004, included a series of predictions about Las Vegas. Some of the safer guesses, such as an increased use of water-efficient landscaping, came to pass. But some of the bolder ones proved woefully off base. For example, I predicted Las Vegas would have a major league sports franchise "in five to ten years." It didn't come close to happening in five years, and it wasn't likely to happen in ten. I also predicted the monorail would be extended "north to downtown by 2007 and east to McCarran Airport by 2012." Yeah, that was a bad bet.

It's well established that few foresaw the real estate bust and Wall Street meltdown, but I should have known better than to predict in the pages of a book that the Las Vegas growth machine would roll on, unchecked, for years on end. But to my credit, I interviewed a local authority on development who offered a wise, if not quite prescient, take on the future of Las Vegas. Greg Borgel, a veteran planning and zoning consultant, said in 2004 that, assuming growth continued at a pace similar to what Las Vegas had experienced over the past decade or so, it would be done in about fifteen years. "We will run up against the limits of growth in a fifteen-year time frame," he said.

The main reason he cited: water. By law, Nevada can get only so much of it from the Colorado River, 300,000 acre-feet per year, and it was already flirting with its limit. Conservation only goes so far, and efforts to obtain water in other ways are costly and logistically difficult.

Another reason, Borgel said, was that Las Vegas's ability to attract evermore tourists was limited. Increasing competition from other states and countries meant that Las Vegas was no longer unique, that it had lost its monopoly as a gambling destination. "I can't imagine we will be able to sustain a population of more than double what we've got now," Borgel said. That meant Las Vegas would top out at around three million people.

In 2004, the prospect of Las Vegas growth stopping dead in its tracks in fifteen years sounded almost cataclysmic. Construction was one of the city's largest industries. But Borgel did not see it in such simple terms. People were

*Sun, Sin & Suburbia: The History of Modern Las Vegas*

moving here in droves, he said, because they desired the quality of life: the jobs, the low taxes, the weather. "We stop growing when people stop perceiving us as having a high quality of life," he explained. "That happens when economic growth stops and we become less desirable environmentally. People have been moving here because they can afford a nice house. When they can't do that anymore, they'll stop moving here."

Borgel saw Las Vegas's quality of life gradually deteriorating. Adapting to a new economic model, in which rapid growth did not play a significant role, undoubtedly would be difficult, leading to high unemployment, business closures and other depressive results.

Although Borgel did not predict the real estate or Wall Street crises, neither did he expect Las Vegas to enjoy never-ending prosperity. A time would come when Las Vegas was no longer the nation's fastest-growing metro area, when it no longer was such a desirable place to relocate. That time arrived sooner than he expected, for sure, but it definitely arrived.

## A fresh forecast

Predictions are precarious, but who can resist them in a city built on betting? At the risk of another round of poor picks, here's a handful of prognostications about Las Vegas.

• The relocation of Zappos.com to downtown Las Vegas will give the urban core a dramatic boost. CEO Tony Hsieh was on a mission that extended far beyond the basic retail objective of selling shoes online. He was intent on reinventing downtown as an economic and cultural force in Las Vegas. Other downtown developments in the '90s and '00s were significant, but Hsieh's plans, if executed, have the potential to transform downtown into a national phenomenon. There's just one nagging question: If, for some reason, Hsieh gets a better offer and leaves town, will his downtown vision be abandoned as well?

• Las Vegas eventually will get its professional sports franchise. People started talking seriously about it in the '90s, but it remained little more than a dream in 2012. The primary reason: no arena or stadium in which to play. But with several serious projects on the drawing boards, it appeared likely that Las Vegas would have a facility worthy of a professional team by 2015.

• Boyd Gaming will resume construction of its Echelon Place resort complex. The west side of the north Strip is in dire need of a boost, and Boyd is best positioned to make it happen. The project, however, will be smaller and built in phases. In the wake of the financial crises that plagued CityCenter's construction, no sane company is going to take a similar risk. The trick for Boyd will be to dream up some clever innovations to make Echelon stand out.

• The monorail will be shut down and dismantled. As much as the Strip needs better mass transit, the monorail was fatally conceived and executed. And its failure will haunt future ideas to move masses of people around the resort corridor.

• Harvey Whittemore's Coyote Springs planned community, sixty miles northeast of Las Vegas, won't get off the ground in our lifetimes. After years of planning and development, the 43,000-acre project consisted of a golf course, a few signs and a lot of well-publicized promises. Then the real estate market collapsed, stalling Whittemore's ambitious plans. Dirt moving continued, however, and Whittemore insisted the project eventually would materialize. But in 2012 Coyote Springs suffered a second strike in the form of legal action by business partners accusing Whittemore of fraud. Thomas and Albert Seeno, home-building brothers from Northern California, claimed Whittemore had misspent more than $40 million. Whittemore countersued, demanding $60 million from the Seenos. The high-stakes legal battle promised to delay the project for years, if not kill it outright. "The collapse of the housing market means Coyote Springs is dead, maybe forever," Las Vegas journalist George Knapp asserted. "Whittemore's dream is toast."

• The proposed nuclear waste dump at Yucca Mountain was declared dead during President Barack Obama's first term, but the zombie will periodically reanimate to menace Southern Nevada. Unable to come up with a more palatable alternative, the nuclear power industry and its political allies will seek every opportunity to revive the project.

• The real estate market will take years to recover, and it's unlikely to ever return to the bubble years. But Las Vegas is not done growing. "Moving west" continues to be a driving force in American culture. Gregg Wolin, whose company intended to develop the Park Highlands planned community in

North Las Vegas, put it this way in 2012: "I don't subscribe to the idea that anything fundamentally has changed in Las Vegas. It's not like people are picking up and moving to St. Louis or Iowa." But development plans drawn up before the recession will be reconfigured to reduce the level of risk. For example, the Inspirada master-planned community in Henderson, which was based on New Urbanist principles, likely will be revised to reflect more conventional neighborhood design. A welcome trend will be the move to larger lots. Rather than squeezing more and more houses onto each acre, even stacking them three stories high, builders will respond to demand and give home buyers a little more breathing room.

• By and large, Las Vegas will not learn from most of its mistakes. When the economy eventually returns to highway speed, Las Vegas is likely to fall back into some of its bad habits. (Lest we forget, Las Vegas was built on bad habits.) But Las Vegas also will benefit from one of its strongest traits: adaptation. Unlike decaying Rust Belt cities, which failed to see the writing on the wall and do something about it, Las Vegas understands it must live in a perpetual state of evolution in order to remain competitive in the global economy.

• Last but not least: A minor author will win a Pulitzer Prize for a book charting the history of Las Vegas. There's your proof about the foolishness of making predictions!

## A little perspective

Las Vegas is a young city. While popular wisdom says it was founded in 1905, Las Vegas didn't really become anything resembling a city until the '30s, or, depending on your criteria, the '50s. By contrast, major cities along the East Coast have their origins in the 1600s. Industrial cities started in the late 1700s and early 1800s.

When you look at Las Vegas's relatively brief history, it's not hard to conclude that the most exciting and prosperous decade was the 1990s. To be sure, Las Vegas had its share of interesting times before then. There was the spasm of growth after the railroad came through town in 1905; the burst of development that accompanied the construction of Hoover Dam in the early '30s; the defense industry infusion and the rise of the Strip in the '40s and '50s; the arrival of billionaire Howard Hughes in the '60s; the tug-of-war between the mob and corporations for control of the resort industry in the '70s and '80s. Except for a few brief lulls, Las Vegas has always been in growth mode. But the town's first eighty-five years paled in comparison with what came next. The '90s really started a year before, in 1989, when Steve Wynn built the Mirage. Wynn's vision of luxury and attractions beyond the casino floor jumpstarted the city's tourism business and triggered a new era in which almost every year brought the implosion of an old hotel and the opening of a bigger, fancier one. Off the Strip, the growth was no less dramatic. Schools couldn't be built fast enough to accommodate all the newcomers, who came to Las Vegas to grab a piece of the well-publicized prosperity. It was an exciting period of activity, progress and, yes, frustration, the latter a result of the community's inability to cope with such rapid growth.

Only now is it possible to begin assessing the '90s in Las Vegas. The picture that is emerging conjures feelings of nostalgia and regret. The nostalgia is for a time when the town, in effect, had the top down, the pedal floored and the music cranked up, racing into the future with a confident and carefree attitude. There was a visceral feeling that Las Vegas was the new center of the universe, the place where big things were happening. The regret is that Las Vegas did not use this good fortune for the benefit of everyone, that in many ways it failed during this period to see the big picture, think of the long term, solidify the community's foundations.

Still, after all the miseries of the economic collapse, Las Vegas remains a vibrant, exciting place to live. Things are constantly in motion. But it's also a place that has yet to become a genuine *community*. Las Vegas is still a congregation of capitalists and consumers in a geographic location, most of them holding tight to the belief that *home* is somewhere else. Until that changes, until Las Vegas becomes a place where money isn't the only object, Las Vegas will be a statistical whipping boy.

If we are to believe planner Greg Borgel's scenario, in which the quality of life in Las Vegas will continue to deteriorate until it no longer attracts newcomers, one has to ask: Why stay? Certainly there are greener pastures, places where the quality of life is higher, where the air is cleaner, the schools better, the traffic lighter.

One answer is that none of those places can touch the spectacle that is Las Vegas. Richard Corliss, cultural critic for *Time* magazine, wrote that "Las Vegas is the great fictional city. It's a page-turning novel told in a million lives and 120,000 hotel rooms; an epic movie with casino chips for special effects; a tragedy of addiction and a burlesque with the smoothest showgirls around." He concluded that Las Vegas is the "most thrilling novel never written."

While Corliss admitted to being a hopeless romantic about the city, there was an underlying truth to what he wrote. You can live a fairly normal life in Las Vegas—beyond the neon—but you can't escape the feverish energy that drives the town. Nor would you want to. Even if you see Las Vegas as a big freeway pileup, you have to admit that you can't avert your gaze.

The novelist John D. MacDonald was best known for his Travis McGee series, chronicling the adventures of a sort-of private eye living in South Florida. In those twenty-one books, MacDonald often diverted from the central narrative to allow McGee to spout off on all manner of topics. These brief editorials often were razor-sharp indictments of the state where he lived. Nevada, especially Southern Nevada, and Florida had much in common, particularly rampant growth and an economy highly dependent on tourism. So what MacDonald said about Florida could just as easily be said of Southern Nevada. And MacDonald effectively answered that nagging question: Why stay?

"Tacky though it might be, its fate uncertain, too much of its destiny in the hands of men whose sole thought was to grab the money and run, cheap little politicians with blow-dried hair, ice-eyed old men from the North with devout claims about their duties to their shareholders, big-rumped good old boys from the cattle counties with their fingers in the till right up to their cologned armpits—it was still my place in the world."

Many residents share the sentiment that there's as much to dislike about Las Vegas as there is to like. Las Vegas isn't a place that elicits middling perspectives. There's plenty to gripe about—the unemployment, the political corruption, the apathy—but that doesn't necessarily equate to contempt for the place. Some people complain because they care.

The economic downturn pounded Las Vegas. But while the city stumbled, it did not fall, even if its bruises would remain tender for many years. Those who stuck it out, who did not cut and run when times got tough, were determined to make the best of a bad situation. If Las Vegas did not experience a collective epiphany about the need to fix its fundamental problems, it did exhibit a remarkable resilience to the psychology of defeat that has afflicted many battered American cities. In short, it continued to be Las Vegas, where sun, sin and suburbia combine to form one of the most interesting, if troubled, cities in America.

*"And so life in Las Vegas goes on. Old familiar landmarks, houses and small shops on Fremont Street ... are being wrecked by cold and disinterested wrecking concerns, and in their places are being erected bigger and more pretentious gambling halls and saloons. The gay Lotharios still come and go, but the once slow tempo of the town is fading into oblivion, giving way to the fast and ever-accelerating crescendo of life today. Only the barren, silent mountains and the sagebrush on the Nevada desert remain the same."*

— Paul Ralli
*Nevada Lawyer*, 1946

*Sun, Sin & Suburbia: The History of Modern Las Vegas*

# Recommended Reading

This book is far from the last word on Las Vegas history. More than 100 books can be found that offer useful or entertaining perspectives on the city's past. The following titles are valuable resources for those who want to learn more about the city. Some are readily available at area bookstores, some are out of print or hard to find.

Barlett, Donald L., and James B. Steele. *Empire: The Life, Legend and Madness of Howard Hughes*. New York: W.W. Norton and Company, 1979.

Cooper, Marc. *The Last Honest Place in America: Paradise and Perdition in the New Las Vegas*. New York: Nation Books, 2004.

Davies, Richard O., ed. *The Maverick Spirit: Building the New Nevada* Reno: University of Nevada Press, 1999.

Denton, Sally, and Roger Morris. *The Money and the Power: The Making of Las Vegas and Its Hold on America, 1947-2000*. New York: Knopf, 2001.

Drosnin, Michael. *Citizen Hughes*. New York: Holt, Rinehart and Winston, 1985.

Earley, Pete. *Super Casino: Inside the "New" Las Vegas*. New York: Bantam Books, 2000.

Gottdiener, M., Claudia Collins and David Dickens. *Las Vegas: The Social Production of an All-American City*. Malden: Blackwell Publishers, 1999.

Green, Michael S., and Eugene P. Moehring. *Las Vegas: A Centennial History*. Reno and Las Vegas: University of Nevada Press, 2005.

Hess, Alan. *Viva Las Vegas: After-Hours Architecture*. San Francisco: Chronicle Books, 1993.

Hopkins, A.D., and K.J. Evans. *The First 100: Portraits of the Men and Women Who Shaped Las Vegas*. Las Vegas: Huntington Press, 1999.

Hurlburt, Brian. *The Las Vegas Country Club: Chronicle of an Icon*. Las Vegas: Stephens Press, 2011.

Moehring, Eugene P. *Resort City in the Sunbelt: Las Vegas 1930-2000*. Reno: University of Nevada Press, 2000 (Second Edition).

O'Brien, Matthew. *Beneath the Neon: Life and Death in the Tunnels of Las Vegas*. Las Vegas: Huntington Press, 2007.

Paher, Stanley W. *Las Vegas: As It Began—As It Grew*. Las Vegas: Nevada Publications, 1971.

Phelan, James. *Howard Hughes: The Hidden Years*. New York: Random House, 1976.

Puzo, Mario. *Inside Las Vegas*. New York: Grosset & Dunlap, 1976.

Reid, Ed, and Ovid Demaris. *The Green Felt Jungle*. New York: Trident Press, 1963.

Roske, Ralph J. *Las Vegas: A Desert Paradise*. Tulsa: Continental Heritage Press, 1986.

Rothman, Hal K. *Neon Metropolis: How Las Vegas Started the Twenty-First Century*. New York: Routledge, 2002.

Rothman, Hal K., and Mike Davis, eds. *The Grit Beneath the Glitter: Tales from the Real Las Vegas*. Berkeley: University of California Press, 2002.

Schumacher, Geoff. *Howard Hughes: Power, Paranoia & Palace Intrigue*. Las Vegas: Stephens Press, 2008.

Schwartz, David G. *Suburban Xanadu: The Casino Resort on the Las Vegas Strip and Beyond*. New York: Routledge, 2003.

Sheehan, Jack. *Forgotten Man: How Circus Circus's Bill Bennett Brought Middle America to Las Vegas*. Las Vegas: Stephens Press, 2010.

Sheehan, Jack, ed. *The Players: The Men Who Made Las Vegas*. Reno: University of Nevada Press, 1997.

Sheehan, Jack. *Quiet Kingmaker of Las Vegas: E. Parry Thomas*. Las Vegas: Stephens Press, 2009.

Simich, Jerry L. and Thomas C. Wright, eds. *The Peoples of Las Vegas: One City, Many Faces*. Reno/Las Vegas: University of Nevada Press, 2005.

Smith, John L. *Running Scared: The Life and Treacherous Times of Las Vegas Casino King Steve Wynn*. New York: Barricade Books, 1995.

Tronnes, Mike, ed. *Literary Las Vegas: The Best Writing About America's Most Fabulous City.* New York: Henry Holt and Company, 1995.

Weatherford, Mike. *Cult Vegas: The Weirdest! The Wildest! The Swingin'est Town on Earth!* Las Vegas: Huntington Press, 2001.

Wilkerson, W.R., III. *The Man Who Invented Las Vegas.* Beverly Hills: Ciro's Books, 2000.

Zanjani, Sally, and Carrie Townley Porter. *Helen J. Stewart: First Lady of Las Vegas.* Las Vegas: Stephens Press, 2011.

# Acknowledgments

The first edition of this book, published in 2004, was the product of many long nights and spoiled weekends. After my kids and wife had gone to bed, I would flip on the trusty Mac and write for hours. Especially in the final months, my home office became, to the untrained eye, a dump, with newspaper clippings, folders, notepads and books scattered on the floor around my desk and chair. Let's not even talk about the desk itself.

Getting this project done would have been impossible without the assistance and understanding of many people. First and foremost, my wife, Tammy, was, as always, the captain of our little ship, taking care of everything that's truly important while I pecked away at the keyboard, oblivious to most everything going on around me. She also was a good sport as I droned on day after day about the things I learned and the roadblocks I encountered in preparing this manuscript.

My daughters, Erin and Sara, were incredibly understanding. Growing up, they never knew a father who didn't have a deadline hanging over his head, but the book was different. It was almost a second full-time job, and they undoubtedly suffered a little in the process. Thankfully, they are now bright, successful young women, so there appears to have been no permanent damage.

Michael Green, my editor, colleague and friend, read every word of the original and revised editions of this book, providing expert and thoughtful guidance on every possible level. His input made it a significantly better book.

The book could not have been completed without the use of the *Las Vegas Review-Journal* library and the assistance of able and amiable librarians Padmini Pai and Pamela Busse. It also would not have been possible without the hard work of the many reporters for the *Review-Journal, Las Vegas Sun* and other newspapers who provide the proverbial first draft of Las Vegas history.

I am indebted to the Las Vegas historians and journalists from whom I learned much and borrowed liberally, especially Michael Green, Eugene Moehring, Alan Hess, A.D. Hopkins, Hal Rothman, David Schwartz, John L. Smith, Stanley Paher, Sally Denton, Pete Earley, Matt Lay and W.R. Wilkerson III.

I talked to more than one hundred people in gathering material for this book, and all of them were helpful in some way. I want to particularly thank Mark Fine, Charles Kubat, Greg Borgel, John Ritter, Tom Warden, Marty Manning, Mark Brandenburg, Bill Boyd, Ray Landry, Bill Thompson, Jan Jones, Bob Fielden, Irwin Molasky, Stephen Crystal, Barry Perea, J.C. Davis, Jeff van Ee, Lorna Kesterson, Lou LaPorta, Joy Bell, John Riordan, Dennis Smith and Mike Dyal.

Thank you to my former bosses in the newspaper business, Sherman Frederick, Allan Fleming and Mike Ferguson, who always supported this book and who gave me incredible opportunities to grow in the journalism field.

Thanks to the following for their support and encouragement over the years: Jon and Sally Schumacher, Barbara Sowards, John and Eulah Wallis, Scott Dickensheets, Steve Sebelius, Sue Campbell, Andrew Kiraly, Andy Taylor, Heidi Walters, Newt Briggs, Jake Highton, George Knapp, Richard Bryan and the late Ralph Denton and Mike O'Callaghan.

Carolyn Hayes Uber, the founding and only publisher of Stephens Press, was a tremendous supporter of all my writing and editing ventures. Over the years she became practically a second mother to me. Her brave and brutal battle with cancer ended in 2014, and Stephens Press ended along with her. I know she would be pleased that the University of Nevada Press has chosen to keep this book available. Thank you to Joanne O'Hare for seeing the value in reprinting the second edition.

# About the Author

Geoff Schumacher is a writer, editor and museum executive in Las Vegas. He is the author of *Sun, Sin & Suburbia: The History of Modern Las Vegas* and *Howard Hughes: Power, Paranoia & Palace Intrigue*. He edited *Nevada: 150 Years in the Silver State*, the official book commemorating the state's sesquicentennial, as well as more than twenty other books. After graduating from the University of Nevada, Reno, Schumacher worked in the newspaper business for twenty-five years before becoming the director of content for the Mob Museum. He was a reporter, editorial writer and city editor for the *Las Vegas Sun*, editor of *Las Vegas CityLife* and the *Las Vegas Mercury*, and director of community publications and weekly columnist for the *Las Vegas Review-Journal*. He culminated his newspaper career as publisher of the *Ames* (Iowa) *Tribune*. Contact him at geoffschumacher.com.

# Index